# FIRST STEPS IN PATCHWORK, QUILTING &

# FIRST STEPS IN
# PATCHWORK, QUILTING & APPLIQUÉ

Introduced by Joen Zinni-Lask

ORBIS · LONDON

**Acknowledgments**
The artwork was drawn by the following artists: Lindsay Blow, Eugene Fleury, Colin Salmon, Amanda Severne, Sue Sharples, Sara Silcock and John Woodcock.
The photographs on the following pages are by courtesy of Camera Press, London: 16, 64, 67, 87 and 89. The remainder of the photographs were taken by the following photographers: Jan Baldwin, Tom Belshaw, Tim Bishop, Allan Grainger, Chris Harvey, Hank Kemme, Di Lewis, Liz McAulay, Polly Mitchell, Spike Powell, Jerry Tubby and Nick Wright.

*Cover:* Hank Kemme
*Half title page:* Hank Kemme
*Title page:* Spike Powell
*Back cover:* Jerry Tubby



First published in Great Britain
by Orbis Publishing Limited, London 1984

This material previously appeared in the partwork *SuperStitch*



Printed in Italy

ISBN: 0-85613-678-6

# Contents

# Introduction

*Patchwork, quilting and appliqué are crafts with an ancient tradition. Sometimes the purpose was one of economy or necessity, such as the patchwork quilts made by the early settlers in America, sometimes it was for decoration, as in the medieval banners and flags, and sometimes for protection or warmth, such as the early quilted fireman's coats of Japan or the quilted petticoats of the eighteenth century. The skills were used either separately or together in clothing, soft furnishings and decorative articles, each providing a challenging opportunity for inventive design linked with necessity and fulfilling an inherent need to make even the most humble article beautiful.*

*The pleasure of redesigning a fabric surface with colour, pattern and form holds a fascination still alive and very active today. The crafts of patchwork, quilting and appliqué appeal to needlewomen as a skill, to sewers as a means of using up their scraps, and to artists as a medium for expressing design. They unite people from all walks of life, training, and background. In the past women often joined together for companionship or for profit to quilt; today they join together to exchange ideas and techniques. It's a revival that's taking place not just in Great Britain and the United States, but in Australia, Norway, Holland, Russia, the Near and Far East, and even in Africa. Everywhere people are drawing on their own design traditions and expressing them in these craft media.*

*The most exciting aspect of this revival is the ease with which these crafts can be practised by everyone. They are all skills easy to master and the doors they open and the creativity they inspire are lovely to see.*

*I hope new doors are opened to each of you reading this book and that the pleasure of these crafts becomes yours.*

*Joen Zinni-Lask, 1984*

# *Patchwork*

*Patchwork, as the name suggests, is the craft of sewing patches or pieces of fabric together. In the days when cloth was expensive or difficult to obtain, needlewomen would save pieces of fabric from worn-out or damaged clothes and furnishings and join them together to make gaily coloured quilts. Frequently, the pieces were cut into different shapes and sewn together to create an amazing variety of patterns which were given intriguing names such as Log Cabin, Streak of Lightning, and Dresden Plate.*

*All you need to start this fascinating hobby is a selection of fabrics and templates. It is the arrangement of the patches which creates the pattern – the simplest square shape can be sub-divided into triangles which are then built up to make larger patterns, hexagonal patches can be pieced to form rosettes, and pieced triangles can be combined with strips to create a pleasing geometric design. Colour choice is vitally important too: a change in the colour mix can totally alter the appearance of a patchwork.*

*Use patchwork to make bedcovers, cushions, place mats or even pictures. Add a dramatic trim to a shirt or blouse. Make up a simple jacket with a quilted patchwork fabric. Patchwork addicts will tell you that this is a wonderful way for needleworkers of all standards to express their sense of colour and design.*

# Colourful creations from fabric scraps

***One of the main pleasures of patchwork is the satisfaction of using humble scraps and remnants to create unique and beautiful results. Combining colours and shapes is a real art, whether you choose the quiet and restful hand-sewing methods, or opt for the quick efficiency of your sewing machine.***

Down the ages, generations of busy seamstresses have pieced and patched with small neat stitches to make quilts which today are collector's items. The earliest patchwork was made from fragments of different fabrics pieced together in a random or 'crazy' design. The craft was born out of the need to make a strong or warm piece of fabric out of whatever came to hand – dressmaking leftovers or pieces of old clothes.

Patchwork became very popular in the early eighteenth century, particularly in America where quilts were often made up by groups of people working together. A young girl and her friends would often sew several patchwork quilts prior to her wedding. These quilts were made up in many patterns and vivid colours. The traditional designs are still popular today, and look every bit as fresh and individual.

The advent of the sewing machine in the mid-nineteenth century revolutionized the craft of patchwork, dramatically reducing the time spent on making up some of the larger and more complicated quilts. However, all forms of patchwork can also be done by hand.

## Traditional methods

The traditional English method of assembling patchwork is to join together many small fabric shapes into striking geometrical designs entirely by hand and sewing over paper patches cut from patterns called "templates". The American way is to hand-sew the various shapes into square units called 'pieced blocks'. A newcomer to patchwork can immediately begin a pretty cushion cover using one of the simple pieced block designs. For the initiated, keen to embark on a more ambitious project, these blocks can be built into a full-size patchwork quilt.

Your patchwork can be as large or as small as you like and range from table-mats and pin cushions to wedding quilts and wall-hangings. Whatever your choice, the secret of success lies above all in colour planning, choice of fabrics, and the accuracy of your pattern-cutting and sewing.

The pleasure of patchwork comes from its colours and patterns which create the attractive finished effect and make each piece a personal masterpiece, as you will see if you make up the pretty pram quilt cover opposite. Patchwork is a matter of colour, hue pattern, shape and texture. It is well worth taking time at the planning stage to achieve a well-balanced design.

## Patchwork materials

Patchwork is traditionally made from fabrics of the same weight, strength, and even age. Heavy patches pull lighter ones out of shape, while very old fabrics may show signs of wear before their neighbours in the design. Dressweight cottons are ideal – use them plain or printed. If you wish to use luxurious silks or velvets, make sure all your patches are compatible in weight and thickness. Keep a lookout for suitable fabrics and try swapping scraps with friends, although for larger pieces of work you may need to buy fabric. Wash and press new pieces of cotton fabric before starting the patchwork to make sure they will not shrink, nor the colours run.

Ideally you need three pairs of scissors for patchwork – a sharp pair for fabric, another for cutting paper patches, and some small embroidery scissors for snipping thread. Sharp steel pins and a thimble are important pieces of equipment as well.

The paper patches that are actually used in the patchwork are cut very carefully from patterns called templates. Many template shapes can be bought commercially but it is easy to make your own – see how in the next chapter.

## Colour planning patchwork

Take some squared graph paper or isometric paper (marked with triangles) depending on the shapes you plan to use. With coloured felt-tip pens or crayons, experiment with combinations of squares, triangles and other geometric shapes. The isometric paper is ideal for designs based on triangles or hexagons. Try

*Above: Patchwork can make cushions, quilts and other furnishings into focal points for any room.*

*Right: A rough sketch shows how, by altering the positions of key colours, you can dramatically alter the effect.*

out several versions – playing around with different dominant colours or light and dark tones of the same colour. You can mix plain and printed patches if you like. Consider adding a border or central medallion in toning or contrasting colours. When you are happy with the scheme, make a scaled-down plan of the whole design as a guide to work from.

# The tradition of patchwork

***Many of the beautiful patchwork quilts made in Victorian times and earlier were stitched together using hundreds of hexagons. This popular six-sided shape makes a decorative honeycomb effect and is a simple and satisfying introduction to English patchwork.***

*Typical English patchwork templates: hexagon, clamshell and diamond.*

Traditional English patchwork is made of patches which are very often all the same shape, such as clamshells, diamonds or hexagons. Each patch is made by covering a paper or card shape with a piece of fabric secured by tacking. The patches are joined by handsewing the edges and the papers are then removed.

## Pins, needles and thread

Fine white cotton thread is usually the best for preparing patches for English patchwork. Use fine matching thread for joining them. Sharps, betweens or crewels in sizes 8, 9 or 10 are the most suitable needles. Make sure your pins are small and slender to minimise the risk of marking the fabric.

## Templates

You can make your own templates. Two methods for hexagon templates are given below. The compass method is the more traditional, but if you can obtain isometric paper, the shape can be drawn more quickly.
You can buy metal or plastic templates in a limited range of sizes. These are long lasting and will not become worn at the corners.
Solid templates are often sold with a corresponding window template. This looks like a frame – an empty or transparent centre portion (actual finished size of patch) bordered by a strip measuring the same as the seam allowance. It is useful for cutting patches – especially on patterned fabric where you may be creating a decorative effect with the motifs, for instance, using the direction of stripes. The finished patch area can be seen through the window.

## Working with hexagons

Traditional hexagon designs such as Grandmother's Flower Garden which is based on rosette shapes make striking heirlooms. Random hexagons of every pattern and hue give a homely look.
Today's patchwork enthusiasts are no less fascinated by the many different effects possible with hexagons. They combine well with squares and triangles in many design variations.

## Making your own hexagonal templates

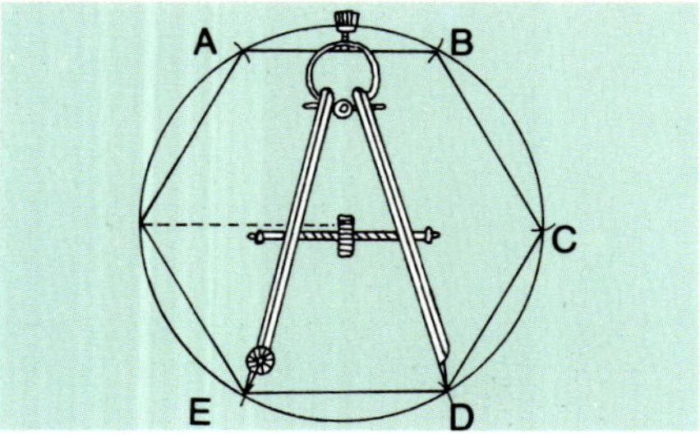

### Using a pair of compasses

You can draw hexagons of any size you like simply and accurately using a pair of compasses. Set the compass width to the measurement of one side of the hexagon, and draw a circle on to a stiff piece of card. Place the point of the compass anywhere along the circle and draw an arc to cut the circle at point A. With the compass point on A, draw another arc to cut the circle at B. Place the point on B and draw another arc. Continue in this way around the circle until you have six points which, when joined up, form a hexagon. Cut out with a craft knife.

### Using isometric paper

On isometric paper (marked out in triangles), draw the outline of the required size of hexagon using a ruler. Stick the isometric paper on to a piece of stiff card and cut out the shape using a craft knife and a metal ruler if you have one.
To make a window template, mark two outlines on the paper, one inside the other, 6mm/¼in (or whatever the seam allowance) apart. Carefully cut out the centre hexagonal portion with the craft knife to leave a frame. The window template is invaluable for cutting fabric patches which include the seam allowance.

## Making papers

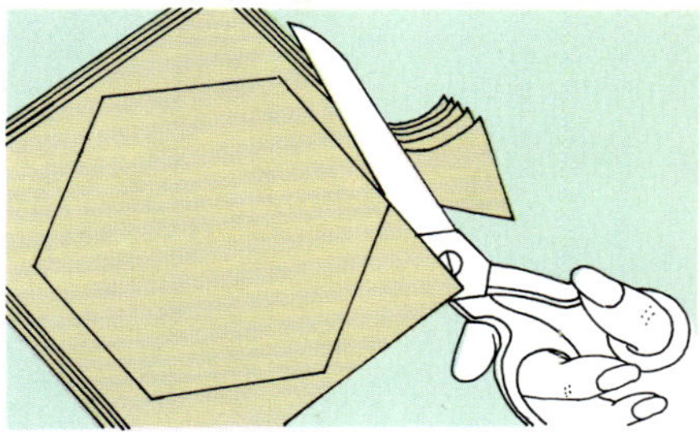

The next step is to use the template for cutting the papers which go into the patches. Use firm paper such as cartridge or writing paper, magazine covers or thin card. Many people use old greetings cards. The choice will depend on the strength of the fabrics. Be very careful to cut accurately – an uneven patch will cause the work to pull out of shape. Lay the template on the paper and draw round it with a hard, sharp pencil. Cut along the pencil lines and check that all the papers are exactly the same. By folding the paper, it is possible to cut several patches at a time.

## Making patches

If you have a window template, hold this against the piece of fabric and cut round the edge, or use it to mark a cutting line. It will help you to get the seam allowance accurate. Otherwise, pin the papers to the wrong side of the fabric, leaving space for turnings, and cut out. Have two sides of the shape on the straight grain unless a particular pattern effect is desired. Pin two opposite sides of the fabric over the paper with fine pins. Fold the seam allowance over the paper all round and tack in place through the paper, catching the folds well down on

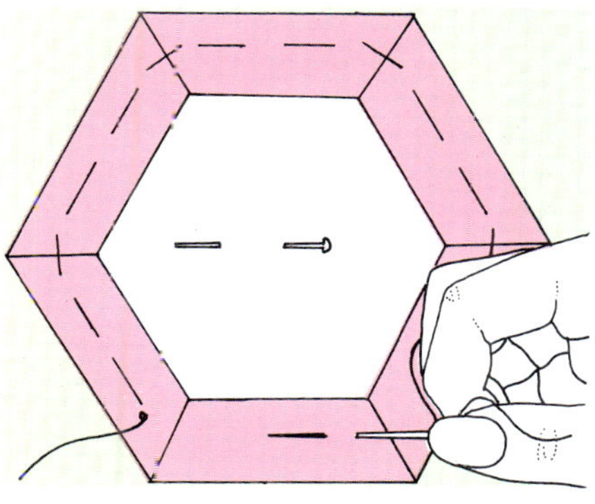

each corner. Press prepared shapes before joining to give crisp edges. Hexagons have wide-angled corners which are easy to work with.

*Above: This beautiful bright bed cover is made up entirely of 2.5cm/1in hexagons. A patchwork like this brings a child's bedroom alive. Red, yellow, blue and multi-coloured patches are assembled in diamond shapes, joined with plain green hexagons and bordered in green. Use scraps left over from a little girl's dresses to make her a cover full of memories. Shortcut idea: Make up some diamond or rosette shapes in plain or printed hexagons and appliqué them on to a plain background for a patchwork effect.*

# *Plump patchwork cushions*

*These pincushions are made up in co-ordinating cotton fabrics – plains and tiny prints are best.*

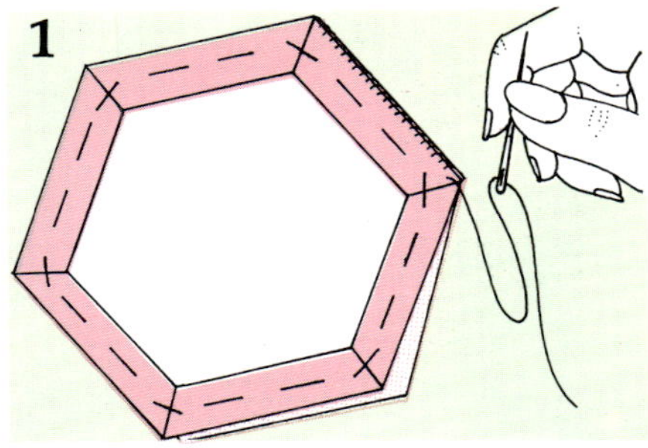



## Rosette pincushion

This slightly smaller pincushion is formed of two rosettes joined around the edges. The centres of each rosette should contrast well with the surrounding patches. It is helpful to make a small diagram of the colour scheme before you start.

The finished diameter of the pincushion is about 12.5cm/5in.

**You will need**
For this pincushion and the rounded pincushion (far right)
Hexagon template, 2.5cm/1in sides
Plain and printed cotton fabric scraps (similar weight)
Scrap of narrow ribbon for rosette pincushion (optional)
Kapok or polyester fibre stuffing
Thin card or stiff paper

**Preparing the rosettes** Using the template, cut 14 hexagons from the card or paper. Make up the 14 patches – seven for each rosette as described.

**1** Take the centre patch and one other. Hold them right sides together and join with tiny overcasting stitches, trying not to catch in the paper. Strengthen each corner with two or three extra stitches.

## Rosette appliqué cushion cover

This quick and simple cushion cover consists of a double rosette in hexagons appliquéd to a plain backing. It fits a 45cm/18in square cushion pad. Suitable fabrics for this and the striped cushion (left) are polyester satin, acetate taffeta or dress lining material – back this with iron-on interfacing if it is very flimsy and note fine fabrics technique below.

**You will need for either cushion**
Hexagon template (4cm/1½in sides)
50cm/½yd fabric (90cm/36in wide) in main colour (used for backing)
20cm/¼yd each of three contrast colours (five for striped cushion)
Matching polyester sewing threads
Thin card or stiff paper

**Making the double rosette** Cut 19 hexagons with 4cm/1½in sides from the card or paper.

Cut out the fabric hexagons with a 1cm/½in seam allowance in colours as follows: 1 cream centre patch, 6 pink inner petals, 12 turquoise outer petals. Make up the patches. When sewing with fine, silky fabrics, use masking tape to

*Left: Plain hexagons in toning colours create a dramatic effect.*

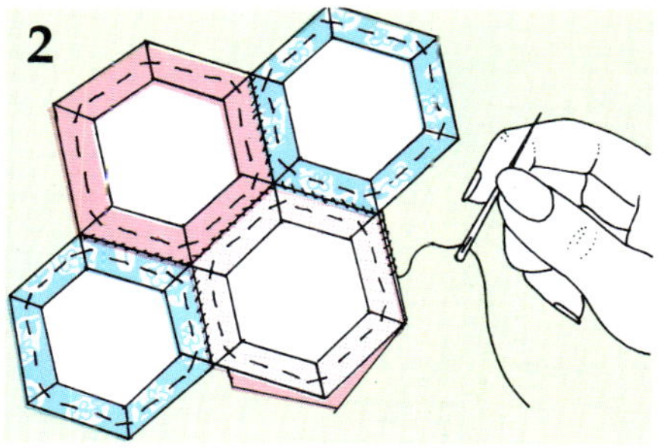


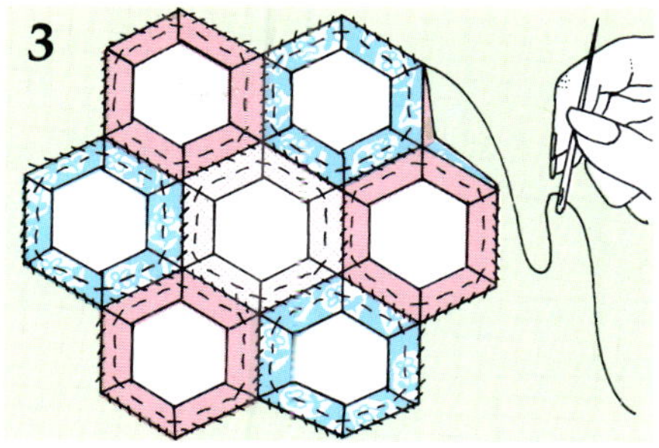


**2** Take a third hexagon and join to the centre hexagon along one edge; join to the other hexagon.
Add the remaining 'petals' in the same way, making sure you have them in the correct order if they are in different fabrics. Make an identical rosette for the other side of the pincushion.
**3** To join the completed rosettes, place them right sides together, and join them round the edge with tiny overcasting stitches, leaving two adjoining edges of the last two petals open for inserting stuffing. If desired, attach a loop of narrow ribbon to the outer edge of one of the petals so that it lies between the two rosettes on the inside, raw ends flush with hexagon edges.
**Finishing off** Remove tacking and papers from all the hexagons. The papers can be used again if the corners are still sharp.
Tack the turnings of the last two petal edges in place, and turn the pincushion right sides out.
Stuff tightly with kapok or polyester fibre, packing it well into all the corners. Sew up the opening neatly on the outside with small stitches and remove the tacking.

## Rounded pincushion

This larger pincushion needs 20 hexagons and six squares, all with 2.5cm/1in sides. There is an extra row of shapes in a new contrast fabric around the centre.
Make two rosettes with contrast centres as for rosette pincushion.
Leaving the papers in, take one of the rosettes and attach six squares and six hexagons to the outer edges of the 'petals' as shown. (Join the shapes with right sides together.)
With right sides together, join on the second rosette, remembering to leave an opening for the stuffing.
Finish off as for rosette pincushion.

stick seam allowances to back of papers to avoid marking the fabric.
Beginning at the centre, join the hexagons into a double rosette.
Remove papers from centre and inner petals. Press carefully on the wrong side using a cloth. Remove papers from outer petals.
**Assembling the cover front** Cut two 45cm/18in squares from blue fabric for the front and back of the cover.
Position the made-up double rosette in the centre of one of the 45cm/18in squares. Pin in place and secure with neat slipstitches round the outer edge.
**Making up the cover** With right sides together, join the back and front with a 1cm/½in seam, leaving a 30cm/12in opening along one edge.
Trim seam (trim corners diagonally) and overcast to prevent fraying.
Neaten raw edges of opening.
Turn to right side, push out corners and insert cushion pad. Sew up the opening with neat slipstitches.

## DESIGN EXTRA

### Hexagon patterns

Sketch your hexagon design ideas on isometric paper. The top two patterns are those you need for the pair of cushions (far left).

**Diagonal-stripe cushion**
The cover front is made up of 56 hexagons (4cm/1½in sides) joined to form the pattern above; you need about 30 papers. To finish, press patchwork carefully on the wrong side.
Press seam allowances out flat on outside hexagons before tacking back of cushion centrally in place, trimming patchwork and seaming.

# Pieced patchwork quilts

***In days gone by, making a beautiful patchwork quilt entailed hours of painstaking hand stitching. Now you can use your sewing machine to join together the square patches to form strips, then quickly seam the strips to make a covetable square or rectangular quilt.***

A pieced quilt is one made of fabric patches seamed by hand or machine. No paper patches are involved. Individual fabric patches are either assembled into square design units, which are joined together as pattern repeats, or else they form a single design covering the quilt area.

Square patches joined randomly can also look effective, especially if several muted-tone patches are interspersed with the odd flash of bright colour such as red or orange.

## Planning the design

Decide on the size of the finished quilt before designing the pattern. Adapting a design may be just a question of altering the size of the patches. You will find that square patches lend themselves to all kinds of striking geometric designs, particularly those which use light and dark shades to create an effect. This type of design has always been popular with the Amish people (a religious sect in Pennsylvania) whose characteristic use of very bright colours with muted ones, sewn in bold geometric patterns, always results in spectacular quilts. One of their favourite designs is *Sunshine and shadow* – sometimes known as *Trip around the world*. The quilt shown overleaf for you to make is a simplified version of *Sunshine and shadow*, which traditionally is made up in at least seven plain, brightly coloured cotton or wool fabrics. The overall design fills a square shape and has the square patches set in a pattern of concentric diamonds.

Another traditional Amish design is *Streak of lightning*. It is always made up in two plain colours – a bright one and a dark contrast – to create a vivid design of diagonal zigzags. This is an all-over design, which you can easily adapt to any size or shape.

Having decided on your design, make a scale drawing with coloured felt-tips on graph (squared) paper and calculate the size the finished squares should be. Colour in the design of the whole quilt – this gives you a good basis on which to calculate the amounts of fabric you need. Square or rectangular shapes are both easy to plan, but if you wish to enlarge or reduce a design, make sure you do it evenly – adding or subtracting the same number of squares from each edge. You can add a plain border of any width you like, to provide a frame for the design, and to cut down on the area of patchwork you need to make up. Or pick out two or three of the colours in the patchwork and plan a striped border. (You can make this by joining strips of the appropriate fabrics.)

## How to estimate fabric

Use cotton or light woollen fabric, plain or patterned. Several firms supply ready-cut cotton squares, up to 12cm/4¾in square, in packs of contrasting colours. To make a rough estimate of the amount of fabric needed for a quilt, divide the area of the finished quilt by the number of colours you plan to use, and add extra for seams. If you use 10cm/4in squares, for example, cut them with 12cm/4¾in sides.

Once you have a scale plan of the design, count up the squares in each colour, then calculate how many squares will fit across one width of the fabric to make an accurate estimate of the fabric requirements.

For example, twelve 9cm/3½in squares fit across 115cm/45in fabric, but only ten across 90cm/36in fabric.

*Left: Joining the squares into strips first makes the patchwork easier to do and helps you form the pattern correctly.*

# Assembling patchwork

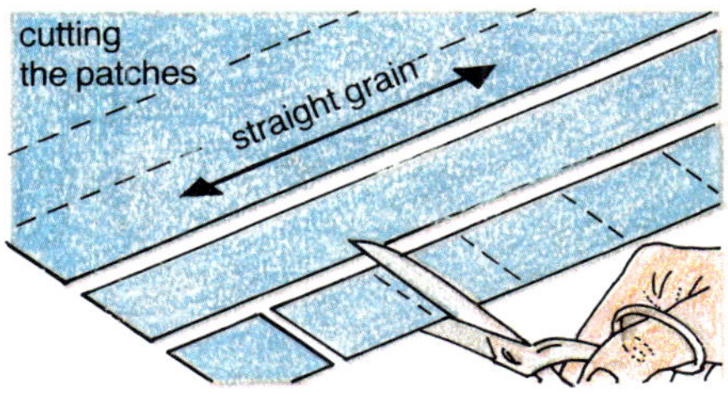


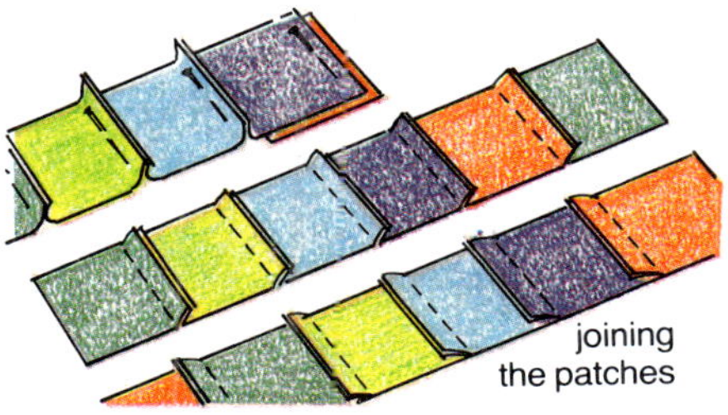

## Cutting the patches

It is important that you cut your patches absolutely accurately. For squares smaller than 4cm/1½in, add 6mm/¼in seam allowances, otherwise add 1cm/½in seam allowances. Cut (or tear) the fabric lengthwise along the straight grain to make strips of the required width, which you then cut into squares.

If you intend to join the patches by hand, or if your machine footplate does not have a 1cm/½in mark, then it is best to mark the cutting lines and seamlines of the squares on to the wrong side of the fabric with a sharp pencil. Make a square window template to mark both the cutting line and the seamline.

## Joining the patches

To avoid confusion, lay out the squares in the correct pattern on a large flat area. At this stage you may decide to make some minor changes to the design. Keep the squares on the flat surface until they are safely sewn.

Pin each square to its neighbour to form widthwise rows, matching raw edges and pencil seamlines if marked. Make sure you join them in the correct order and the right way up for one-way designs.

When a complete strip has been pinned, machine along the seamlines, using the 1cm/½in mark on the machine footplate. Press all the seams in the same direction with a hot iron. This makes the finished work stronger.

Now pin the next strip and machine in the same way. Press the seams in the opposite direction to those on the first strip. Pressing in alternate directions lessens the bulk where the seams meet.

## Joining the strips

Once all the squares have been joined into strips in the correct order, join the strips along long edges, beginning at the top of the quilt and working downwards. Be careful to join the strips accurately so that the corners of the squares meet neatly. Press all horizontal seams in the same direction.

# Traditional designs and borders

A scheme is shown below for a square quilt made up in the *Streak of lightning* pattern. It makes a stunning wall-hanging. Add a plain border made up of four strips of fabric – two long and two shorter, as shown.

The pattern on the right shows how squares and rectangles of different sizes can be used to make a colourful and effective border, creating a large pieced quilt around a smaller piece of patchworked squares.

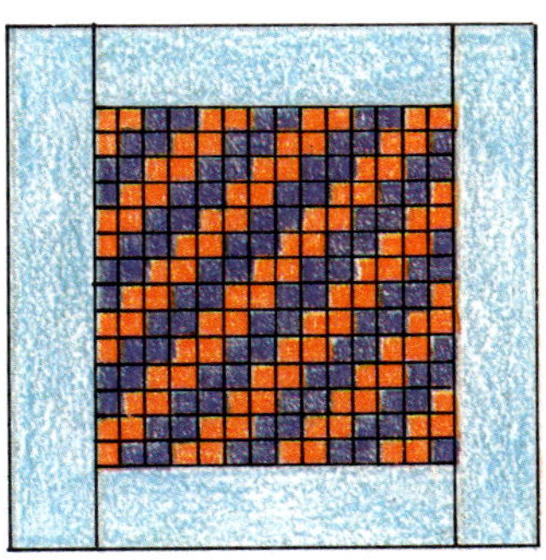

*Above and right: Quilt designs made from squares, showing two different methods of dealing with the border.*

# Elegant quilt in machined squares

A patchwork quilt in a bedroom is an inspiring finishing touch to the rest of the furnishings. Make one that incorporates curtain and cushion fabrics, or the colours of the carpet. The pattern of squares used here is created with four printed fabrics and one plain.

Amounts are given here for both standard single and double quilt sizes. If you want to adjust the basic plan, remember that this design must have an odd number of squares both ways. First measure the bed, deciding on the drop you want, and measuring the length and width of the area on top of the bed. Then work out the design, based on 10cm/4in finished squares.

To add extra warmth and body, and to make the cover reversible, you can invest in some pre-quilted fabric for the lining.

*Below: Brown and white is refreshing, but you could choose any colour scheme – make a scaled-down colour plan first.*

**You will need**
**For a single quilt** 170cm×250cm/67in×98in:
1.10m/1¼yd each of five different cotton fabrics, 120cm/48in wide
*or* 1.60m/1¾yd each of five 90cm/36in wide fabrics
Matching sewing cotton
5.10m/5⅝yd lining fabric (any width) or pre-quilted fabric
1 sheet graph (squared) paper
**For a double quilt** 250cm×250cm/99in×99in:
1.50m/1⅝yd each of five different cotton fabrics, 120cm/48in wide
*or* 2.30m/2½yd each of five 90cm/36in wide fabrics
7.60m/8⅜yd lining fabric (any width) or pre-quilted fabric
Matching sewing cotton
1 sheet graph (squared) paper

## Making up the patchwork

First choose your fabrics and colour scheme, then make a scaled plan on the graph paper with the help of the chart. Planning and measuring will be easy if you make each square on the plan represent 10cm/4in.
Alternate the diagonal rows of dark, light and plain patches to create the prettiest effect.
Cut the patches as described on page 15, remembering to allow for the seams. Join the patches in strips, beginning with the top horizontal row of the plan and working downwards.

## Finishing a quilt

Consider whether you would like to add a border to the patchwork, or whether it is already the right size.
**Adding a border** Join strips of plain or patterned fabric to each edge of the patchwork with right sides together, pressing seams towards the border. Many traditional quilts have large squares and rectangles in contrasting colours incorporated in their borders, which help to set off the finished patchwork.
**Lining a quilt** Back the quilt with plain, patterned, or ready quilted fabric for extra weight and warmth. You will probably have to join two or more widths of lining fabric.
Lay the patchwork on the lining, wrong sides together, and turn in both raw edges 1cm/½in. Tack, and machine round close to the edge. This is the traditional English method of finishing a quilt.

## Chart for double and single quilts

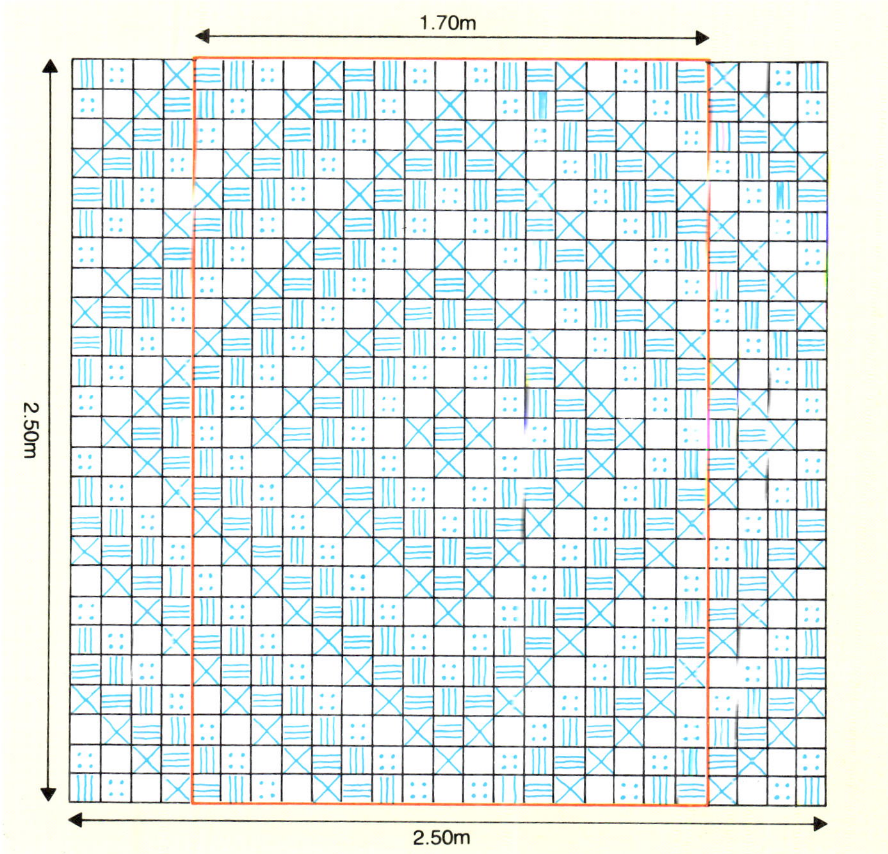


### Working from the chart

Use the chart for the single and double version of the patchwork quilt. The single version is outlined in red. The five fabrics are denoted by different symbols on the chart. Cut patches 12cm/5in square to give 10cm/4in finished squares, and count the number you need in each fabric from the chart.

## Quick mitred corners

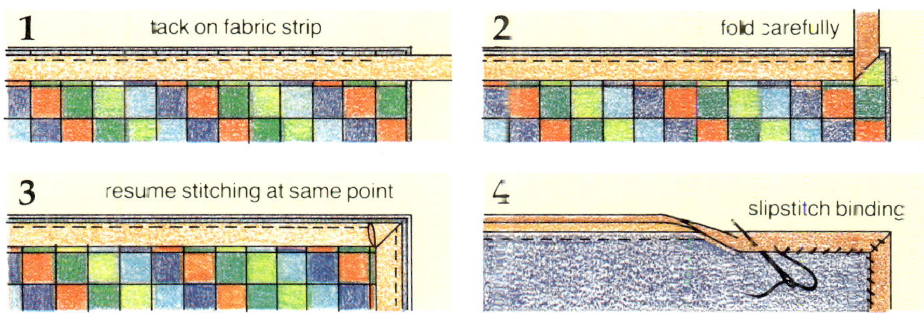


**1** To make a bound edge with neat mitred corners, cut a strip of plain fabric 7cm/2¾in wide and a little longer than the quilt's perimeter. Tack this round the edge, right sides together, raw edges of strip, patchwork and lining matching.
**2** When you reach a corner (1cm/½in from two edges), stop sewing and fold fabric strip diagonally up, and down again so that top fold lies flush with raw edges of strip and quilt. Now the continuation of the strip is parallel with next quilt edge.
**3** Resume stitching at exactly the same point on the other side of the fold. Repeat at each corner.
**4** Remove tacking and turn strip round to wrong side. Turn raw edge of strip over and slipstitch neatly in place, pushing corner folds to inside and slipstitching the diagonal corner openings on both front and back of quilt.

# *Stick-and-stitch pram quilt*

Modern materials and methods have revolutionized patchwork. To achieve an effect quickly, you can now assemble patches directly on to iron-on Vilene – a light and versatile fabric normally sold for interfacing in dressmaking. One side of the Vilene will bond with another fabric when the two layers are pressed with a hot iron.

By arranging fabric patches in a patchwork design on Vilene, pressing, and oversewing the joins with a zigzag machine stitch, you can make beautiful 'patchwork' much more quickly than by traditional methods.

If you need to put any shapes on to larger ones, you can fix them in place using small pieces of Vilene Wundaweb – a light adhesive tape which bonds two layers of fabrics together when pressed.

Experiment with the stick and stitch technique by making up this pretty cover for a standard pram quilt. The cover is shown here in pink, blue and white, but you could adapt the design to any colour combination you choose using your colour planning know-how.

The shade of the thread you choose for the machine stitching will make quite a difference to the overall colour effect of the finished article. The patches in the photograph are oversewn in blue thread to tone with the border.

You can use the stick-and-stitch method for making cushion covers, tablecloths, wall hangings – anything where you want a patchwork effect in next to no time. The addition of the Vilene adds body and keeps the patchwork looking crisp and smart.

## You will need

For a quilt cover 50×58cm/20×23in:

Cotton fabric colour A 60×120cm/24×48in (Cut 52×60cm/20×24in for back of cover.)

30cm/12in colour B (Cut 2 pieces 30×60cm/12×24in – one for patches and one for the border strips.)

20cm/8in colour C

10cm/4in colour D

1m/1yd lightest iron-on Vilene (Light Supershape) width 84cm/33in. (Cut 2 pieces – one 40×48cm/16×19in and one 50×58cm/20×23in.)

3 standard reels polyester thread in chosen colour for oversewing

Card, 8×16cm/3×6in (not too stiff)

1 pack Vilene Wundaweb *or* tacking thread

Sewing machine (zigzag function)

2 plastic press studs *or* 25cm/10in piece white Velcro

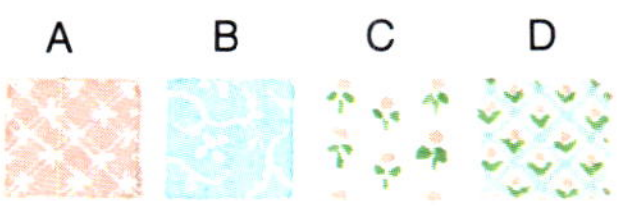


*Above: Use this colour code to position the patchwork pieces as in the diagram, or choose a colour scheme from the suggestions above right.*

*Left: This charming pram quilt covered in quick Vilene stick-and-stitch patchwork will keep baby snug in his pram. It is shown here made up in the following Laura Ashley furnishing cottons:*
*A: L571 white/rose*
*B: R143 white/sky blue*
*C: P767 rose/moss/white*
*D: P754 sky blue/ multi/white*

## Preparing the patchwork pieces

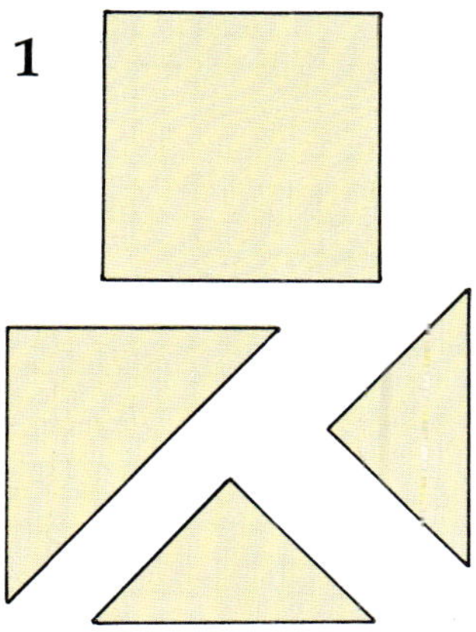


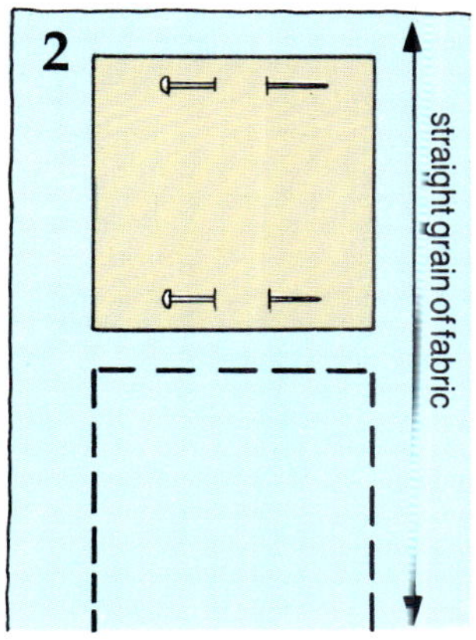


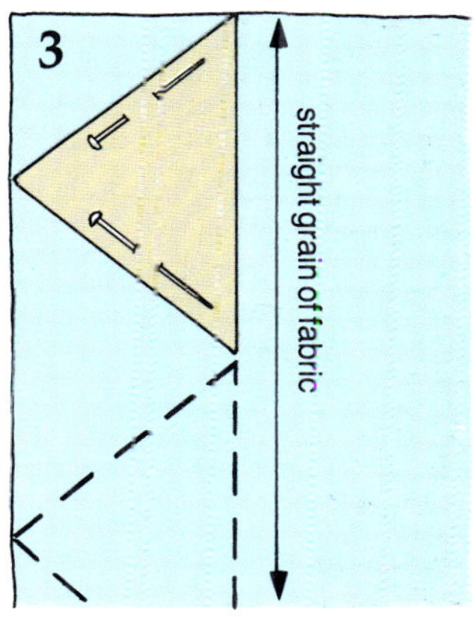


**1 Making the templates**
Cut 2 squares 8cm×8cm/ 3in×3in from card. Cut one of these in half diagonally to form 2 triangles, and cut one of these triangles in half again to make 2 smaller triangles. These form the templates from which you cut the fabric pieces.

**2 Squares (30 in all)**
Pin the square template on to colour A, making sure that two of the edges are parallel with the straight grain of the fabric. Cut round the card, allowing 1mm extra all round for a tiny overlap. Remove the card and repeat until you have 8 squares in colour A. Cut out 16 squares in colour C, and 6 squares in colour B.

**3 Triangles (22 in all)**
Pin the large triangle on to colour C, making sure one of the sides lies along the straight grain of the fabric, and cut round it. This time leave no extra allowance. If it suits the design of your fabric, you may prefer to place the longest side of the triangle so it runs across the straight grain.
Remove the card and repeat with each shape facing the same way, until you have 4 large triangles. Cut 18 small triangles from colour D in the same way.

## Assembling the patches

**Positioning the squares** Pin squares on to Vilene 40×48cm/16×19in (adhesive side up), arranging them to form the pattern as on the chart on page 19. If you find this tricky, use a ruler and tailor's chalk or a pencil to mark the shapes on the Vilene. Use only one pin per piece, placing it in the centre. Overlap the patches by 1mm at the edges to make neat joins and prevent gaps.

**Bonding the fabrics** With a warm iron (set for wool/rayon), press lightly on the fabric side over a damp cloth to bond the fabric and Vilene together. Remove pins and press again firmly on the Vilene side with a hot iron (set for cotton). Now position all the triangles as in the diagram. Lightly fix in position using small pieces of Wundaweb between the two layers of fabric and pressed with a hot iron. Alternatively, pin in place and tack around the edges.

**Joining the pieces** Programme your sewing machine to close zigzag for a satin stitch effect (stitch width 3mm/⅛in). Test this on a scrap of fabric first to check that it will cover the seams nicely without being too dense and bulky. Machine along the joins with polyester thread.
Sew along all the long straight seams first, in the same direction each time. Now sew all the crosswise ones, also in the same direction. Next sew the long diagonal sides of the large triangles and finally the short sides of the small triangles. (These can be sewn in a continuous line.) Keep the fabric taut as you sew but do not stretch the patches.

*Right: Zigzag stitch gives a neat finish.*

## Adding the border

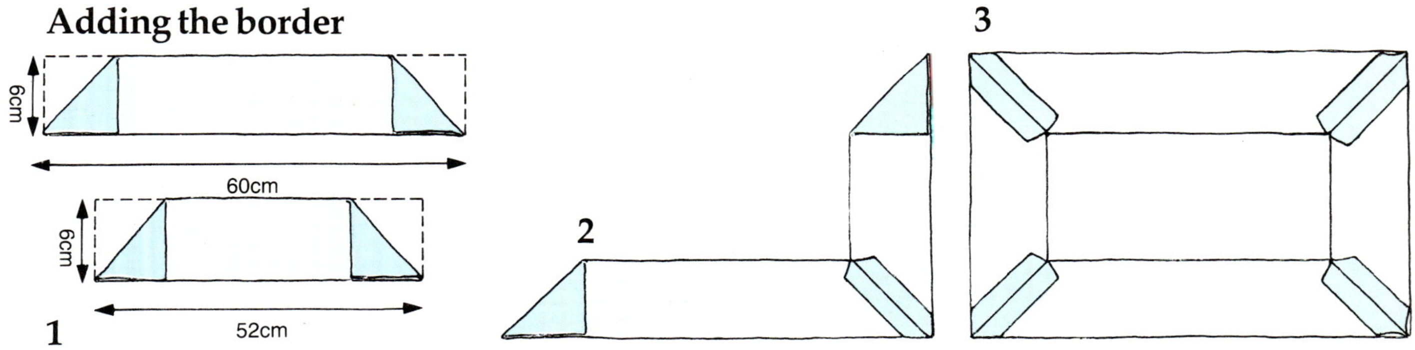


**1** Cut two strips of fabric B 6cm×52cm/2¼in×21in, and two strips 6cm×60cm/2¼in×24in. At each end of each strip, fold the corners on one side to the opposite edge as shown, forming a diagonal fold. Press flat. The resulting fold lines will be the seamlines for joining the pieces together.
**2** Pin one of the short strips to one of the long strips along the seamline fold with right sides together. Tack the seam and sew along it so that the two pieces form an L-shape. Trim seam allowance to 1.5cm/⅝in and press the seam flat. This diagonally seamed corner is called a 'mitred corner'.
**3** Join the other two pieces in the same way and join the two L-shapes to form an oblong frame.
Lay the made-up patchwork section on to the centre of the other piece of Vilene (50×58cm/20×23in) leaving a 5cm/2in border. Vilene should be placed adhesive side up.
Then lay your border 'frame' in place. It should just overlap the patchwork by 1–2mm/⅛in. Press to secure. Then sew all round the inner edge of the border with zigzag stitch using the machine as before.

## Backing the cover

Take the piece of backing fabric A. Place it on the front of the quilt cover with right sides together. Sew around edge with a 1cm/½in seam allowance. Leave a 25cm/10in opening in the centre of one of the shorter sides. Trim the corners diagonally and neaten the raw edges with zigzag stitch.
Turn through to right side and press seams carefully, gently pushing out the corners with a closed pair of scissors. Neaten the raw edges of the opening and close with two medium size plastic press-studs (see diagram right) or pieces of Velcro sewn along the opening edges.

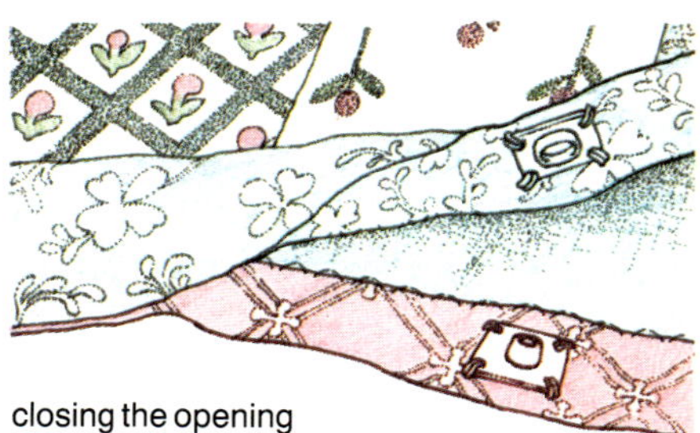

closing the opening
with plastic press studs

# Geometric wallhanging from simple pieced blocks

***Many patchworks are made up from units called pieced blocks – usually identical squares of patchwork. When they are joined together, the most beautiful geometric patterns appear, suitable for quilts, cushions or wallhangings such as the one featured here.***

One of the most rewarding aspects of patchwork is that you can 'paint' a geometric masterpiece in fabric squares, even if you've never painted a picture in your life. Even the most simple of shapes can be combined to make conversation pieces.

Sometimes pieced blocks are made up by hand from patches tacked over papers. Sometimes the patches are seamed together by hand or machined without using papers. (The advantage of pieced blocks is that they do not use cornered seams, so papers are not essential.)

The simple blocks in the wallhanging shown below are made up from two basic shapes – a triangle and a series of strips of equal width which are joined by machine. They could also be sewn by hand, without papers, using running stitch.

The square pieced blocks can be treated like regular square patches – joined into long horizontal strips, then seamed together along their length.

## Choosing colours

Colour plays an important part, as always in patchwork – particularly when you are working with strips. The way each strip interacts with the one next to it can make a big difference to the look of the finished work. For predominant colours and wide borders, it is a good idea to choose a muted colour – black, grey or beige, for instance – which will not fight brighter shades such as the vivid diagonal stripes in the design shown below.

*Below: Traditional American patchwork designs can have a contemporary look*

# *Striking geometric wallhanging*

This wallhanging in a dramatic colour combination looks contemporary but in fact, it is based on a traditional *Amish* design called Roman stripes, with its typical combination of bright and muted colours in plain cotton fabrics. The hanging is machine pieced and hand quilted and measures 83cm/32¾in square but you could make it whatever size you like by planning the design on graph paper and marking the measurements of squares and border.

### You will need

1.30m/1⅜yd firm cotton fabric in black (A)
1.30m/1⅜yd in purple (E)
0.50m/½yd in red (B)
0.50m/½yd in deep pink (C)
0.50m/½yd in pale pink (D)
0.50m/½yd in mid brown (F)
0.30m/⅜yd in light brown (G)
1m/1yd black cotton lawn for lining
Note: all fabric requirements are based on 90cm/36in-wide fabric
1 large reel Sylko 40 thread (black)
Card *or* thin plastic sheet

**For the quilting**

0.90m/1yd polyester wadding (1oz or 2oz weight)
1 ball DMC pearl cotton size 12 (black) if hand quilting
1 reel black poly cotton thread if machine quilting
Betweens needles size 7
Tailor's chalk or pale crayon

### Making the templates

You need one right-angled triangle with two 12cm/4¾in sides, and one strip 1.5cm/⅝in wide and 19cm/7½in long for cutting the coloured stripes. To obtain the triangle shape, either use a set-square, or graph paper, draw two 12cm/4¾in lines at right angles and join.
Cut out the shapes from card, or thin plastic sheet, using a craft knife. Some patchwork specialist suppliers stock transparent plastic sheets with a square grid marked on them, specially for making templates.

### Preparing the patches

Wash and press the cotton fabrics to remove any excess dye or finishing. Mark the triangle and stripe shapes on the wrong side of the fabrics by drawing round the templates with a soft lead pencil. This pencil line will be the seamline. Allow for a generous seam of 1.5cm/⅝in (to be trimmed later) all round each shape – do not cut along the pencil lines.
Draw the triangles with one of the 12cm/4¾in sides on the straight grain, and draw the stripes running diagonally across the grain. The finished piece will then hang straight.
**Following the cutting layout** for the black fabric (A), draw two border strips 85cm×7cm/33½in×2¾in, two 75cm×7cm/29½in×2¾in and 25 triangles. Again, allow generous 1.5cm/⅝in seams.

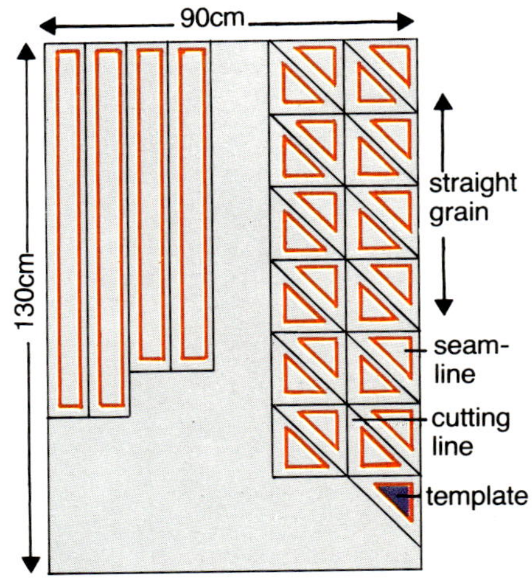


## Assembling the wallhanging

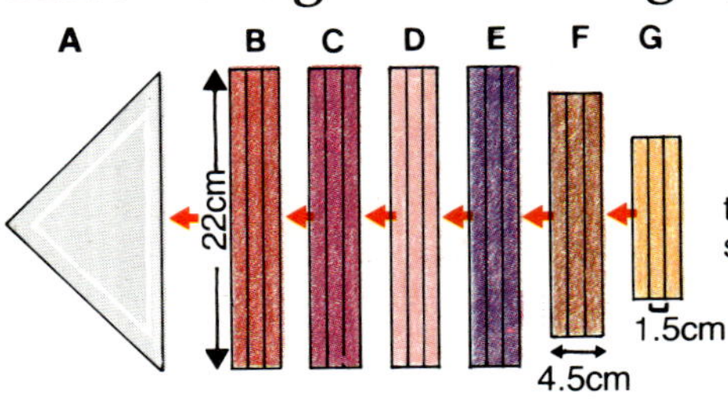


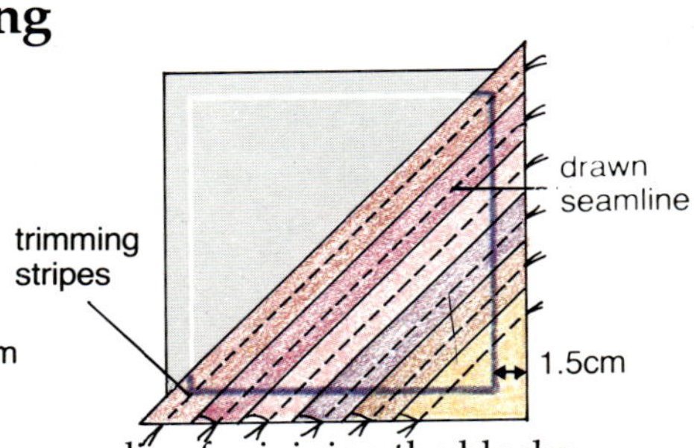


The wallhanging is made up of 25 identical square pieced blocks joined together in a square surrounded by a double border and edged with binding. To make up each block use a straight machine stitch. Pin the black triangle A to stripe B matching marked seam lines and seam, taking care not to stretch the stripes. Join B to C, C to D, D to E, E to F and F to G, as shown. Trim seams to about 8mm/⅜in and press each towards black triangle. Using the triangular template as a guide, draw another triangle on the wrong side of the sewn pieced stripes to complete the square block. This pencil line is the seamline for joining the blocks. Trim stripe edges of block to within 1.5cm/⅝in of pencil line. Assemble 24 more blocks in this way.

### Making up the panel

Machine five blocks together to form a strip, making sure that all the coloured stripes are lying in the same direction. Press all the seams towards the black triangles. Make four identical strips of five blocks each. Join all the strips together along the long edges, to make a large square. Be careful to align the corners accurately – uneven joins will affect the straightness of the diagonal lines. Trim seams and press towards black triangles. Press the entire panel well, unpicking and adjusting any points that do not meet properly.

making up the panel

### Adding the borders

Join the two shorter purple side border strips (fabric E) to the sides of the patchwork along marked seamlines. Trim seams and press outwards.
Now attach the longer top and bottom border strips along marked seamlines. Again, trim seams and press outwards. Repeat with the

Next, mark and cut the purple pieces (E) – see cutting layout. This fabric is used for the thinner border strips and for binding the finished work, as well as for one of the stripes.

Draw four border strips – two 70cm×3cm/27½in×1¼in and two 65cm×3cm/25½in×1¼in (add seam allowances). Mark the binding strips – 12cm/4¾in wide. You will need about 3.50m/3¾yd in length, so cut two strips the full length of the fabric and a third strip 1m/40in long. Cut the ends diagonally for mitred seams. Now mark 25 stripes, across the grain of the fabric in this and each of the other five colours. Make the stripes longer than you need – they can be trimmed to the required size. Obviously the red and pink ones need to be slightly longer than the brown and purple ones. Leave 3cm/1¼in between the marked seamlines (for two seam allowances). Cut out all the pieces.

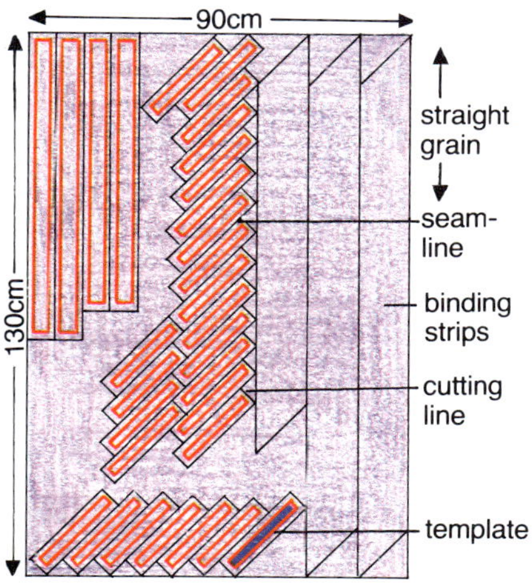


guide to quilting lines

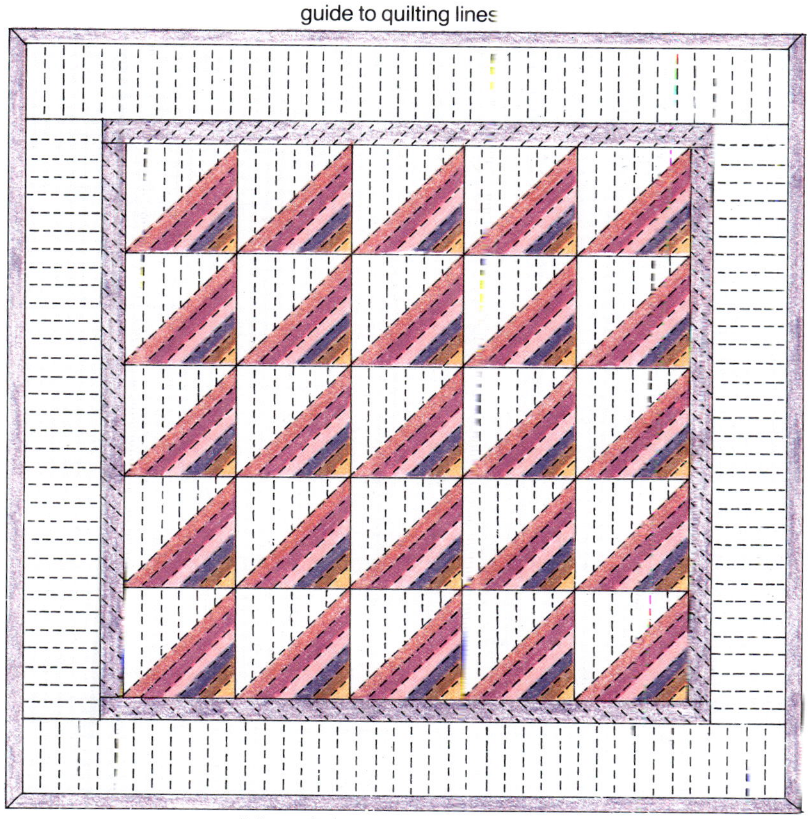

quilting stitches

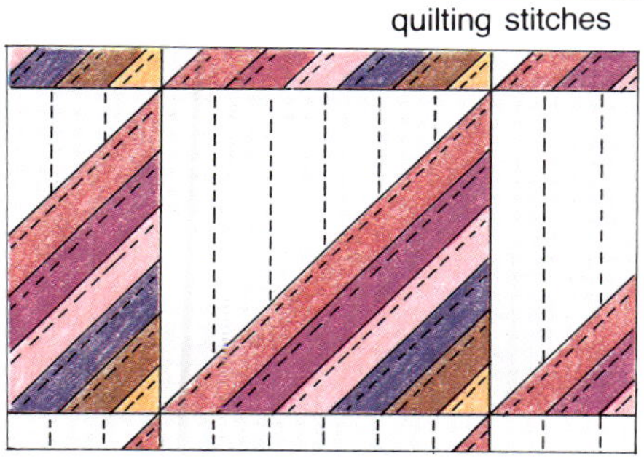

four black border strips, joining the two shorter ones to the sides, and finally adding the two longer ones to the top and bottom edges. The pieced top is now complete. Press it well on both sides.

## Quilting the hanging

Cut the lining and wadding slightly larger than the pieced top. Tack the three layers together, beginning at the centre and working outwards, smoothing out the wrinkles as you go. The quilting can be worked by hand (using black pearl cotton thread) or by machine (using black poly cotton thread).

**By hand** Mount the tacked layers on a frame if you have one, otherwise support the work on your lap. Run the lengths of pearl cotton through a block of beeswax for extra strength.

The lines of quilting which follow each stripe should run very close to the seams on the stripes – about 2mm/⅛in away on the lower (non-seam allowance side). On the black triangles, the quilting lines should run in five equally spaced vertical lines (2cm/¾in apart).

Mark the quilting lines on the black fabric with a ruler and tailor's chalk pencil or a pale crayon. The lines on the coloured stripes can be easily judged without marking. On the purple border, the quilting lines run diagonally and are 2cm/¾in apart. On the black border, the lines run straight – vertically at the top and bottom, horizontally at the sides. Remove the work from the frame and brush off quilting marks. Remove all tacking stitches. Trim lining and wadding flush with the patchwork top.

**By machine** Position the lines of quilting as described for the handstitched method. Set the machine to a medium straight stitch, and begin quilting in the middle of the work. When the quilting is complete, work any loose thread ends in to the back of the work with a needle.

## Binding the edges

Join purple binding strips with diagonal seams to obtain a long strip slightly longer than the perimeter (length all round) of the quilt. Fold the strip in half lengthwise so that its width is 6cm/2¼in, and press. Stitch binding to right side of quilt with raw edges matching, and allowing a 1.5cm/⅝in seam. Mitre the corners (see Quick mitred corners, page 17), and slipstitch folded edge in place on the back.

**To hang** Attach two small rings, or fabric tabs to the back of the quilt through which you can insert a piece of dowel for hanging.

# Dresden Plate: a patchwork pattern in a circle

***This old American patchwork design is so called because the circular motifs worked in floral prints remind one of china plates. One motif pieced and quilted makes a striking place mat while several motifs backed on squares make a traditional quilt.***

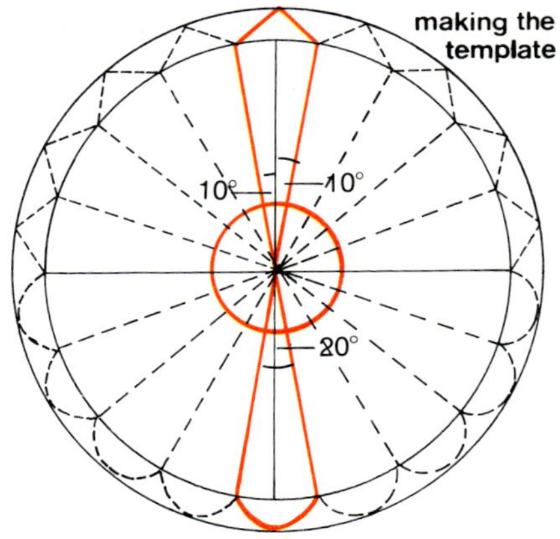


This American pattern is a combination of pieced patchwork and appliqué and was particularly popular in the 1930s. It derives from an older pattern called Friendship Ring, so named because people used to exchange bits of fabric to make up their designs.
The circular Dresden Plate motif can be divided into as many petals (segments) as you like. The petal tips can be rounded or pointed and the ends are covered by a central circle of fabric which is stitched on last. Any number of different patterns can be used within the motif – tiny patterned prints are most effective – and the central circle is sometimes cut from a plain fabric for contrast. The petals can be stitched by hand or machine and traditionally the flower shapes are then appliquéd by hand on to squares of backing fabric to form blocks which can be made up into a quilt.

**Making your own template**
Dresden Plate templates are available from craft shops but only in a limited number of sizes.
To cut your own accurate templates first decide on the size of the circle you want. If you are making a quilt you should also consider the size of the square blocks you plan to use.
Take a piece of strong card and draw a circle to the required size using compasses and a hard, sharp pencil. With the same centre point draw a smaller circle about 1cm/½in within the first circle.
Using a metal ruler draw horizontal and vertical lines at right angles to each other through the central point to cut the circle into quarters.
Decide on the number of petals you wish to divide the circle into. There are 360° in a circle so it is a good idea to choose a number which divides easily into 360, such as 18. This would mean that each petal requires 20°. Using a protractor, measure and mark 10° either side of the central vertical line. Draw two lines from the centre through the two marks to the outer circle. Re-set the compasses and draw a small circle for the centre.
The petals can be pointed or curved. Join the edges of the petal where they cut the inner circle to the central line at the edge of the outer circle for pointed petals, or draw a freehand curve to touch the outer circle at the same point for curved petals.
To increase or decrease the overall size of the circle lengthen or shorten the outside edges of the petal.
Carefully cut out the two templates using a craft knife. Mark the straight grain along the central line of the petal template.

*Right: These red and white prints make pretty, fresh-looking mats but you could equally well use a selection of multi-coloured cotton scraps.*

## Dresden Plate place mats

Each of these mats is made from one Dresden Plate motif using two pretty matching prints, one light, one dark. Of course, you could use several different prints if you like. The 20cm/8in diameter mats are machine pieced, quilted, and the edges neatly bound with bias strips of the darker fabric, so there is no need to finish the outer edges of the petals before you join them together.

**You will need for a pair of mats**
30cm/⅜yd light printed cotton fabric A
50cm/½yd dark printed cotton fabric B
30cm/⅜yd white cotton fabric
30cm/⅜yd of 4oz polyester wadding *or* 60cm/⅝yd cotton wadding (used double thickness)
Note: fabric and wadding requirements are based on 90cm/36in width fabric
Matching sewing thread
Firm card and soft pencil
Tracing paper, scrap of plain paper

**You will need for four mats**
50cm/½yd fabric A
80cm/1yd fabric B
60cm/⅝yd white cotton fabric
60cm/⅝yd polyester wadding *or* 90cm/1yd cotton wadding
Other materials as above

**Preparing the patches**
Make your own templates or trace the petal and circle template shapes from the page and cut them out in firm card – an old greetings card is ideal.
Place the petal template on the wrong side of fabric A, positioning it upright on the straight grain of the fabric. Draw carefully round the edge of the template with a soft pencil.
Allowing a 1cm/½in seam allowance all round, mark five more petals on fabric A for each mat and six petals on fabric B.

**Cutting out the patches**
Carefully cut out six petals from fabric A and six from fabric B. The outlines drawn round the templates on the wrong side of the fabric will be the seamlines.

## Assembling the mat

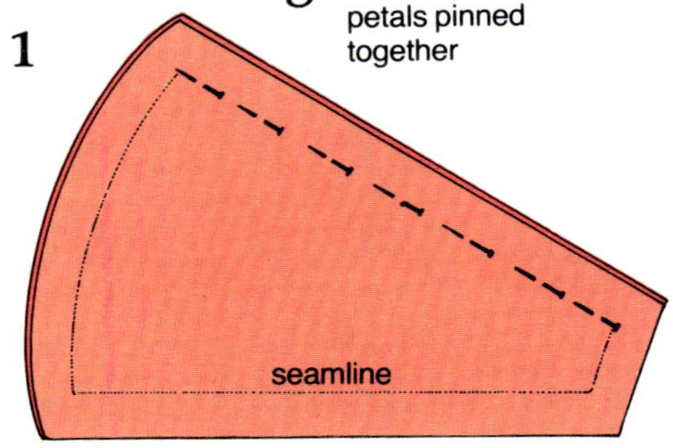


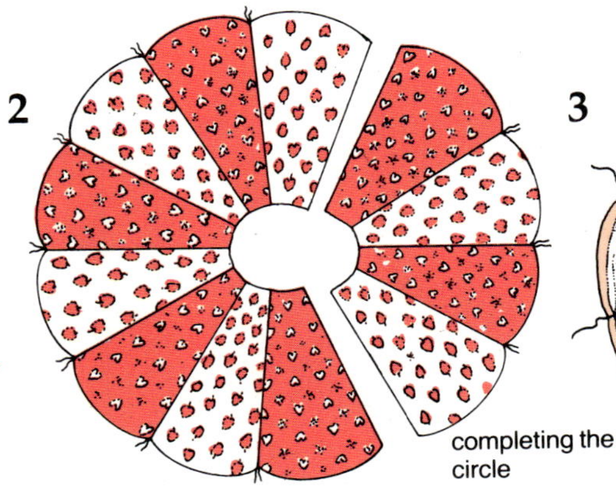


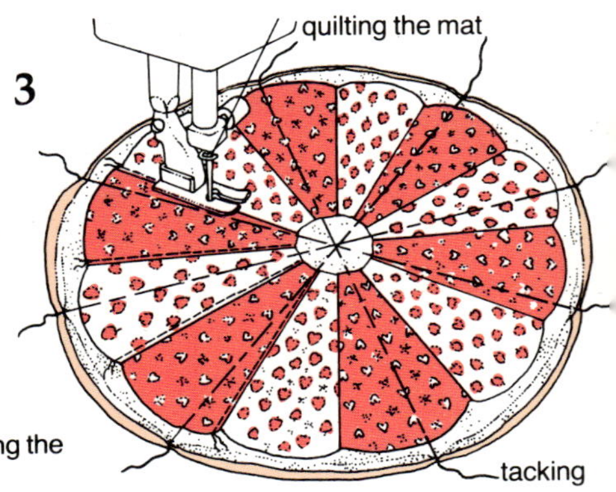


**1** With right sides together, pin the petals in pairs along long edges. Each pair has one fabric A piece and one fabric B piece. Make sure the pencil lines are aligned as you pin. Machine each pair along one seamline using a small stitch. Each mat needs six pairs of petals.
**2** Join the pairs into fours in the same way, then join the three sets of four into the 12-piece circle. Press seams in the same direction.

**Quilting the mat** Use the pieced motif as a guide to cut a circle of wadding and a circle of white fabric, both a little larger than the motif. Make a sandwich of the wadding between the motif and the backing. Pin and tack the three layers.
**3** Using a small machine stitch, quilt along each petal seam on the top (patchwork) side. Work from the outside to the centre and keep as close to the join as possible, without catching in either of the neighbouring petals, so that the quilting line is 'sunk' between the petals. Stop stitching 1cm/½in from inner edges and fasten off threads.
**Adding the centre circles** Using the circle template, cut out two circles in fabric A remembering to leave a 1cm/½in seam allowance. Use the same template to cut out two paper circles without seam allowance.

## DESIGN EXTRA

### Dresden Plate quilt blocks

The appliqué motif is prepared slightly differently from the method used to prepare a motif on its own. To ensure a firm and symmetrical block, the petals are stitched to the ground fabric at the same time as they are joined to each other.

**Making a quilt block**
Cut out a background square, allowing for turnings. Mark it into quarters by tacking.
**1** Prepare a paper pattern the size of the finished circle and divide into quarters by folding. Matching the quarter lines, pin it in place on the square, tack round the edge and remove pattern. Mark the small centre circle in the same way. Cut out the petals for a motif, adding seam allowances as described for the mats. The ends of the petals on the quilt shown below right are pointed instead of curved. Fold under and tack seam allowances on outer pointed edge of each petal.
**2** Take a prepared petal and turn under seam allowance along one long edge. Place it right side up on square with the vertical quarter line running through the centre line of petal and the point touching the tacked circle. Tack in place. Lay the second petal over the first, right sides together, and stitch with small running stitches along seamline through all layers.
Open out petal and press. Continue round in this manner, tucking raw edge of last petal under neatened edge of first petal and stitching. Slipstitch round outer edge of motif and remove tacking.
Add a centre circle as given for the mats. You can slip a small circle of wadding under the circle to add emphasis.

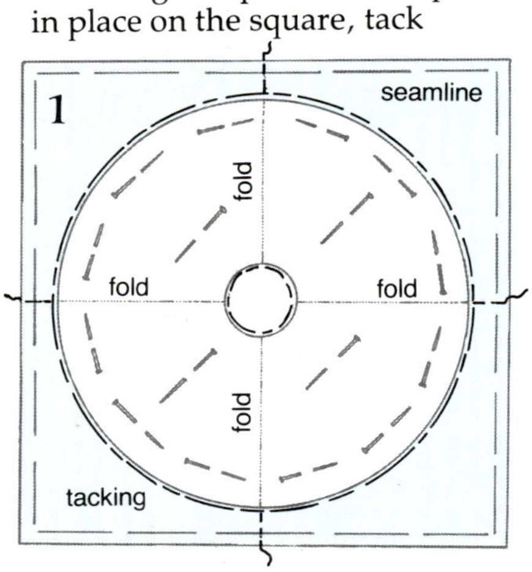

paper pattern aligned to backing

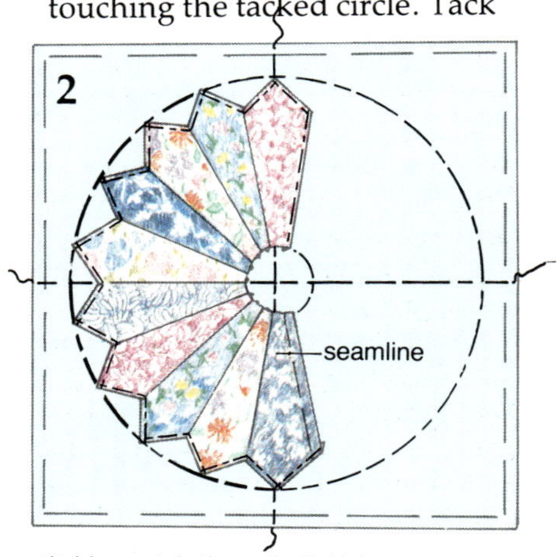

stitching petals through all thicknesses

*A homely quilt with fan-shaped corners.*

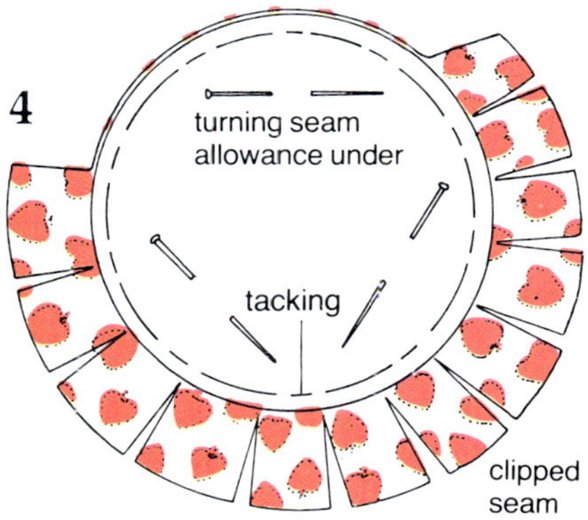


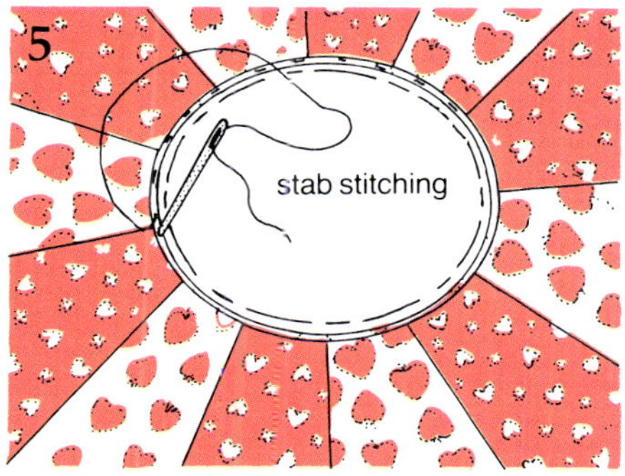


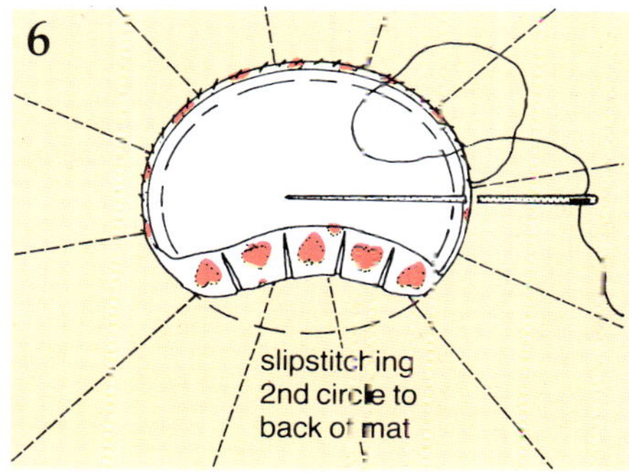


**4** Centre a paper circle on the right side of a fabric circle. Pin and tack round the edge. Clip the seam allowance almost to the edge of the paper and press allowance to the wrong side. Tack down the seam allowance using the edge of the paper circle as a guide to ensure a neat circular edge. Press with a hot iron.

Tack a neatened circle to the centre front of the mat to cover the raw inner petal edges and seam ends.

**5** Stab stitch close to the edge of the appliquéd circle.

**To work stab stitch** make tiny invisible running stitches on the top layer of fabric, and longer ones on the back, stabbing the needle vertically up and down through all layers. Remove all tacking and paper.

**6** Prepare a second circle in the same way and slipstitch to the centre back of the mat. Remove tacking and paper.

**Binding the edges** Cut bias strips from a 30cm/12in deep piece of fabric B. Each strip should be 3cm/1¼in wide. You need about 90cm/36in of binding per mat so join strips diagonally. To join two strips, fold under a corner of each at 45° and press. Place strips right sides facing. Match creases, stitch and trim.

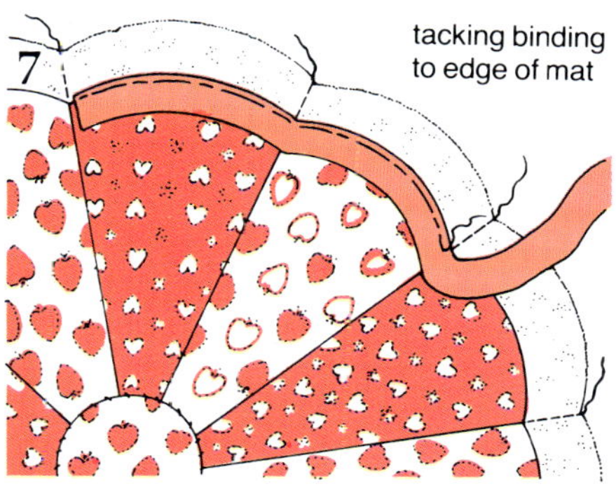


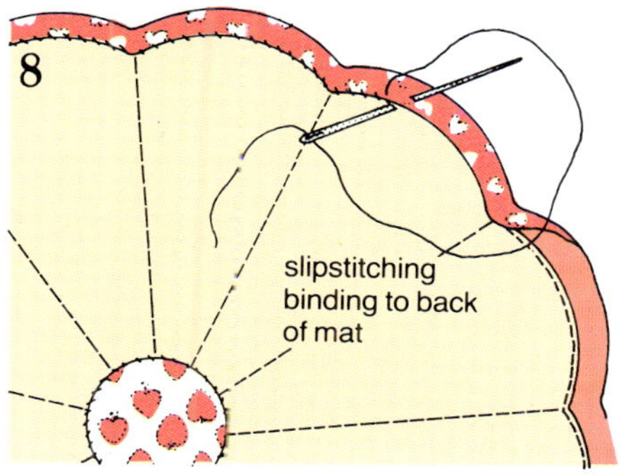


**7** With right sides together, tack binding round top edge of mat, easing it carefully round the scalloped edge as you go. Machine stitch all round, about 6mm/¼in from the edge of the patches. Trim off surplus wadding and backing neatly, flush with the patchwork.

**8** Fold binding to the back of the mat, turn under raw edge and slipstitch in place.

## Matching basket cosy

Make a matching basket cosy to cover an existing basket, adjusting the two templates as described below.

### You will need

20cm/¼yd fabric A
30cm/⅜yd fabric B
50cm/½yd wadding
50cm/½yd white cotton fabric
All other materials as given for mats

### Making up the cosy

Cut templates and patches to the required size. The finished motif is larger than the place mats, but has the same number of petals, so extend the long edges of the template accordingly at both ends. The circular template is also larger. Make up in exactly the same way as the place mats, except for the top centre patch. To make a padded button for picking up the cosy, hem one of the larger circles with small tacking stitches, using a doubled thread. Draw the thread up slightly, insert pieces of chopped wadding to pad firmly, and draw it up tight into a knob. Stitch in place to cover all raw edges at centre.

## Trace pattern for templates

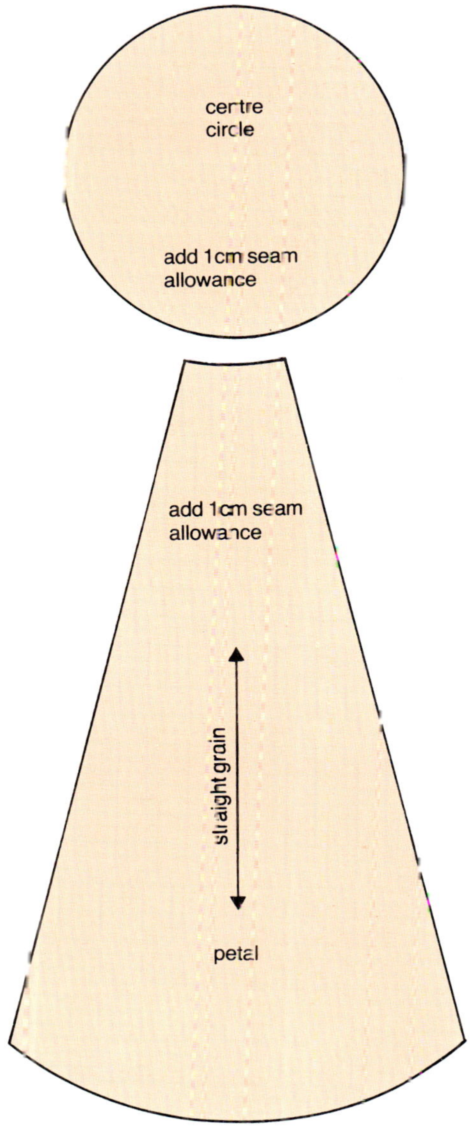

*Use fabrics with tiny prints and same-sized designs for patchwork cushions.*

# Patchwork cushions from pieced triangles

***Here is a method for joining triangular patchwork which ensures a neat finish for those tricky corners. At the same time, learn how to mix and match fabric remnants to make this set of pretty colour co-ordinated cushions in traditional designs.***

Part of the skill of professional-looking patchwork is knowing how to choose the right colours, prints and weights of fabric. For cushion covers such as the ones shown here, make sure you use good-quality cotton fabrics which are completely non-stretchy and do not fray easily.
Remember to wash and press all the fabrics before using them in case of shrinkage.

### Choosing the colours

There's an art in mixing patchwork prints – tiny prints are more suitable than large, bold ones. These cushions have a predominant colour in pale and dark tones, plus two secondary colours.
The predominant-colour prints each include a little of the secondary colours giving a harmonious effect – each of the blue prints here has a little pink and green in it.
Instructions are given in this chapter for a pair of cushions in pinwheel and lattice designs with all the small triangles in pale and dark blues, and pale green outer triangles. By switching the colours around and substituting the pale for dark fabrics, different parts of the design predominate and a totally different effect is produced.
A pair of cushions can be made up to match a room's colour scheme and it is worth taking the trouble to make a coloured sketch of the design first. You may need to change the colours round to get the best effect.

*Right: Carefully chosen prints combined in pairs for toning patchwork cushions will add softness and style to a bedroom or sitting room. Or you could make up just one of them for a pretty present.*

## Pinwheel and lattice-patterned patchwork cushions

This pair of cushions, one of each design, are made up in the same fabrics and look most effective together. Alternative colourways are shown right.
The cushions are machine sewn and machine quilted. The quilting is not essential but it is simple to do and does make all the difference to the finished patchwork.

### You will need

For a pair of cushions, one lattice and one pinwheel design
25cm/¼yd each of four 90cm/36in cotton print fabrics dark blue, pale blue, pale green and pink
50cm/½yd extra of one of these or a plain toning fabric for cushion backs
50cm/½yd polyester wadding (4oz weight)
Cotton threads to match each print
Two 40cm/15in cushion pads
Two 30cm/12in zips in a colour to match cushion backs
Graph paper and stiff card, at least 20cm×30cm/8in×12in
Pencil, ruler, craft knife and glue

## Making templates and cutting out

making the templates

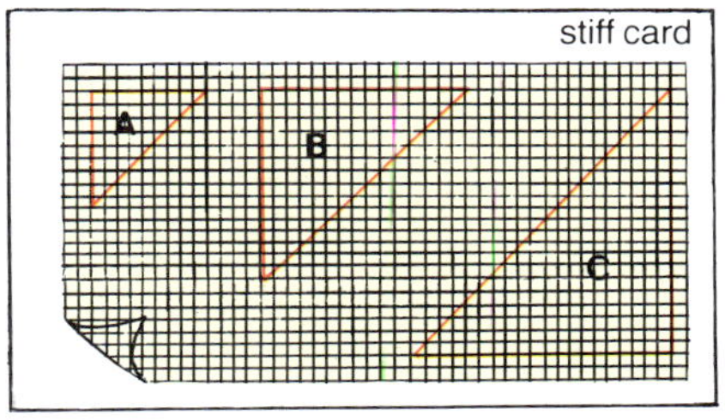


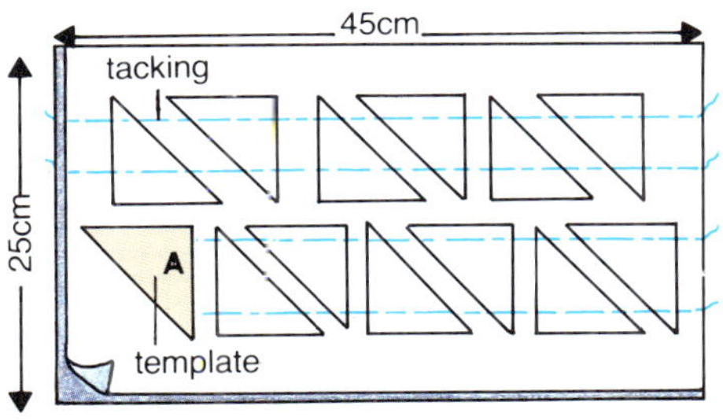


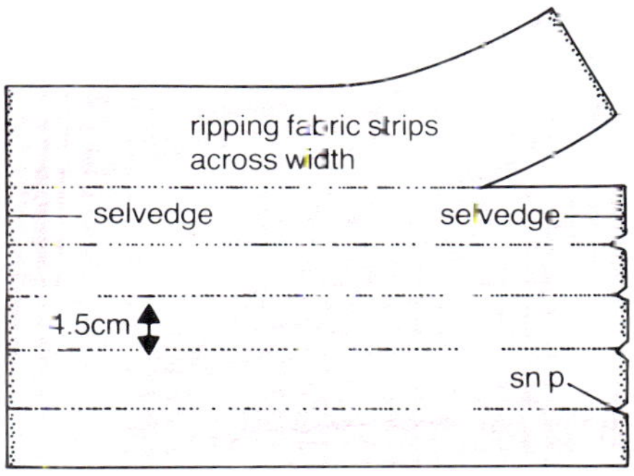


**The templates**
You need three triangular templates of varying sizes. On graph (squared) paper, mark three isosceles triangles – each with one right angle and two equal sides of 9cm/3⅝in (A), 15cm/5⅞in (B), and 20cm/8in (C).
Paste these on to stiff card and cut out very carefully using a ruler and craft knife. These templates include a seam allowance of 6mm/¼in.

**Triangles** Cut one piece 45cm/18in wide from the lengths of pale and dark blue fabric. With right sides together, press and work four rows of tacking about 7cm/3in apart. Trace 13 times round template A on the wrong side of the paler fabric, using a ball-point pen or pencil. These are the cutting lines and will not show on the front of the patchwork. Be very accurate and do not pull the fabric.
Cut out all the triangles using sharp scissors – do not remove the tacking. From template C, trace and cut eight corner triangles in the green fabric, using a single fabric thickness. For the pinwheel design only, cut four B triangles in pale blue.

**Strips** For both of the designs you need lengths of pink strips 4.5cm/1¾in wide and totalling 3m/120in. For the pinwheel design only you also need 1.25m/50in of strips the same width in dark blue. Three widths of the remaining 25cm × 45cm/10in × 18in piece of blue fabric should be sufficient. Mark 4.5cm/1¾in intervals along the fabric selvedge. You may have to waste the first few centimetres at the top to get the first strip straight. Snip the marks with scissors and rip quickly and firmly across the width of the fabric – you may have to snip through the other selvedge, too. Steam press the strips to flatten the edges.

## Assembling the pinwheel design

1
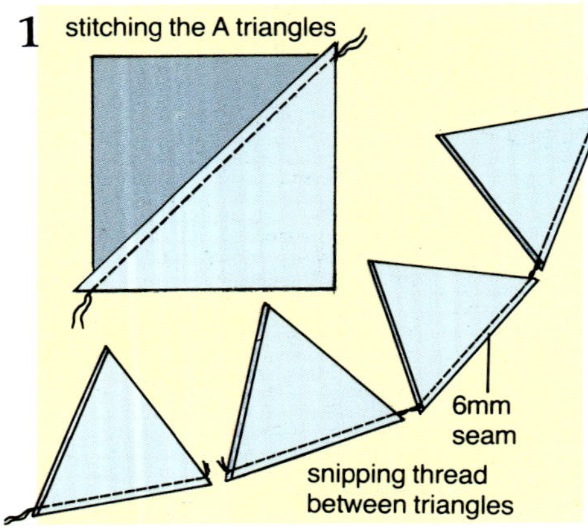


2
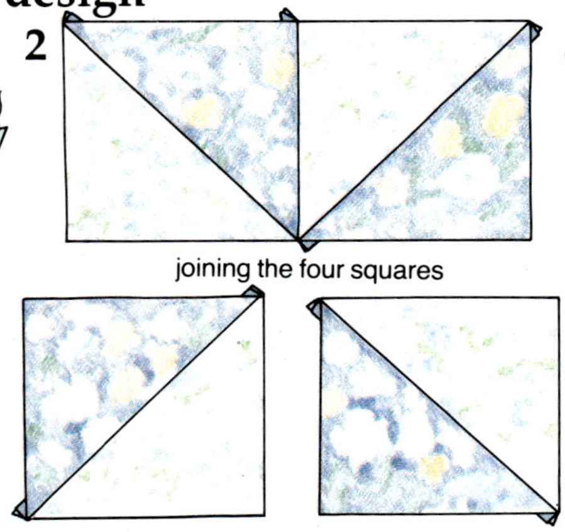


3
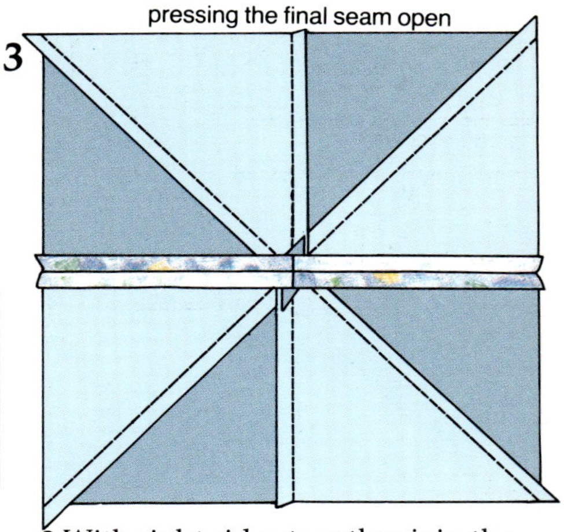


### Triangles

**1** Take four of the 13 pairs of A triangles. With dark blue thread in the machine needle and bobbin, stitch each pair together along long edges, with a 6mm/¼in seam. It is most important to keep the seam an even 6mm/¼in but it is not necessary to snip off the thread between each pair – just stitch them in a 'chain'.

Cut the four pieces apart, remove tacking and press seams towards the darker triangles.

**2** You now have four squares – arrange them on the table in a pinwheel. Stitch them together in two pairs, with right sides together, again taking a 6mm/¼in seam. Press seams towards the darker triangles.

**3** With right sides together join the two pairs, matching centre seams exactly to give a neat centre where the eight seams meet. This is more important than matching edges. Press this final seam open on the wrong side. Steam press the whole piece on the right side, pulling it into a perfect square shape if necessary.

7
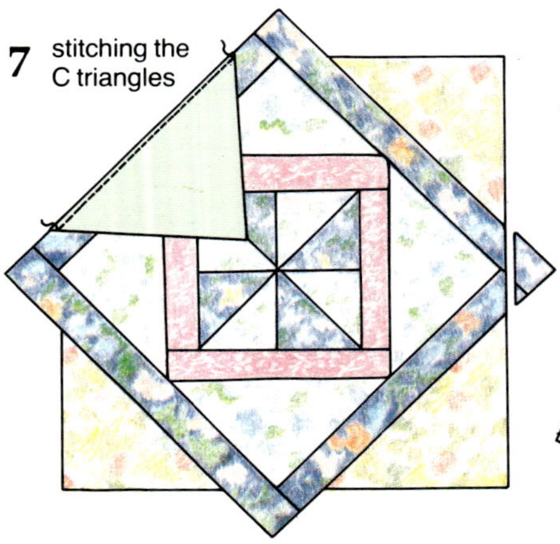


**7** Finish off by adding the four large green C triangles. The patchwork now measures about 43cm/17in square. Snip off the protruding corners of the blue strips, steam press and spray starch the patchwork, ready for quilting.

## Assembling the lattice design

1
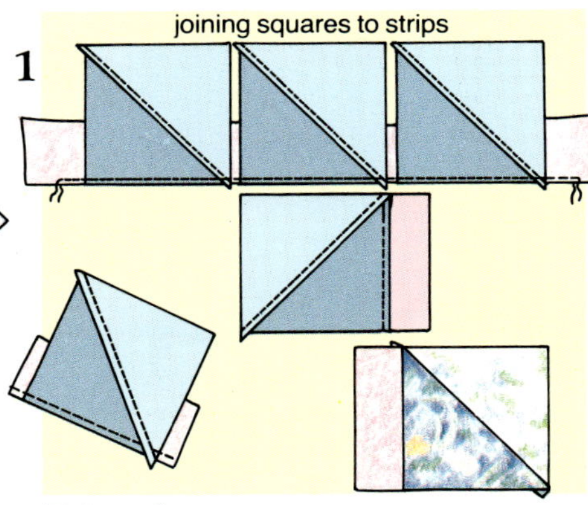


2
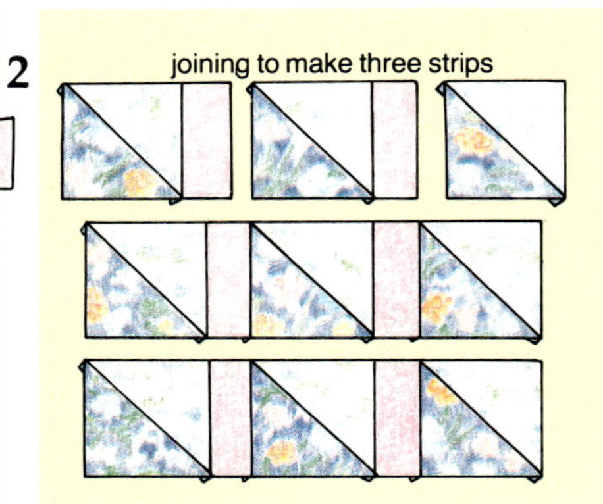


### Triangles

Take the remaining nine pairs of A triangles and stitch each pair together as for the pinwheel design. Open out and press seams towards dark triangles to form nine squares.

**1** Take a length of pink strip and right sides together, stitch six squares along the edge, taking a 6mm/¼in seam. The squares should be close to each other but not overlapping, with all the dark triangles in the same position. Cut the strip between each square, open out and press seams towards strip.

**2** You now have six squares with pink strip borders, and three without. Join these nine pieces into three strips, taking 6mm/¼in seams as usual and pressing seams towards pink strips. Take care to keep all the squares the same way up.

4

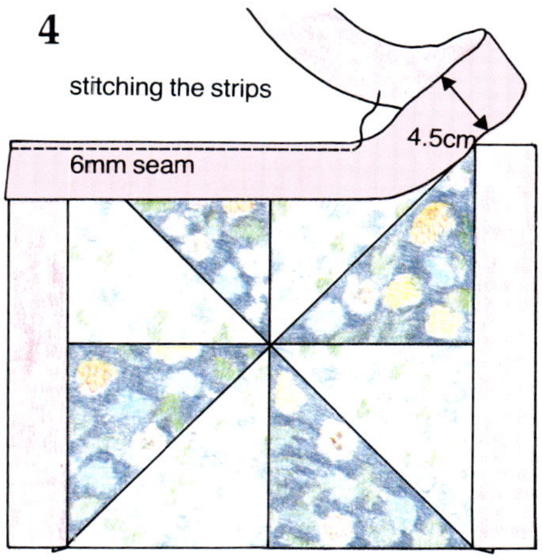


## Strips

Take one of the pink strips and lay it right sides together along one of the edges of the square. Sew the strips with a 6mm/¼in seam, then cut the strip off flush with the patchwork before opening it out.

**4** Join the strip to the opposite edge in the same way and cut it off. Press seams outwards. Now sew the strip to the other two sides as shown, trim ends flush with first strips, and press seams outwards.

5

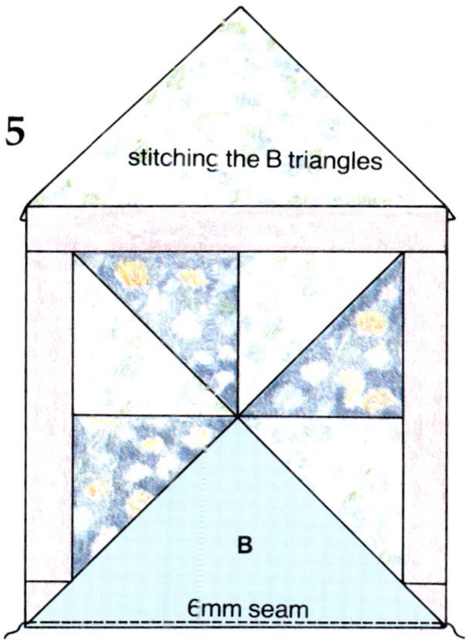


## Outer strips and triangles

**5** Join on the pale blue B triangles two at a time, on opposite sides of the square. Make sure you keep the outer points of the triangles in line with the central seams of the pinwheel square. Press the first two seams outwards (towards the triangle) before adding the other two triangles.

6

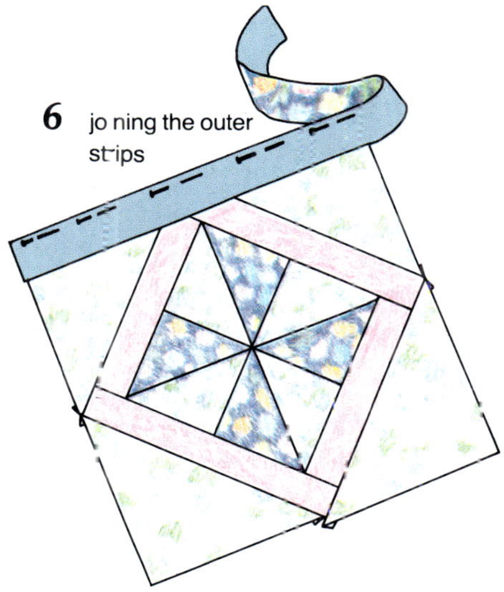


**6** At this point, you may find that the edges of the patchwork do not look absolutely straight. Do not worry about this, but continue by adding the dark blue strips to the edges of this larger square. Proceed exactly as before, but cut and pin the strips in place *before* stitching to make sure all the pieces align correctly. In some places, the seam allowance may need to be wider than 6mm/¼in. Make sure you sew each strip parallel to the one opposite. Press seams outwards as you sew each strip.

3

**3** Cut four pink strips to the same length as these pieced strips, and stitch strips and squares alternately to form a large rectangle. Keep the squares aligned across the rectangle and make sure that all the pale and dark triangles are in the same position in each row. Press all seams towards pink strips.

*Right: Here's the lattice design worked in apricot and rust with a touch of blue. Notice how the paler triangles stand out from the other prints.*

### Outer strips and triangles

**4** Cut two more lengths of the pink strip to the length of the longer side of the rectangle and join these on as shown. Press seams outwards.

**5** Add the four green C triangles to each edge as for the pinwheel design, making sure the outer points are centred. Open out the triangles and press seams outwards. Snip off the protruding pink corners. The finished square measures about 43cm/17in. Steam press and spray starch.

**4** joining outer strip to make a square

**5** stitching the C triangles

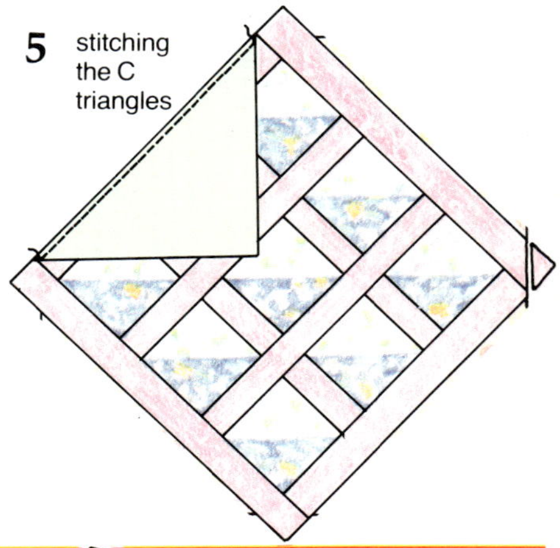

## Quilting the cushions

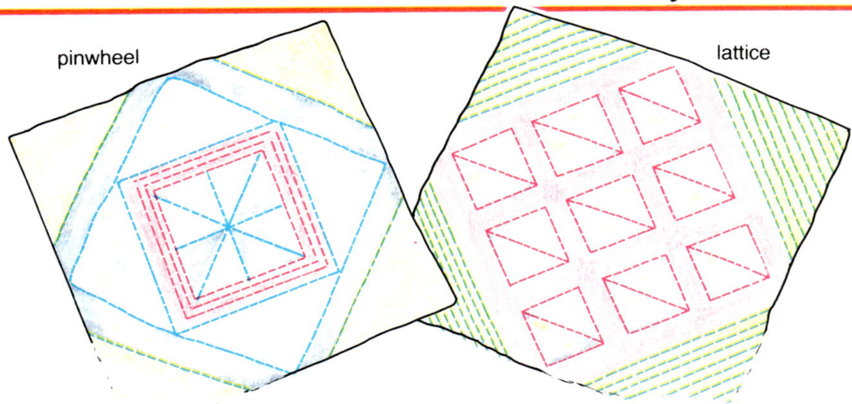


For each cushion, cut a square of wadding the same size as the patchwork. Pin the patchwork pieces over the wadding. Quilt the parts in the same colour on both cushions at the same time to save having to change the colour of thread too often.

It is a good idea to test the machine tension on a scrap of fabric and wadding before quilting the actual covers.

**Using pale blue thread** in the needle (the bobbin colour does not matter) set the stitch to a medium straight stitch.

Beginning at the centre of the pinwheel cushion, quilt along each seam of the central wheel.

Quilt in the seamline, stitching steadily and taking care not to waver over to the bulkier side of the seam. Finish off by pulling the needle threads through to the back and tying the four ends together. Now quilt the inner square formed by the long edges of the larger pale blue triangles and finally the outer square formed by the other two edges. Finish off the ends on the back as before.

**Using pink thread** in the needle, add three or four parallel lines round the square pink strips on the pinwheel cushion. Now quilt round each of the nine squares on the lattice design, and along the diagonals.

**Using green thread** in the needle, quilt across the long edges of the green corner triangles on both cushions. If you like, carry on quilting to the outer corners in parallel lines about 8mm/3/8in apart to give added relief and texture. There's no need to tie off the ends as they will be caught in the seam when the back is attached.

## Making up

Cut a piece of fabric measuring 42cm×45cm/16½in×17½in for each cushion back. Fold over a third of the fabric, right sides together, along the longer edge.

Mark and stitch a 1.5cm/½in seam leaving a central gap of 30cm/12in for inserting the zip. Cut right across on fold and press seam open. Set zip into opening using a zip foot if your machine has one. Steam press the back.

**Joining back and front** Using a light pencil or water-erasable marker, draw a 38cm/15in square on the wrong side of the back. This is the seamline. (A square template cut from card is useful for doing this.) Open the zip a little and place the

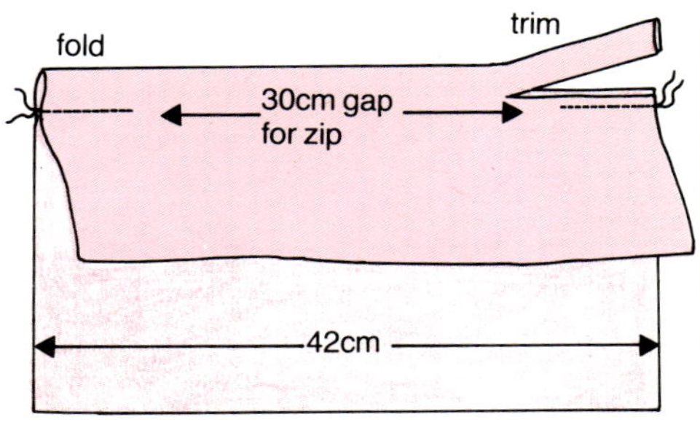


cushion back and front right sides together, centring the design carefully on the backing. Pin, and sew round on the seamlines, rounding off the corners a little if you wish. Make sure there is no puckering on the patchwork. Trim seam to about 6mm/¼in to reduce bulk of wadding. Turn, steam press edges lightly and insert cushion pad.

### Alternative quilting

If your machine has a decorative machine embroidery feature, this can be used instead of a straight-line stitch for the quilting. Worked in a contrasting colour, it really adds a professional touch to the work (see below).

Check that the bobbin is full before starting to quilt because thread is used up very quickly in decorative stitches.

# Pictorial patchwork from pieced blocks

***Instead of abstract patchwork patterns, try a pictorial design using the same basic shapes and methods. Pieced blocks can represent houses, baskets or boats, as on this charming quilt or wall hanging for a child.***

*Left: If you prefer plain fabrics, try a scheme such as red boats and blue sails.*

This fresh-looking quilt with its bold design of different-coloured sailing boats is built up from traditional patchwork shapes. It measures 87cm×124cm/34in×49in and is suitable for a cot or child-sized bed. It also looks stunning hung on a nursery wall and is quick to assemble using your sewing machine. Each pieced block has a sailing boat cut from different colourways of the same furnishing cotton, but you could make them all the same colour if you prefer. The quilt shown here has a hand-sewn quilting design which includes a shining sun and waves in each block but you could equally well machine-quilt the design. A gay, striped binding finishes the edges.

**You will need**
1m/1yd white cotton fabric
30cm/⅜yd six different pattern or colour fabrics *or* 1m/1yd in the same colour or pattern
1.15m/1¼yd royal blue cotton fabric
80cm/1yd blue and white striped cotton fabric for binding
84cm × 130cm/36in × 1½yd nylon foam wadding (1oz weight)
1.30m/1½yd lining fabric
1 reel white Sylko thread
1 ball DMC coton perlé No. 50
Quilting needles (betweens, size 7-9)
Card or plastic sheet for templates
Soft pencil
**Note:** all fabric requirements are based on 90cm/36in wide fabric

**Cutting the patchwork pieces**
To make the six sailing boat blocks, you need three different templates which should be cut from stiff card or plastic sheet. (See page 29 – Making templates and cutting out.)
You will need a 7.5cm/3in square, a 7.5cm/3in right-angled triangle, and a 7.5cm × 30.5cm/3in × 12in rectangle. Each block requires four white squares, six white triangles, two patterned squares, six patterned triangles and one white rectangle.
**Following the cutting layouts** (right), draw round the templates on the wrong side of the fabric, allowing seams of 1cm/½in all round. Cut all the pieces with at least one edge on the straight grain of the fabric.

*Left: Ideal for children, the quilt is warm and light.*

## Cutting layout for white fabric

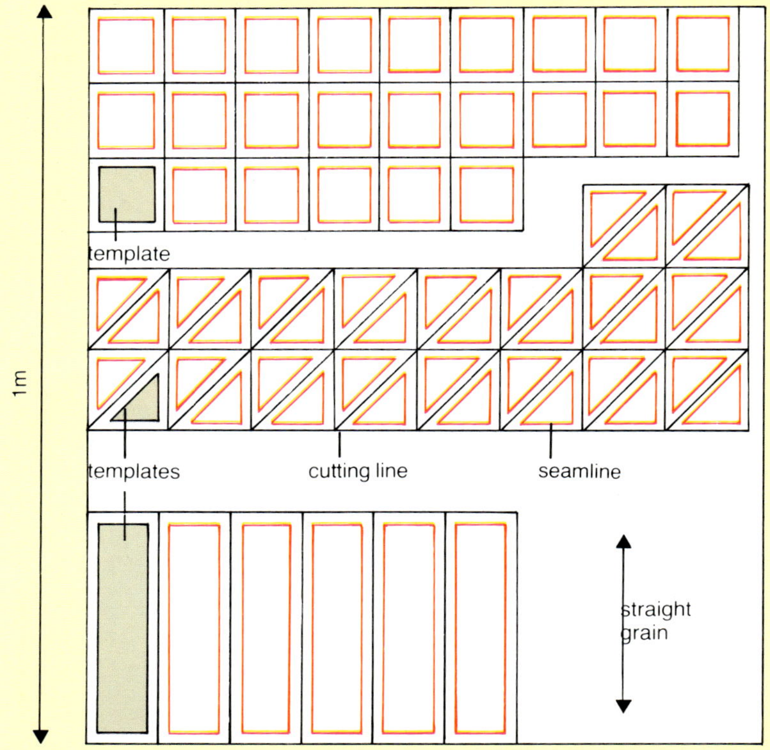


## Cutting layout for patterned fabric

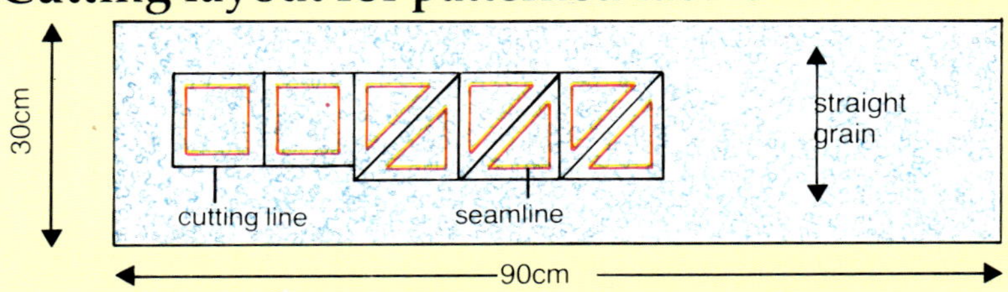


## Assembling a block

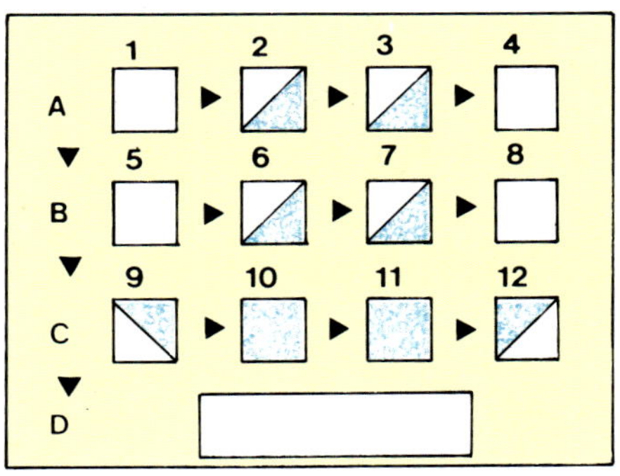


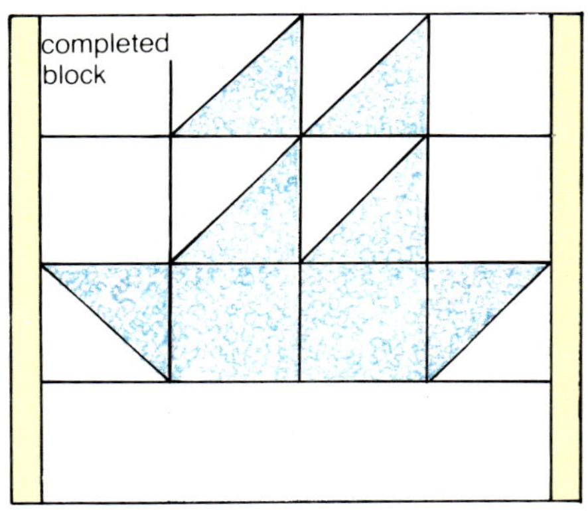


Join each of the patterned triangles to one of the white triangles, along the long edges, making six 7.5cm/3in squares. (See page 30, top left – Triangles – for a quick machine method.) Trim seams to 6mm/¼in, press towards patterned triangles. You now have 12 squares and are ready to assemble one block. Join the pieces to make the boat design in the order shown in the diagram, making three strips. Trim seams and press in alternate directions on each horizontal strip to reduce bulk (see page 15 – Joining the patches). Now join the three strips of squares horizontally and join the white rectangle to the lowest row. Trim and press these seams, and make the other five identical blocks.

## Making the borders and dividers

All the borders and dividing strips are 7.5cm/3in wide and have seam allowances of 1cm/½in. Keep seam allowances accurate so that the blue strips are all of equal width on the right side of the finished work.
Mark out the strips on the wrong side of the royal blue fabric, using a pencil and ruler.
You will need four strips measuring 7.5cm×30cm/3in×12in (strips 1-4), three measuring 7.5cm×104cm/3in×41in (strips 5-7), and two measuring 7.5cm×81cm/3in×32in (strips 8-9).
It is a good idea to cut the strips a little longer than specified to allow a margin for error – remember to add 1cm/½in seam allowances to the measurements given.
Arrange the six sailing boat blocks flat on the table, (if they are each a different colour make sure they are in the positions you intend them to occupy in the finished quilt).
**Positioning the dividers and border strips** Join strip 1 to the bottom of block A, then join on block B, strip 2, and block C. Similarly join strip 3 to block D, following with block E, strip 4, and block F. Trim all seams, and press towards the royal blue strips (being the darker colour).
You now have two vertical strips of sailing boat blocks. Join strip 5 to one long edge of one of these strips A, B, C, join strip 6 to the other edge, and join on the other sailing boat strip D, E, F. Add strip 7 to the remaining edge. Trim and press seams towards the blue strips.
Finally, join on the top and bottom strips, 8 and 9. Trim and press seams.

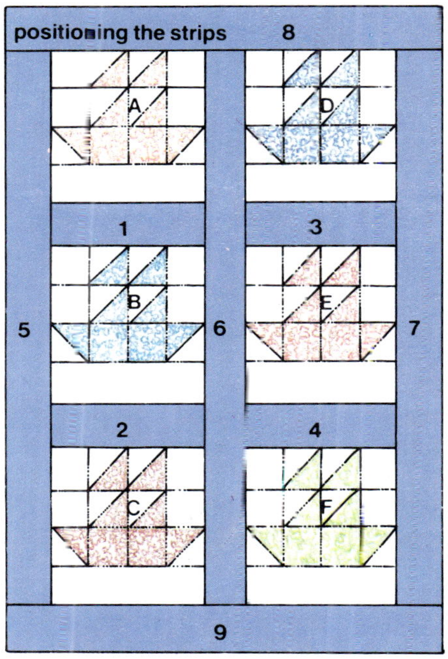


## Quilting the patchwork

Make a sandwich of the patchwork top, the nylon wadding and the lining fabric. Tack these firmly together with lines radiating out from the centre.
It is possible to quilt this patchwork on your lap but if you find it easier, mount it in a large quilting hoop, moving the hoop as each part is completed, or stretch it in a rectangular quilting frame.

### Quilting lines for each block

The pattern of the quilting stitches enhances the seaside design. In each block, the sea has its own quilted waves and a sun has been stitched in the top right hand corner. Follow the diagram given to mark these on to the fabric with a dressmaker's chalk pencil or a water-erasable marker. Quilt the rest of the block in a lattice design. The lines of quilting should cross at the centre of each square.

Begin quilting in the top left-hand corner of each block and quilt diagonally across the squares to the edge of the rectangle. Next begin at the bottom left-hand corner and quilt diagonally up to the top right. You will need to quilt close to the seamlines between the triangles. Continue the quilting, working outwards, from these two lines in alternate directions, until the whole lattice pattern is finished. Repeat the quilting on each of the five other sailing boat blocks.
Next work parallel diagonal lines of quilting about 2.5cm/1in apart, over all the blue dividers and border strips. The lines run diagonally upwards from the bottom left and bottom right-hand corners to meet in a V down the centre of the middle dividing strip.

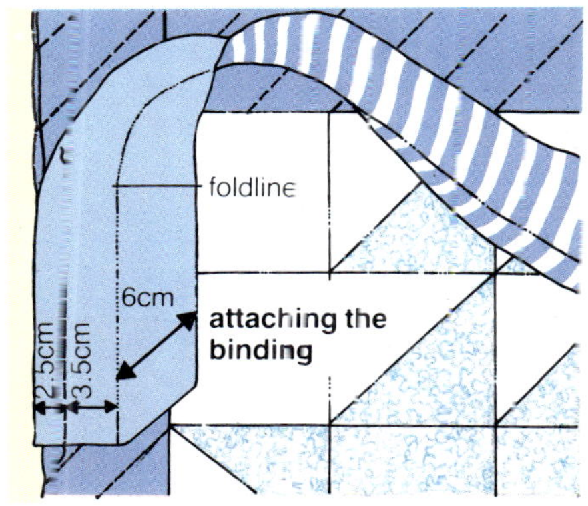


### Binding the edges

The sailing boats quilt looks most effective bound with strips cut from the striped fabric. Cut the strips across the straight grain so that the stripes run crosswise. You need a 4.5m/5yd strip 12cm/4½in wide and will have to join it with three or four seams according to the width of the fabric. After joining the strips, fold the whole length in half lengthwise and press. Lay the strip along the edge of the quilt, raw edges matching and right sides together. Machine round 2.5cm/1in away from the edge, mitring corners. Turn the binding strip to the back of the quilt and slipstitch in place.
**Finishing touches** Sign and date your work on the back, using running stitch. If you wish to hang the quilt on the wall of a child's bedroom, sew loops of lining fabric to the back of the top edge and insert dowelling through the loops.

# Log cabin pattern for patchwork

***Log cabin originated in Britain, but is an important part of the North American patchwork tradition. The simple strip shapes create stunning colour effects which can be combined to make a variety of overall patterns for quilts, cushions and clothes.***

Log cabin is a very well-known pieced block patchwork pattern which is built up by laying strips – the cabin logs – around a central square patch. The use of dark and light strips in the same block is strikingly effective. Usually, half the block is worked in dark colours and half in light creating an effect of light and shadow.

The finished blocks can be joined together to produce a number of different overall patterns, and many of the early American patchwork quilts use this pattern in delightfully original ways.

Traditionally the patches were stitched together by hand, but they can also be pieced together quickly by machine. Although templates were not normally used, a quick method using a template strip guide to make the blocks is given right.

*Below: Single block in toning colours.*

## Choosing fabrics

Dressweight cottons are the most suitable for this kind of patchwork. For the strips you will need an equal number of dark and light fabrics with the colours shading from light to medium in the first group and medium to dark in the second.

The central square should be plain and unrelated to the strip fabrics to help highlight the design.

## Constructing a basic block

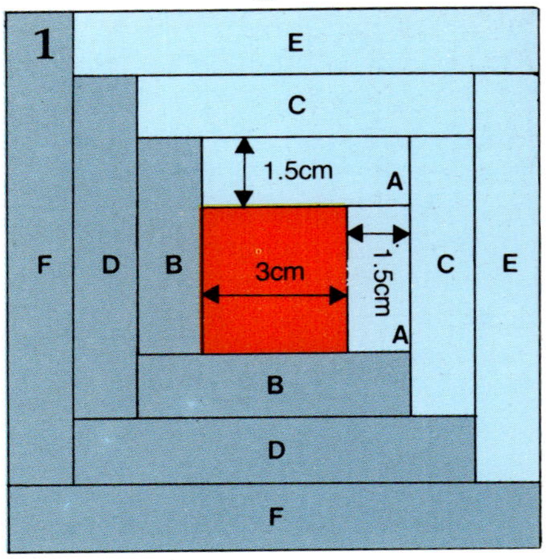


This quick method is ideal for large projects as several blocks can be under construction at once which saves time.

**1** Make a simple diagram of a finished block to help you calculate the ideal strip size. The centre square can be any size but twice the width of a strip looks about right. The block in the example has three strips each side of the centre square. Cut two templates from card or plastic, one 3cm/1¼in square and one 1.5cm/⅝in wide and the length of the block – in this case 12cm/5in.

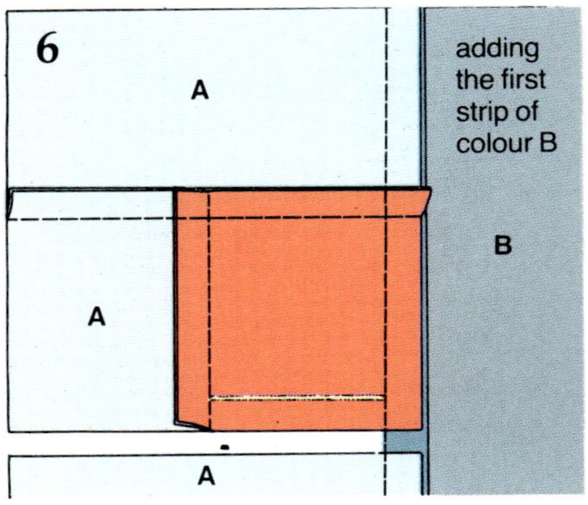


**6** Now take a strip of colour B (the first of the darker colour group) and lay several of the three-piece blocks along it as before, right sides together, edges matching. The side laid flush to the long edge of the strip of colour B should be the side of the block with the centre colour and the *second* strip of colour A. Mark the seamline and machine along it. Join on as many blocks as necessary, cut apart and trim edges flush.

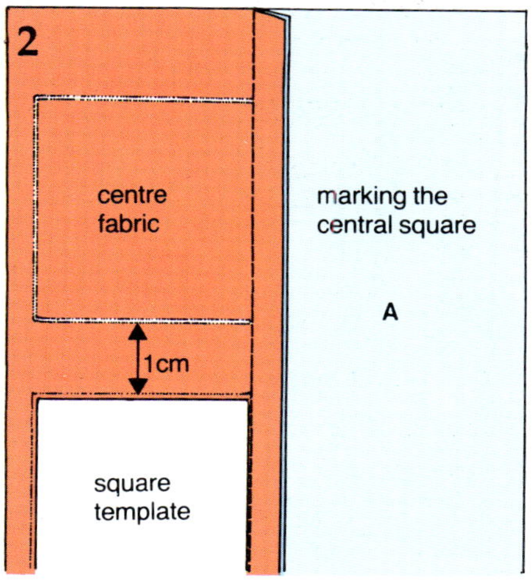


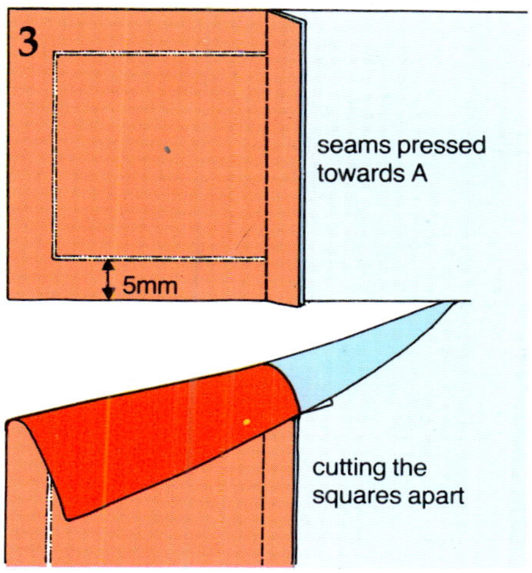


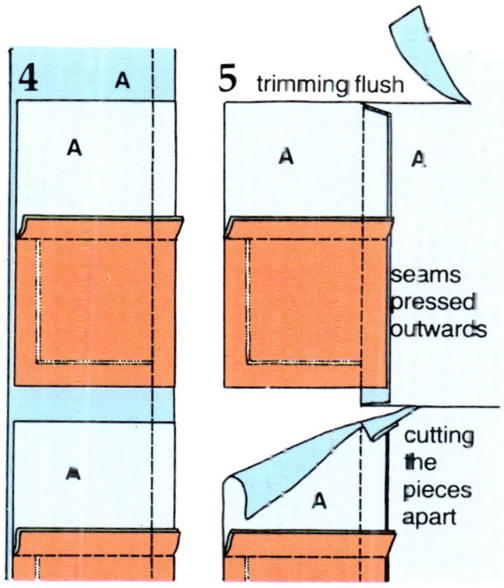


The block is made up of six different fabrics, A-F, plus the contrast fabric for the centre square. Divide them into two colour groups, A, C and E are the lighter fabrics and B, D and F are the darker fabrics.
Cut a series of strips 4cm/1½in wide across the grain using the whole width of the fabric. This includes seam allowances. Cut strips from all the fabrics including the centre square fabric.
Take one of the strips of colour A and lay it right sides together on a strip of the centre colour, matching the edges. Using a ruler and a washable embroidery marker, draw a line along the strip, 5mm/¼in from one long edge and machine along this line. Press seam towards colour A.

**2** Lay the square template on the wrong side of the centre colour strip with one side of the template butting up to the machined seamline. Mark out a series of squares at 1cm/½in intervals along the whole length of the strip.

**3** Cut the squares apart, exactly halfway between each one. You will now have a series of pieces made up of the centre colour and colour A.

**4** Lay up to four of these two-colour pieces right sides together on a further strip of colour A making sure one of the two-coloured sides is flush with one long edge of the new strip. Extend the marked line on the centre square across the pieces and machine in place.
Continue adding pieces along the strip as necessary.

**5** Cut the pieces apart as before, trimming the edges flush with the first two pieces to be joined. Press seams outwards from the centre.

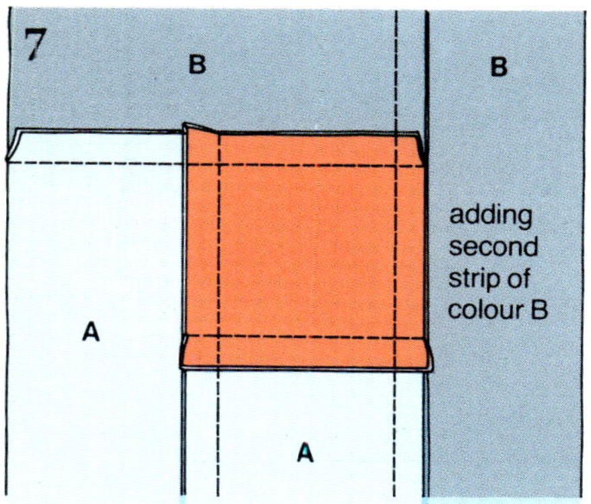


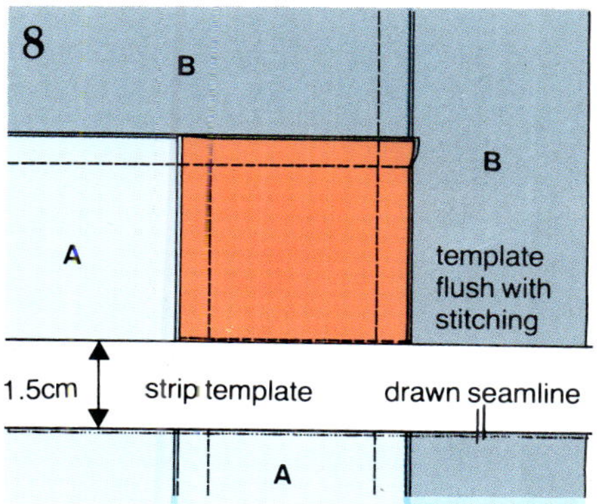


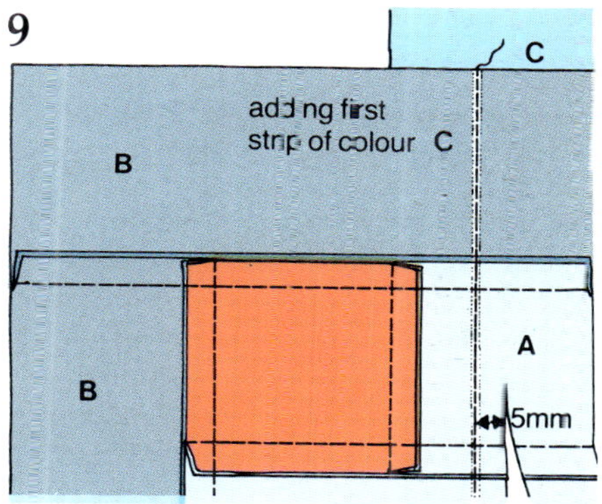


**7** Lay the last edge of centre colour on a further strip of colour B, mark, machine and cut apart. Press seams outwards and trim the finished pieces to a square. The centre square is now completely surrounded.

**8** Take the strip template and lay it on the wrong side of the block, with one edge along the stitched line of the centre square and on the side of the block with *three* patches and two seams. Draw a line along the other edge of the template. This gives the seamline for the next strip to be added.

**9** Lay two or three blocks on to a strip of colour C, right sides together and edges matching and machine along the marked seamline. Cut blocks apart, trim seam to 5mm/¼in pieces and press outwards. Add a second strip of colour C in exactly the same way using the template strip to mark the seamline.
Continue adding on strips outwards, working round the square and trimming and pressing seams outwards after stitching until you have completed the block. There should be the same number of strips on all sides of the centre square. Always remember that the first strip of a new round should be added to the side with *two* seams, using the template strip to mark the seamline.

### Joining the blocks

When joining log cabin blocks try to avoid joining two identically coloured outer strips together. Either vary the outer strip fabrics or simply use a single outer strip to join the blocks together.

# Chunky kimono-style jacket

The edges of this cosy quilted jacket are bound with the brilliant red fabric used for the centre square patches. It is worked almost entirely by machine, with a little hand finishing. The jacket shown here is made up in the largest size, for a medium/large jacket, make smaller blocks using colours A to J only (J and I will be the dividing strips) and for a small/medium jacket, make blocks with colours A to H only (H and G will be the dividing strips). The instructions are based on making up the large jacket, you may need to add an extra row of blocks to the ends of the sleeves and bottom of the jacket to obtain the required length for the small size. This can easily be calculated by using the diagram right.

## Calculating fabric

The log cabin blocks used in this jacket have strips with a finished width of 1.5cm/⅝in. The centre square is 3cm/1¼in wide.

Draw an accurate diagram of one log cabin block for whatever size you are making to calculate how much fabric you need in each colour. Multiply the length of strips required for each colour (add about 9cm/3½in for seams) by the total number of blocks in the jacket (48). Now divide by 90cm/36in (being the width of the fabric) and multiply by 4cm/1½in (the width of each strip including seam allowances). The result will be the length of 90cm/36in-wide fabric you need. Round it up to the nearest 5cm/⅛yd.

## You will need

For a large jacket:
1m/1⅛yd plain fabric in contrast tone for block centres and trim
2½m/2¾yd extra of one of the strip fabrics for lining
**Light fabrics** A: 30cm/⅜yd, C: 40cm/½yd, E: 55cm/⅝yd, G: 70cm/¾yd, I: 75cm/⅞yd, K: 80cm/⅞yd
**Dark fabrics** B: 35cm/⅜yd, D: 50cm/½yd, F: 60cm/⅝yd, H: 75cm/⅞yd, J: 85cm/1yd, L: 80cm/⅞yd
(All fabric allowances are based on 90cm/36in wide fabric)
3m/3¼yd Terylene 2oz wadding
3m/3¼yd firm Vilene interfacing
1 reel Sericum mercerised machine twist No 60 (1000 metres) in medium shade of main colour
1 reel thread to match lining fabric
65cm/25½in open-ended zip

## Making a pattern for the jacket

Cut the piece of Vilene in half, widthwise and join the two pieces halfway (for centre back) with a 1cm/½in seam. Mark and cut out the jacket cross shape to full size using the diagram to help you. Pin the side and underarm seams and try on to check size and sleeve and jacket length. Adjust as necessary. Open out pattern and mark the position of each log cabin block in pencil on the Vilene. You can then pin the finished blocks on to the Vilene as they are completed.

The jacket front and back each have sixteen blocks and each sleeve has eight blocks. Four blocks make up a pattern square.

*Above: The log cabin pattern is an ideal choice for square-cut garments like this jacket. It is made up from tones of blue cotton prints, with a contrasting centre square.*

## Making up the blocks

Cut out all the 4cm/1¼in wide strips across the grain of the fabric. Lay out strips to see how the finished square will look. You may wish to change a fabric or alter the order. Make two card or plastic templates – one 3cm/1¼in square and one strip 1.5cm/⅝in wide and the length of one block, in this case 21cm/8¼in. Thread up a number of machine bobbins with the medium-shade thread – log cabin uses a great deal of thread. Stitch the fabric strips together using a fine needle and following the sequence given on the previous page until you have four blocks completed as far as colour J.

## Joining the blocks together

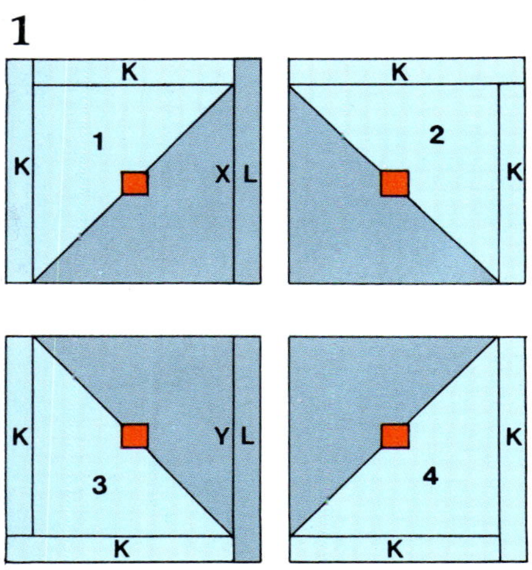


adding the K strips

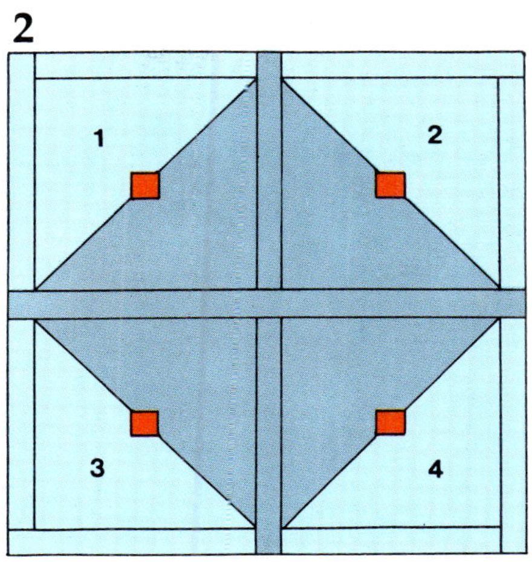


adding the long L strips

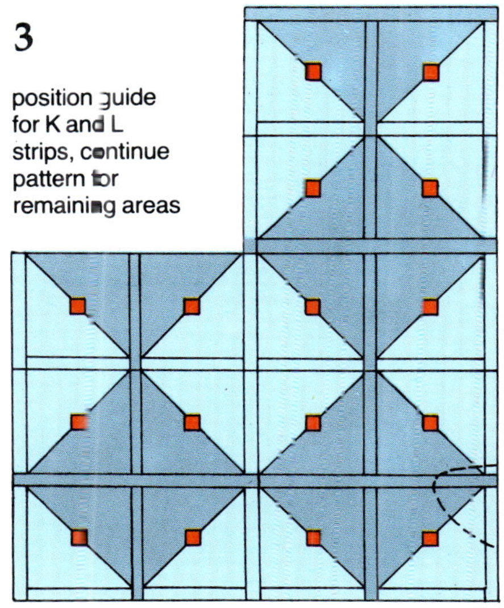


These blocks are to be joined into a square with the dark corners on the inside. To avoid having a double band of colour L only one strip is added to join the blocks together.

**1** Add colour K on two sides of each block in the usual way. Lay the blocks out in a square as shown. Blocks 1 and 2 are separated by a single strip of colour L and similarly blocks 3 and 4.

Add a strip of colour L to block 1 on the side marked X and to block 3 on the side marked Y.

Lay the strip template on the wrong side of block 1 with the edge along the seamline joining strips J and L. Mark the new seamline on strip L.

With right sides together, match inner seamline of strip J, block 2, to outer seamline of strip J, block 1, and stitch along marked seamline on strip L.

Join block 3 and 4 in the same way, trim and press seams outwards.

**2** Now join a long strip of colour L to the bottom of blocks 1 and 2 along the second colour strips J. Mark with the template, machine and press. Join this strip to blocks 3 and 4 by marking and stitching as before. You now have a block of four squares with a dark cross in the centre.

Similarly, when joining four light corners, join on only a single strip of colour K (the darkest of the light colours) between blocks.

**3** Make up all remaining blocks as far as colour J, and pin out on the Vilene jacket shape to see where the single strips of colours K and L are needed. The dividing strips of colour L (the darkest blue) should run continuously vertically and horizontally across the patchwork, interrupting the dividing strips of colour K. So join the K strips first. When you have assembled the completed blocks in a cross shape, remembering to leave centre front open, cut away half of the two blocks along each underarm edge as shown using the Vilene as a guide.

## Positioning guide for strips

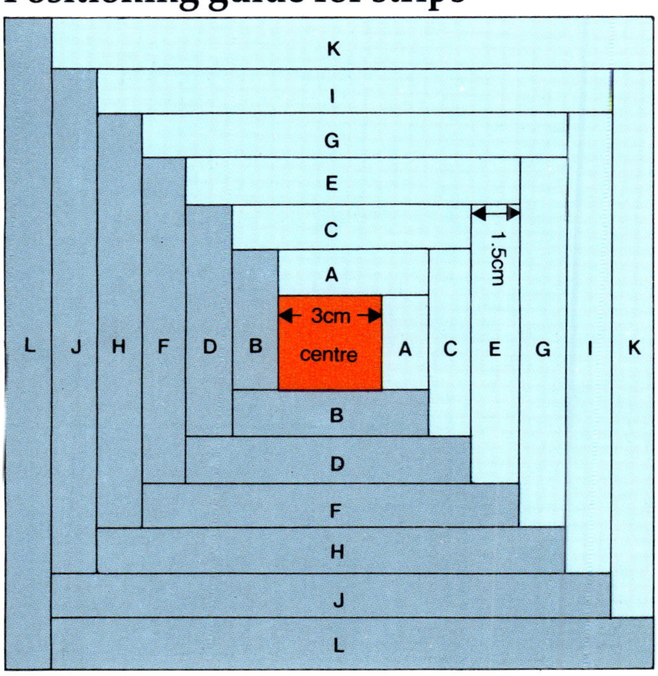


## Positioning guide for blocks

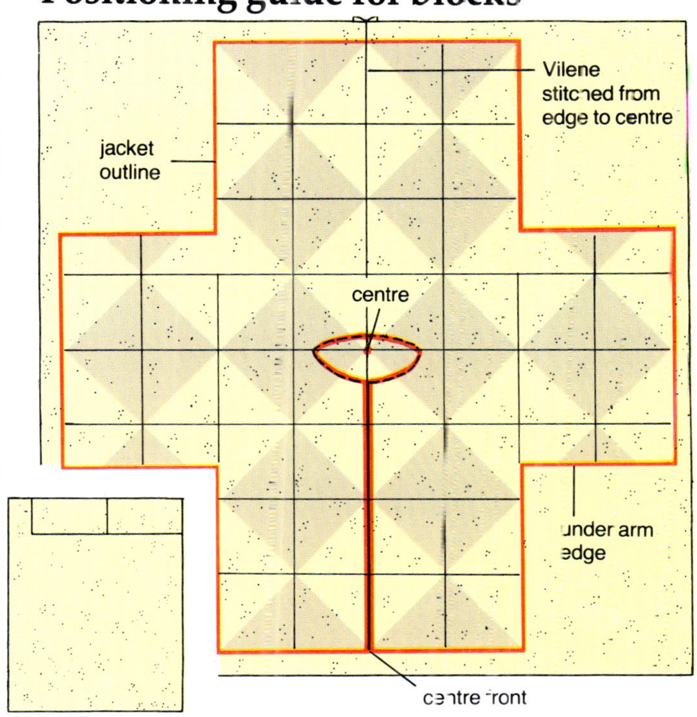

## Making up the jacket

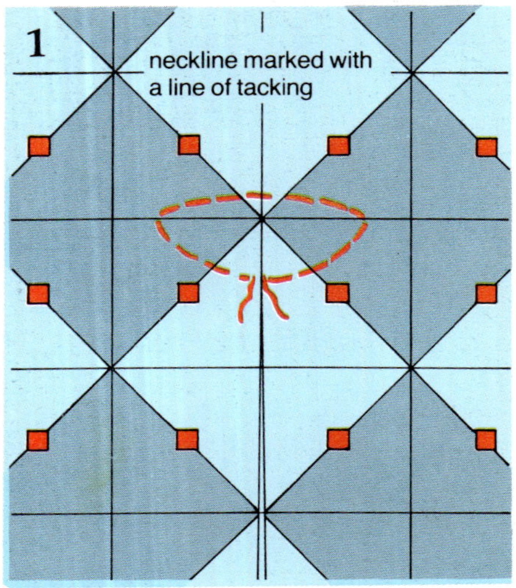


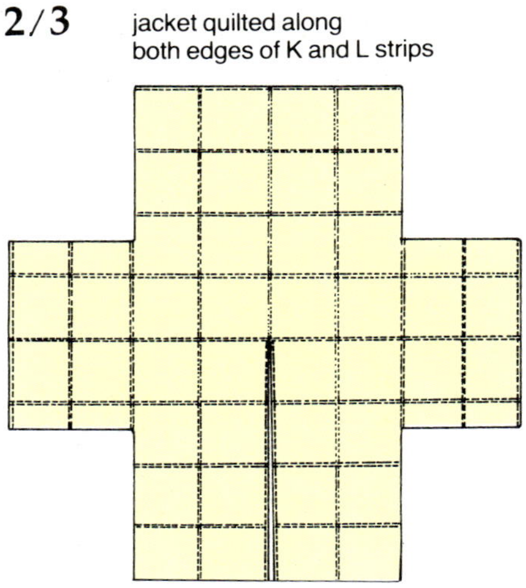


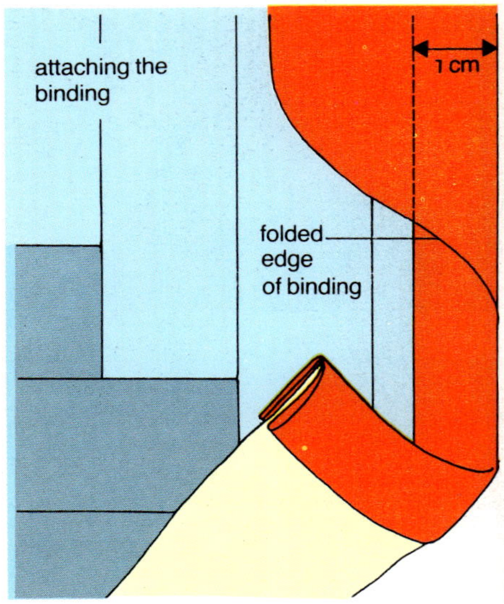


**1** Mark the position of the neck edge with tacking. Mark a gentle curve from the centre top to the centre side of the two upper centre front blocks. Dip neckline down slightly at back. Use the Vilene pattern to cut out the jacket shape in lining fabric and wadding. Lay out the lining, wrong side up, and place the wadding and patchwork, right side up, on top. Pin carefully in the centre of each block, tack all layers securely together with a series of diagonal lines.

**2** Thread the bobbin with thread to match the lining, set a medium stitch and quilt along all the horizontal strips of colours K and L on both edges of each strip, except for the outer edges of the lower edge strips. You will have to roll up part of the jacket under the machine arm to do this.

**3** When the horizontal quilting is complete, begin at the centre back and quilt along both edges of all the vertical strips of colours K and L except for the outer edges of the front and sleeve edge strips. You can also quilt round the edges of each centre square by hand if you wish to.

Remove tacking, trim edges neatly and trim neck edge to within 1cm/½in of tacked edge. Fold jacket in half along shoulder line so that front and back right sides are together and tack the two side and underarm seams. Try on and make any fitting adjustments at this stage. Machine side/underarm seams with a 1.5cm/⅝in seam. Trim all fabrics close to stitching except back seam allowance of lining. Lap back lining allowance over raw seam and hem.

Trim centre front, cuffs and bottom edge to neaten.

### Finishing off

Cut bias strips of centre square fabric 6cm/2¼in wide and fold and press in half. Apply bias trim round bottom edge by tacking binding to jacket with raw edges matching, and machining 1cm/½in from the edge. Hem folded edge to seamline on inside. Repeat for neck, front and cuff edges.

To close the front, use an open-ended zip (or see Design Extra). Tack zip in place so that bias-trimmed edges meet exactly when it is closed. Stitch zip in place by hand along bias trim seamlines. Hem edges of zip webbing to jacket lining on inside.

## DESIGN EXTRA

### Log cabin pattern variations

You can assemble finished log cabin blocks in all kinds of ways. Many traditional quilts are made up in patterns which radiate out from the centre point – these are not so suitable for smaller items.

If you think of each block being made up of a light and a dark triangle, you can design your own jacket pattern. Here are three ideas which show how you can give an effect of diagonal stripes, bold zigzags, or all-over triangles.

Instead of an open-ended zip you could use fabric ties to close the jacket – or simply wrap it over and tie with a bold sash.

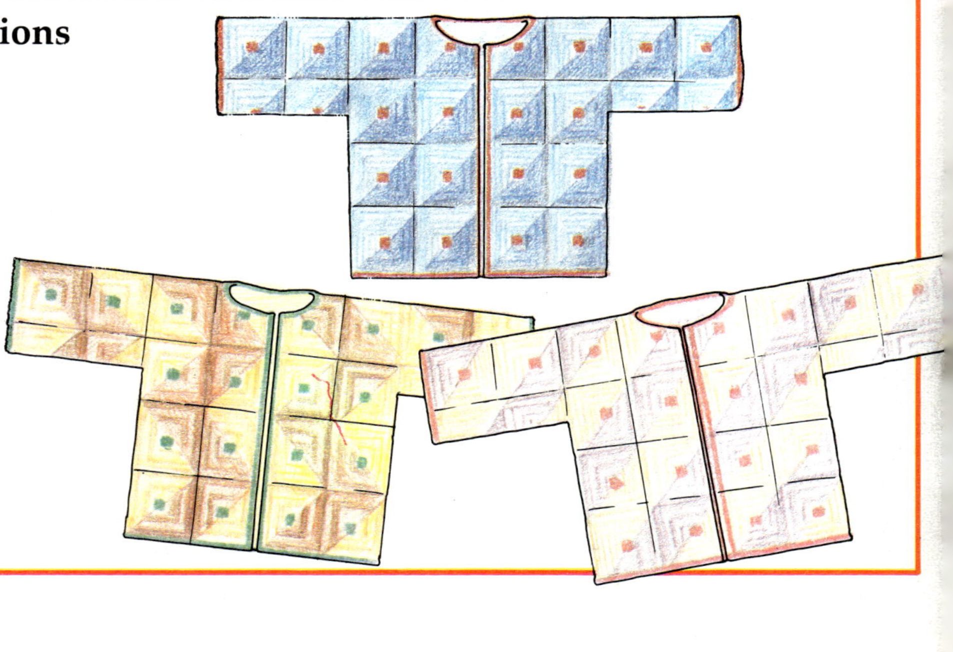

# Pattern variations in Seminole patchwork

***This traditional form of patchwork can be speedily assembled by machine although accurate measuring and cutting are essential. Simply by joining straight strips of fabric, cutting and rearranging them you can create a wealth of dramatic geometric patterning.***

Although Seminole patchwork is based on traditional designs, it has always been a technique most suited to the machine. By joining together strips of bright fabric, cutting the strips into pieces and reassembling them in an offset position, a wide range of decorative bands of patchwork can be created.

The Seminole Indians used this form of patchwork to decorate clothing and it is best used for straight bands of decoration either inserted in or applied to a garment.

By varying the number and width of the strips and the way in which you cut and reassemble the pieces, you can make numerous patterns.

Join a series of different bands together with banding strips to form a panel for the bib front of a child's dress or dungarees. Try incorporating ribbon or narrow lace on your fabric strips and as well as clothing, use Seminole patchwork on all kinds of bags, cushions, quilts, purses, pincushions, tablemats and other home projects.

### Equipment

Apart from your sewing machine, you need an iron, pins, sharp scissors, a clear plastic ruler and a fabric marker – either a soft pencil, dressmaker's chalk pencil or a water-erasable marker.

**Fabrics** should be non-stretchy and firmly woven. Choose non-slip fabrics of a similar weight. Do not choose fabrics which are bulky when seamed together, or difficult to press. Pure cotton, Tana lawn and cotton/polyester blends are all suitable. For best results, use strongly contrasting fabric – plain colours and small, all-over prints.

### Cutting and marking the fabric

Press the fabric and fold with right sides together, selvedge to selvedge. Use a ruler to mark the straight crosswise grain at right angles to the selvedges. This will help you to cut all the strips straight from that piece of fabric.

Stitch all pieces with 5mm/¼in seams (this means you should cut all strips 1cm/½in wider than the required finished size.) Check the width of your machine presser foot as these often measure 5mm/¼in and can be used as a seaming guide.

It is very important to cut fabric accurately and make all seams straight.

### Chain sewing

When machining pieces together, save time by chain sewing (see pages 30-31, Assembling the pinwheel design). When all the cut pieces are joined in pairs, snip the joining threads and join pairs of pairs together in the same way. Proceed with this method until you have assembled a complete Seminole band.

Careful pressing is essential. Wherever possible, press all seams in one direction and check that the right side of the patchwork is perfectly smooth.

### Finishing the patchwork

As your pieced strips will end up with jagged edges, you need banding strips to finish and neaten them. This provides a firm edge along which to attach the patchwork. Always cut banding strips on the straight grain of the fabric.

*Right: The ideal way to match up your separates: add a Seminole patchwork trim made from co-ordinating prints. The top and trousers make a smart, but casual, outfit.*

## Stitching a simple Seminole pattern

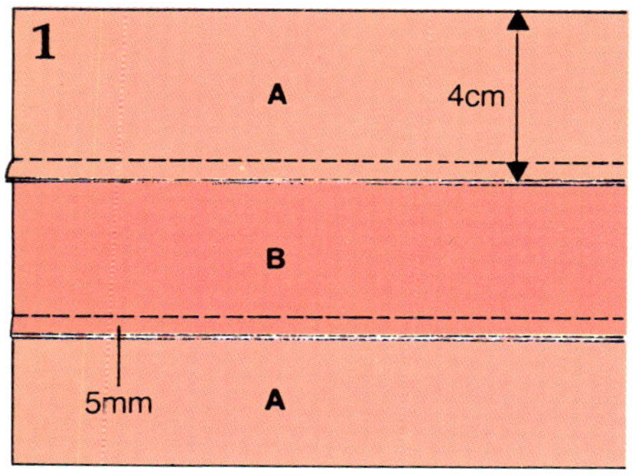


**1** On the crosswise grain of both fabrics, cut two strips of fabric A, 4cm/1½in wide and one strip of fabric B, also 4cm/1½in wide. Seam these three strips together with fabric B in the centre, taking 5mm/¼in seams, and press both seams in the same direction.

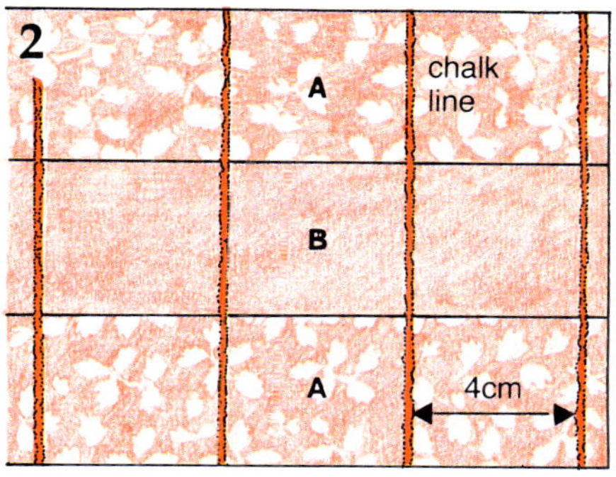


**2** On the right side of the fabric, mark strips at 4cm/1½in intervals. Make sure your marked lines are at exact right angles to the seamlines. Cut along all the marked lines.

**3** Place two joined pieces with long sides together, right sides facing. Slide the top piece along so that the

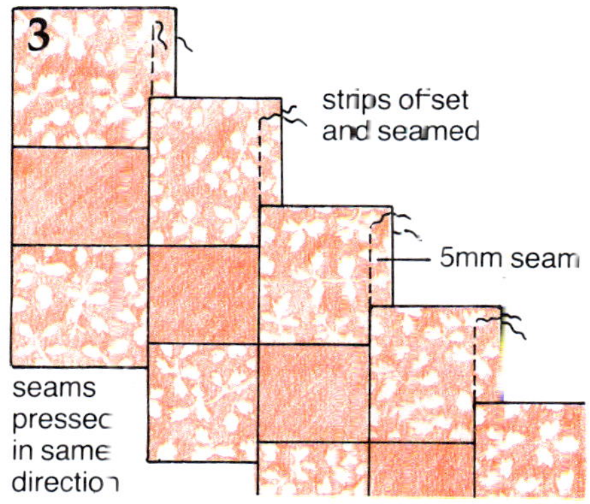


area of colour B diagonally adjoins the area of colour B on the lower piece. Seam the pieces together in this position and chain sew all the other pairs at the same time. Continue joining until the required length is reached. Press all seams in the same direction.

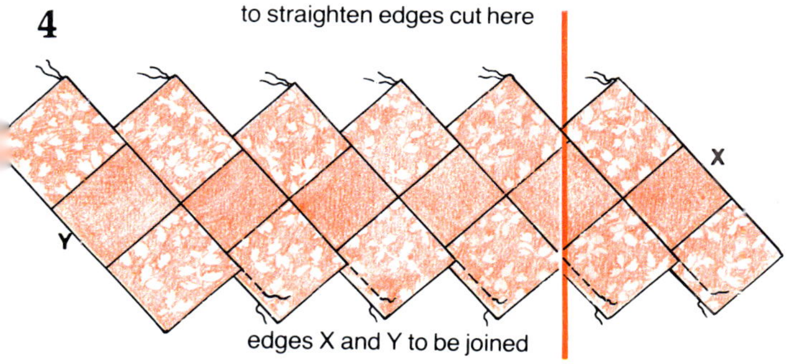


**4** To straighten the ends of the strip cut straight across the strip cutting one of the colour B squares diagonally in half. Now join the two diagonal-edged ends together, leaving the two straight edges at either end of the patchwork.

**5** Cut two banding strips in colour C, the length of the patchwork. Lay one strip along one side of the patchwork, right sides together and stitch in place. The stitching line

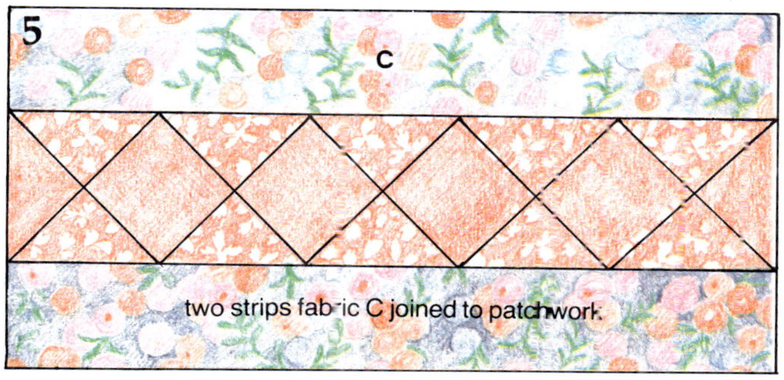


should touch each outer corner of the colour B squares. Repeat on opposite side and trim away points of colours A and B. Press these seams outwards.

## Chevron pattern variation

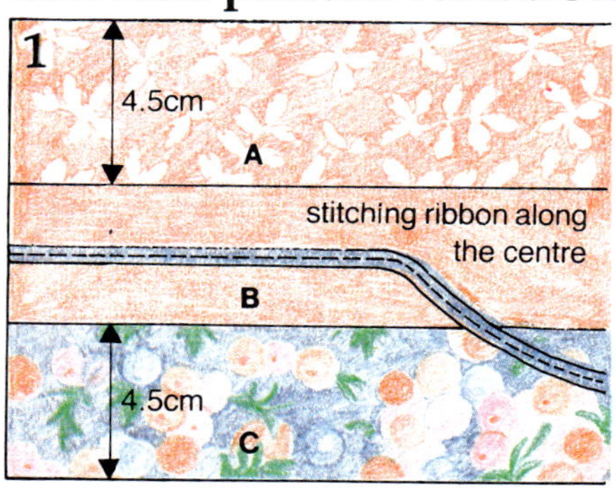


**1** Cut strips of colours A and C, 5cm/2in wide. Cut a 4cm/1½in wide strip of colour B and join the three strips together with colour B in the centre. Appliqué a length of contrasting 3mm/⅛in ribbon along the centre of the strip of colour B for added decoration. Press seams.

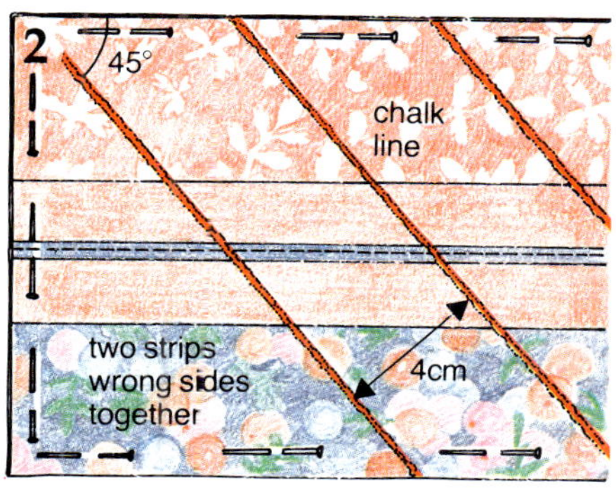


Make a second identical pieced strip in this way.

**2** Lay one pieced strip on top of the other, wrong sides together, matching seamlines, and pin in place. Mark a 45° angle across the top strip and then mark a series of parallel lines, 4cm/1½in apart. Cut

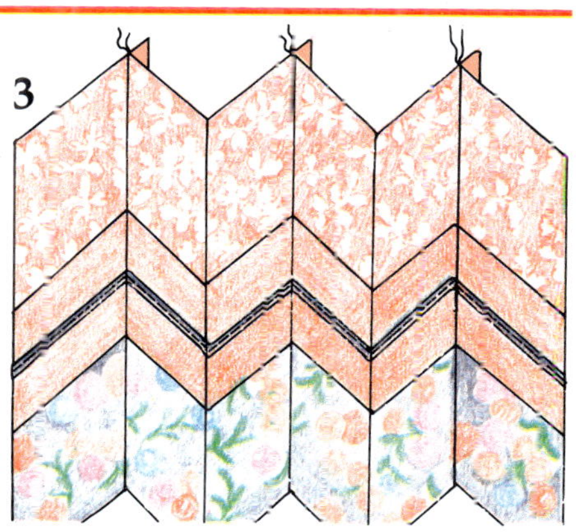


along all the marked lines, giving mirror-image pairs of strips.

**3** Join the pairs along their long edges, matching seams and ribbon carefully, to produce a striking zigzag pattern band. Trim the outer edges to straighten and apply banding strips of colour B.

## Diamond pattern variations

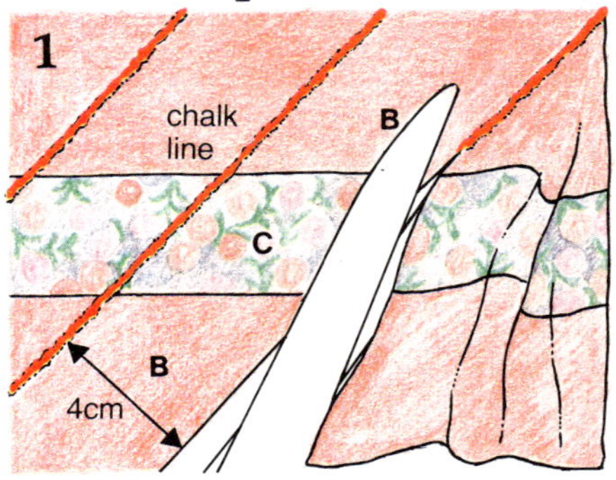


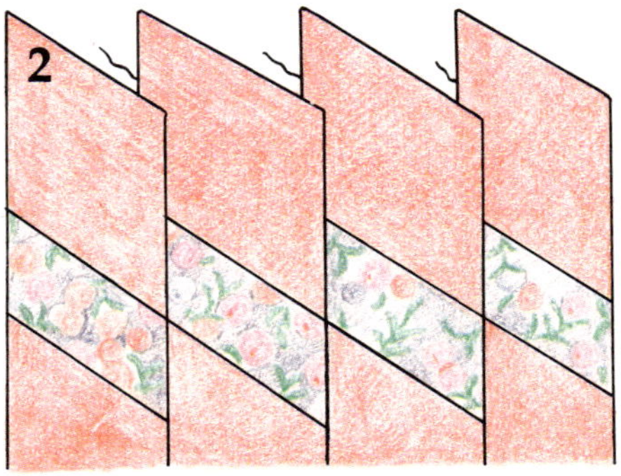


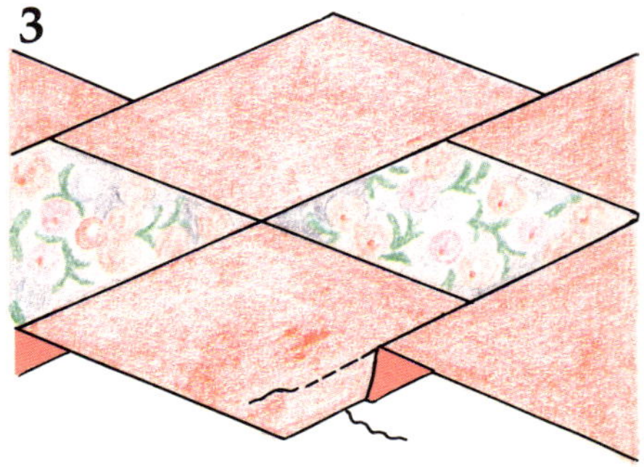


Using only two colours, it is possible to create some pretty diamond effects. It is very important to be accurate with these patterns, so pin horizontally along seamlines before stitching.

**1** Cut two strips of colour B, width 4cm/1½in, and one strip of colour C, width 3cm/1¼in. Join the strips with colour C in the centre.

Mark a 45° angle as before. Mark a series of strips 4cm/1½in wide and cut out.

**2** There are several different ways in which you could offset the pieces to make patterns. To make a wide border, join strips along long edges so that pointed ends are level along both sides. Colour C appears as a series of parallelograms in the centre.

**3** Alternatively, join the strips so that the upper corner of one strip of colour C coincides with the lower corner of the next one. This gives a much narrower border with colour C appearing as a row of horizontal diamonds in the centre.

## Up-and-down blocks design

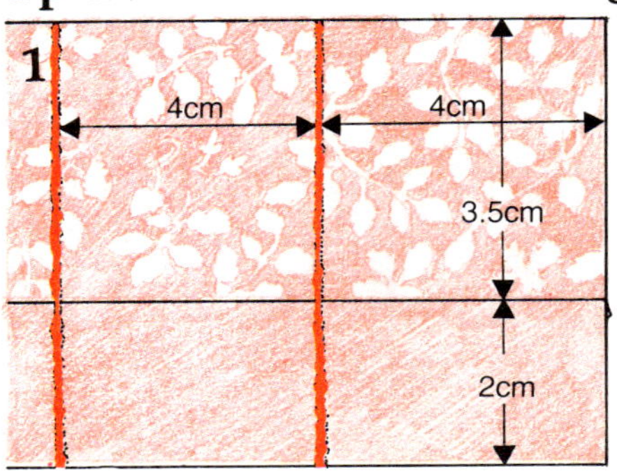


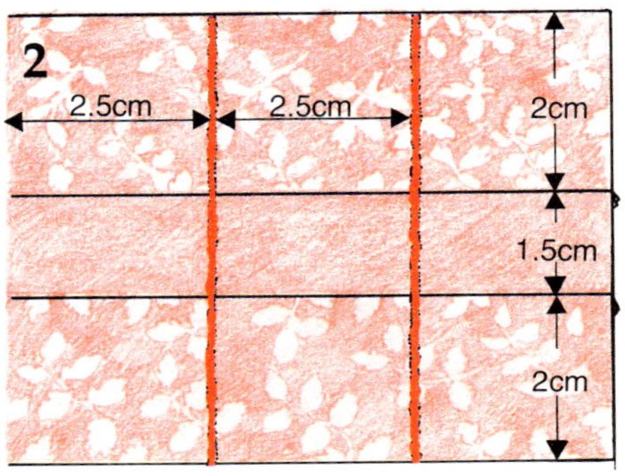


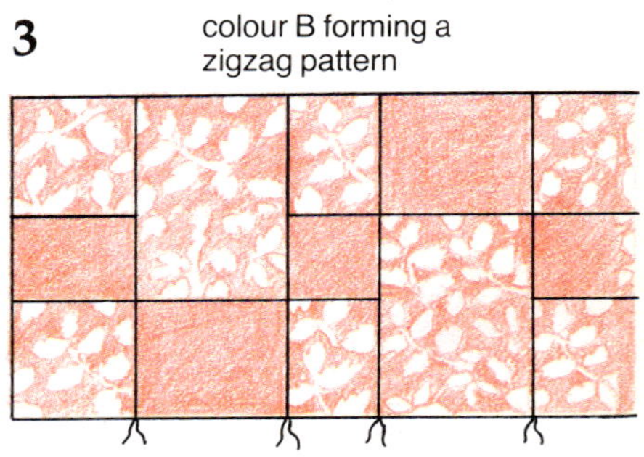


This simple pattern uses two sets of joined strips.

**1** Cut a 4cm/1½in strip of colour A and a 2.5cm/1in strip of colour B. Seam together and press. Mark and cut into pieces 4cm/1½in wide.

**2** Cut two 2.5cm/1in strips of colour A and one of colour B. Seam together with colour B in the centre. Press seams, mark and cut into pieces 2.5cm/1in wide.

**3** Turn alternate pieces of the first strip upside down, placing pieces of the second strip between them. Seam together, carefully matching corners of colour B so that a zigzag pattern of boxes forms. Press all seams in the same direction.

# *Seminole trim for blouse and skirt*

An attractive bib-fronted blouse and lightly gathered skirt are the perfect partners for the simple Seminole patchwork band trim. Try to choose patchwork fabrics which introduce a new shade, as well as providing a link with the main colour of the outfit. Two small-scale prints and a plain lawn have been used to make this Seminole trim.

The amount of patchwork you need to make depends on the garment you are trimming. The pattern shown here makes a 76cm/30in long band from strips cut from 90cm/36in wide fabric (ie 15cm/6in approximately are lost). The skirt shown here has a band of patchwork set in about 9cm/3½in from the hem. Measure round the skirt to find out how much patchwork you need. Measure the shirt front, yokes, cuffs etc in the same way. You may wish to join completed strips together to cover a larger area. Make outer seams of patchwork panel equal to those on the pattern.

### You will need

30cm/⅜yd each of three fabrics, width 90cm/36in
Soft pencil, ruler, sharp scissors
2m/2⅛yd matching prepared piping

### Preparing the patchwork

Read the instructions for Seminole patchwork first. This design is similar except that three different fabrics are used instead of two. The centre colour is also used for the banding. Cut all strips 4cm/1½in wide, except the outer colour strips which should be cut 5cm/2in wide.

*Choose simply constructed clothes for adding Seminole patchwork. You could use any of the patterns shown here for bands on a skirt. Add banding strips to reach required width for a blouse panel.*

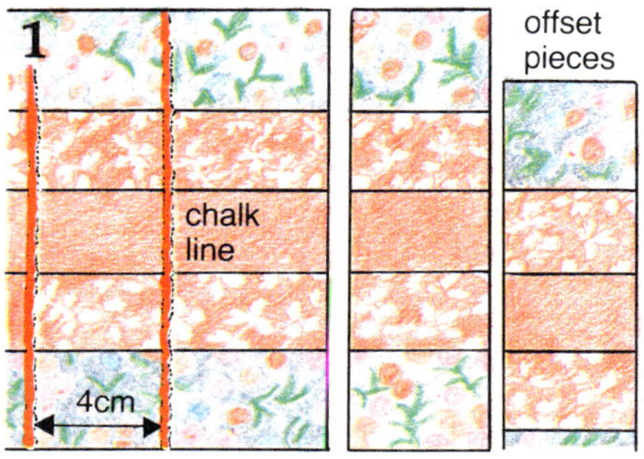


**1** Join strips of centre, second and outer colours with 5mm/¼in seams. Press all the seams in the same direction.

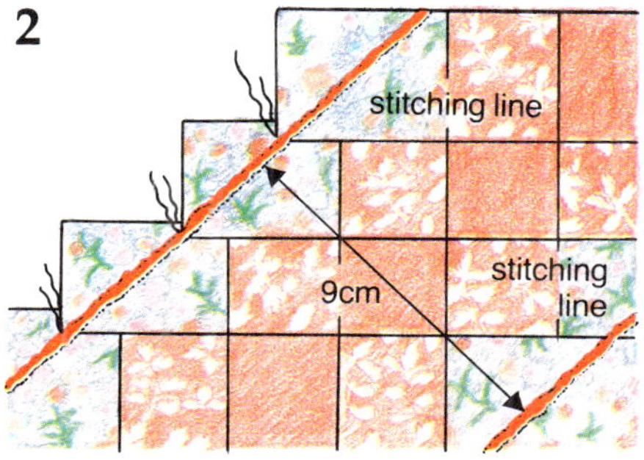


Mark and cut crosswise strips of 4cm/1½in width. Offset the pieces and stitch with 5mm/¼in seams so that the centre colour squares touch at the corners. Continue joining pieces until you have the required length. Straighten ends of strips as described on page 43.

Press all seams in the same direction.

**2** Now mark a stitching line along either side of the strip to give a strip 9cm/3½in wide. Join banding strips of the centre colour to either side, using this seam line.

Appliqué or set in patchwork to blouse and skirt as required, using prepared piping along all seams except neck edge.

# Patchwork picture ideas

Many traditional patchwork patterns have romantic-sounding names which are suggested by the shapes in the pattern. Sometimes the link between the pattern and its name is not so obvious and it takes imagination to fit the two together.

There is a group of patterns which are bold pictorial representations of everyday items – boats, houses, tulips, baskets of fruit and flowers. These are all built up from popular patchwork template shapes – squares, triangles, rectangles, parallelograms, and trapezoids.

Apart from some of the basket designs, the patterns are entirely pieced together into blocks before being made up into a finished item. Sometimes there are dividing strips between the blocks and often they have a border. Basket of flowers blocks usually include a pieced basket and appliquéd handle and flowers – a combination of two techniques.

Some pictorial patchwork designs are more suitable for childrens' projects, but several such as tulips and baskets of fruit can make beautiful quilts, cushions and wallhangings for any room in the house. You can make the designs as large as you like. A square cushion cover could be made up of one pieced block, or four joined together. Quilting the finished work by stitching round each motif adds emphasis.

appliqué pieces

*Below: Two more colourful quilts.*

# Quilting

*The ancient craft of quilting was devised to add warmth to bed covers and clothes. A layer of soft wadding was sandwiched between two layers of fabric and anchored with lines of basic stitches. In time stitching patterns were created to add interest and texture to the quilting, and elaborate, all-over designs can be found on many of the old English quilts.*

*Today traditional hand-sewn methods can be replaced by the sewing machine, and the introduction of lightweight, synthetic wadding means you can wash quilted fabrics more easily so that the techniques are available for a far wider range of items, including fashion jackets and waistcoats, table linen and cushions. Quick-to-make projects with small amounts of quilting can be just as effective as the traditional, full-scale bed cover. Try making some simple quilted bags or add some quilted relief to a garment by emphasising the pattern on a dress fabric.*

*Explore quilting variations such as trapunto, where varied amounts of wadding are inserted into a stitched design to give a subtle, three-dimensional effect, Italian quilting, where a cord is inserted between parallel lines of stitching to create a raised, linear design, or contour quilting, which uses the design printed on the fabric as a stitching guide. Quilting also combines well with both patchwork and appliqué, adding texture to a background area or relief to a motif.*

*Cosy quilted items are always expensive in the shops. But with only a little time and the minimum of equipment you can quilt and make up your own fabrics into a wonderful variety of articles for your home, your family and yourself.*

# Quick quilting on a sewing machine

***Wadded machine quilting is fun to do and gives a luxurious padded look to both clothes and home items. Try making some of these deliciously pretty bags for a bathroom or dressing table. Pick a fabric with ready-made lines to sew along, and make the job fast and easy.***

Quilting is the stitching together of two or more layers of fabric. It is decorative and adds another dimension to the fabric by altering the surface, giving it texture and relief. It is also of practical use, providing warmth, strength and body for clothing and household articles.

One of the most popular uses of quilting is as an enhancement for bed covers, often those worked in patchwork or appliqué. The quilting makes them thicker, warmer and more hardwearing.

### Wadded quilting

There are several different types of quilting, but one of the most useful is wadded quilting. The method involves making a sandwich of a top layer which can be plain or patterned fabric, a middle layer of wadding, and a bottom layer of lining fabric. The sandwich of three layers is tacked securely and then quilted – either on your lap or on a frame. Once tacked, the three layers can be quilted by hand or by machine in a series of small running stitches.

### Machine quilting

This chapter deals with wadded machine quilting – a quick technique which gives a professional finish. The fabric is quilted first and then made up into the finished item.

Although quilted fabrics are available commercially, colour ranges are limited. Using your machine and a little imagination, you can make your own individually quilted fabrics.

Once you have perfected the technique, you can make tablecloths, mats, bags, jackets, cushions and all sorts of small household accessories and gifts like those in the picture.

**Fabrics, threads and wadding** The top fabric for a quilted layer is usually cotton, cotton blend, silk, satin or wool, with similar lining fabric.

Use a matching shade of Sylko machine twist, or silk twist for silk fabrics. The fabrics in this chapter have been quilted with transparent nylon thread, which is almost invisible. It should be used only for machine quilting.

Most people use bonded terylene wadding available in 2oz, 4oz and 8oz weights, which can be bought in 1m/1yd wide rolls in most fabric departments. Cotton and wool domette (a soft interfacing) is sometimes used for machine quilting and is less bulky to use.

*Right: These quilted bags look expensive but are economical to make (see instructions overleaf).*

## Step-by-step machine quilting

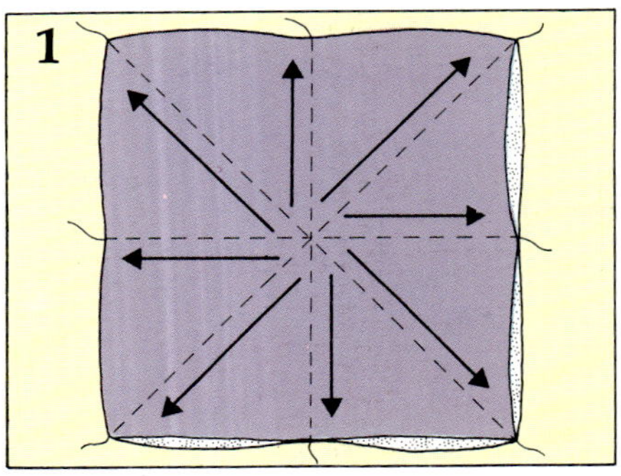


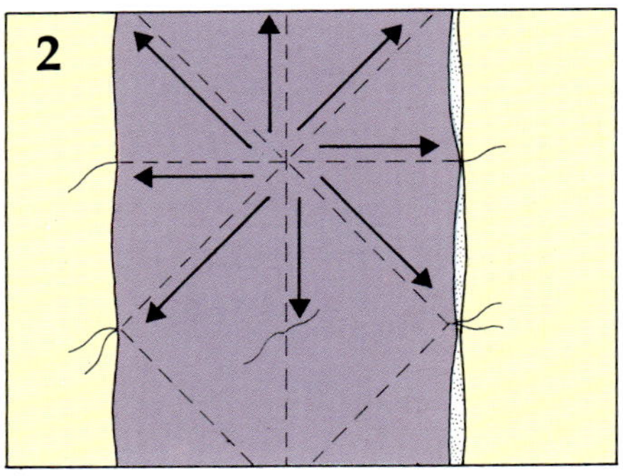


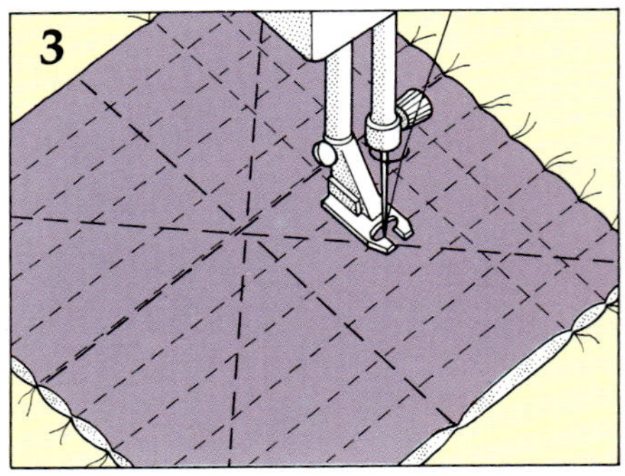


### Preparing the fabric

Take a piece of fabric at least 5cm/2in larger all round than the amount needed for the pattern pieces of the project. Cut lining and wadding to same size. Press fabric to remove wrinkles. Lay the lining fabric flat with the wadding on top. Next lay down the top fabric, right side up, and smooth out, keeping all layers aligned.

### Tacking fabrics and wadding

**1** Tack through all layers using a contrasting thread, which is easy to spot when removing. Stitch in a starburst pattern – first sew centred horizontal and vertical lines, then sew equidistant lines radiating from the centre to the outer edges. Use long running stitches. The spokes should be no more than 15cm/6in apart along outer edges of fabric.

**2** If the piece of fabric is long and narrow, you may need to tack several smaller starbursts along its length.

This tacking distributes the wadding evenly and prevents it from bunching. Do not tack round the outer edges of the fabric – this can cause puckering during quilting.

### Stitching

Loosen tension and pressure on the sewing machine. Set a medium stitch length and try out on a scrap 'sandwich' of fabric and wadding.

**3** Small pieces of fabric can be quilted with consecutive rows of stitching, beginning at one side. All the rows must be stitched in the same direction. If quilting a grid pattern, work parallel rows, turn

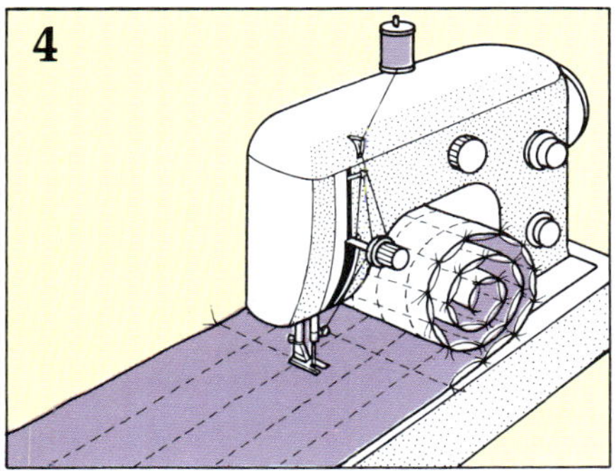


fabric and work the crossing rows. Begin stitching with the bulk of the fabric on the left of the needle.

**4** If quilting a long length of fabric, roll the quilted portion of the fabric up under the machine arm to keep it out of the way while you are working the remaining portion. Leave a short length of thread at the end of each line of stitching to prevent unravelling. These threads do not need finishing off – they will be secured by seams or bound edges.

## Machine quilting designs

Fabrics quilted by machine are often stitched in straight-line or grid patterns. These include diamonds, squares, vertical or diagonal stripes, and zigzags, which divide the fabric into neat, padded compartments.

A quilting guide-bar on your machine will place the stitching accurately. Stitch one straight guide-line, set the guide-bar to a suitable width, and stitch the second row with the bar following the first row. Work successive rows in the same way.

Quilting lines can be marked on to fabrics using a ruler and chalk pencil (brushes off after stitching) or a water-erasable marker (easily removed from most fabrics with a little water – test on fabric scrap first).

Simplest of all, use the design of a geometric print fabric to place the quilting lines. Stripes, trellis designs and checks are ideal, teamed with a plain or non-geometric print fabric as the backing.

*Above: A selection of effective quilting patterns for plain or printed fabrics.*

# *Quilted bags make perfect gifts*

All-over machine quilting is particularly suitable for small items such as these pretty cosmetic bags.
The four bags described in this chapter are made up in trellis fabrics specially chosen to give a suitable quilting design of diamonds or squares. For each bag, first quilt the fabric as described on page 48.
Graph patterns are given for the small and larger cases. To enlarge, copy on a grid of 5cm/2in squares. Cut required pattern pieces first from paper, then use these to cut shapes from quilted fabric or plastic lining. For sewing linings with plastic, see below. All seam allowances are 1cm/½in unless otherwise indicated, and are included in the pattern pieces.

Buy top fabric and lining of any width. They should tone in colour.

## Two drawstring bags

These come in two sizes and each bag incorporates a pair of eyelet holes. Follow the kit manufacturer's instructions for inserting the eyelets.

### You will need

40cm/½yd printed cotton fabric
40cm/½yd polyester wadding (4oz)
40cm/½yd cotton lining fabric
2 large eyelets (12mm/⅝in available in kit with insertion tool)
1m/1yd cotton cord to fit eyelets
1 card bias binding (25mm/1in wide or buy 12mm width and join)
Transparent nylon thread or matching sewing cotton

### Making up the bag

Cut fabric pieces as follows:
Large bag, one rectangle 40.5cm×28.5cm/16in×11in. Small bag, one rectangle 40.5cm×18cm/16in×7in. Both bags one circle radius 7.3cm/2⅞in. Cut drawstring casing strip from leftover lining fabric 3.4cm ×40.5cm/1¼in×16in. Tack close to edge of quilted pieces to reduce bulk. Insert eyelets 2.5cm/1in apart in centre front of main bag piece, 9cm/3½in from top (long edge) of large bag, 5.5cm/2¼in from top of small bag. Join short edges of main piece; neaten seam allowance with bias binding. Press seam open.
Turn in 7mm/⅜in seam allowance along both edges of casing and tack. Join ends to make a circle. Turn bag to wrong side and tack

## Small cosmetics case

One flat pattern piece folds up into an envelope-style case. The pattern is given far right, 1 square = 5cm/2in.

### You will need

25cm/¼yd printed cotton fabric
25cm/¼yd polyester wadding (4oz)
25cm/¼yd cotton lining fabric
25cm/¼yd opaque shower curtaining
5cm/2in strip of Velcro (20mm/¾in wide)
1 card bias binding (12mm/½in wide)
Transparent nylon thread or matching sewing cotton

### Making up the case

Cut one pattern piece from quilted fabric and one from plastic lining. Stitch loopy side of Velcro strip to centre front of quilted fabric piece, 2cm/¾in from the straight end of the fabric. Stitch fuzzy side of Velcro strip to plastic lining, 2cm/¾in away from rounded end of the plastic. Place lining on fabric with right sides facing. With a fine needle, tack together 5mm/⅜in in from edge. Machine the tacked pieces together along seamlines leaving one of the case side seams unstitched.
Carefully clip to stitching at each inward corner. Trim allowances close to stitching on all but the open edge of the case. Turn to right side and push out all corners with closed scissors. Tuck in edges of unstitched side along seamline and tack close to edge. Topstitch all round 6mm/¼in from edge. To assemble, place side and

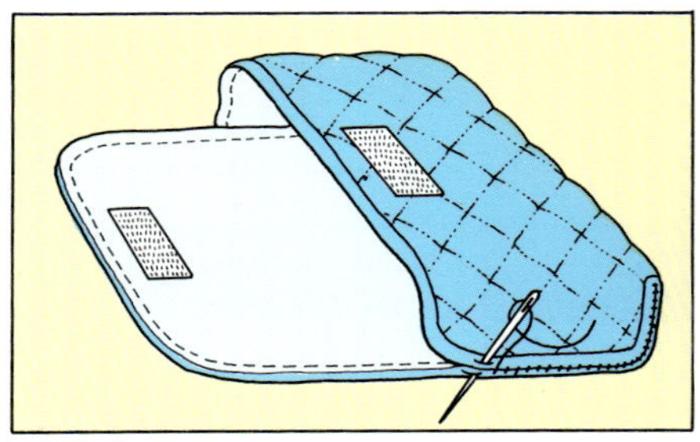

bottom edges together and join by hand with overcasting stitches. Continue up side seams and finish off at top of bag. Stitch over first stitching, reversing direction. Make tie with 65cm/25in of bias binding. Stitch to centre of front flap on stitching line so that 20cm/7¼in extends below flap, 40cm/15¼in above it. To seal case, close Velcro and tie bow.

PROFESSIONAL TOUCH

## Sewing with plastic

Give your cosmetic bags a practical and professional-looking plastic lining with a soft, pliable plastic such as shower curtaining.
Once a puncture is made in plastic, it's there to stay, so avoid using pins on it. Cut out pattern pieces by fixing the pattern to the plastic with adhesive tape. When tacking, use a fine needle and stitch along the *outer* edges of seam allowances.
Use transparent nylon thread and a medium stitch – a small stitch could cause the plastic to tear between perforations.
Plastics may pull under the machine's presser foot. If this happens, sandwich the article you are sewing between sheets of tissue paper, stitch through all layers. When the sewing is completed, simply tear away from the seams.

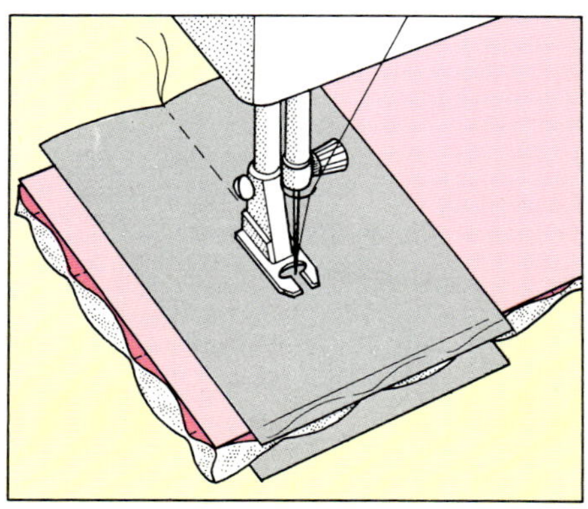

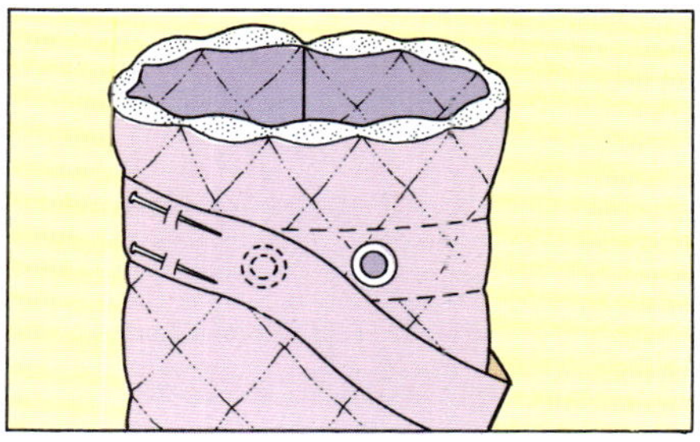

casing in place, centring over eyelets and matching seams. Machine stitch close to edges. Pin bag bottom to bag body with right sides together. Tack and stitch. seam. Finish with binding or overcast. Apply binding to top edge of bag. Insert cord through casing.
For tassels, knot cord 10cm/4in from ends, unravel below knot and trim.

*The drawstring bag and small cosmetics case are cut on the straight grain, but the larger cosmetics case has been cut on the cross to give a pattern of squares.*

## Larger cosmetics case

This larger sized cosmetics case has a convenient Velcro closure at the top and a plastic lining. The pattern is given below, 1 square=5cm/2in.

### You will need

20cm/¼yd printed cotton fabric
20cm/¼yd polyester wadding (4oz)
20cm/¼yd cotton lining fabric
20cm/¼yd transparent shower curtaining
22.5cm/¼yd strip of Velcro (20mm/¾in wide)
1 card bias binding (12mm/½in wide)
Transparent nylon thread or matching sewing cotton

### Making up the case

Cut paper pattern from graph. Cut two fabric and two plastic pieces from this pattern.
Trim 6mm/¼in off top edge of each piece of plastic. Aligning bottom edges, tack a piece of plastic to wrong side of each quilted piece, sewing close to outer edges and along top edge of plastic. Fold top 6mm/¼in of quilted fabric to back and tack it down; stitch through all layers. Separate Velcro strip and tack each piece near top edge of case pieces on wrong sides. Stitch top and bottom edges. On right side of each case piece, tack bias binding so the top edge aligns with the bottom edge of the Velcro (on wrong side of case piece). Stitch binding in place.

Position a strip of 12mm/½in bias binding flush with curved outer edge of each case piece. The binding should run along each outer edge and extend 4cm/1½in at each top edge. Stitch inner edge of binding. Trim away fabric and lining below the newly-stitched edge. Turn top ends of binding to wrong side of each piece, turn under when level with bottom edge of Velcro on inside, and tack in place. With wrong sides together, tack case pieces together, sealing Velcro and aligning outer binding edges.

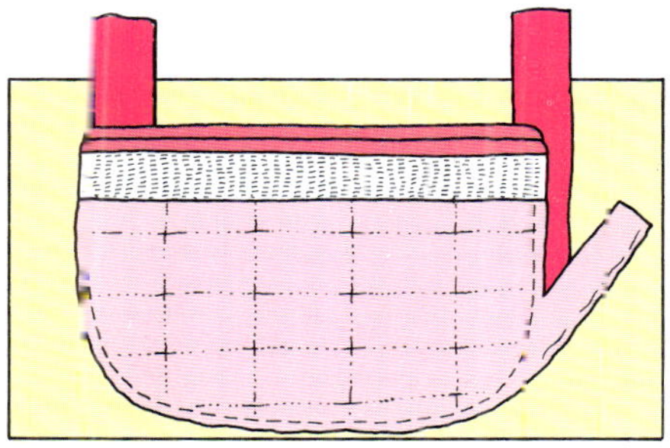

Stitch along outer edges of binding. For bow trim, cut a 28cm/11in strip of 12mm/½in binding. Fold in half lengthwise. Sew along open edge. Knot ends, trim excess, tie bow and hand sew to case front.

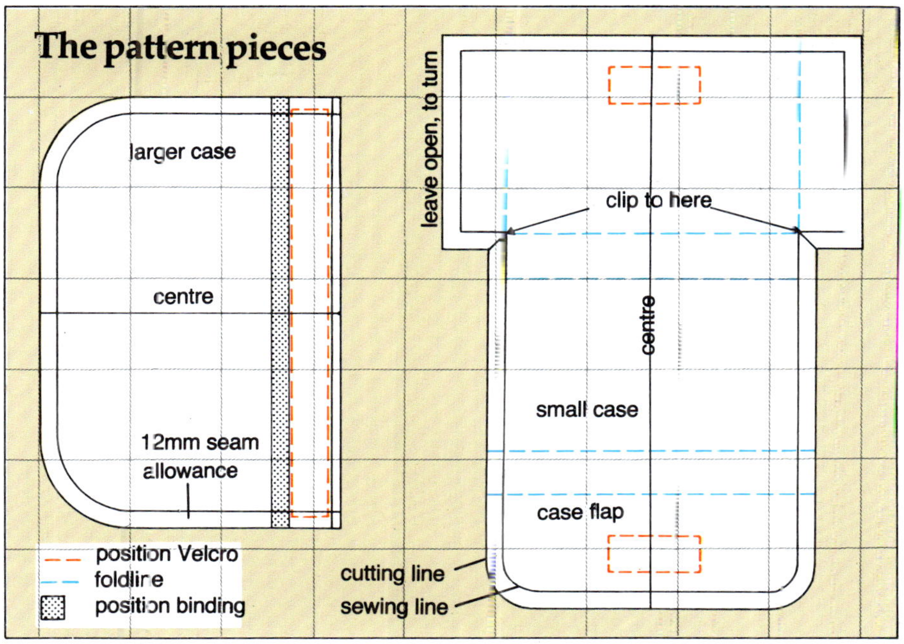

# English quilting: a hand-stitched technique

*Quilting was originated for the purely practical purpose of adding warmth, but its effect is so decorative that top designers now use it to decorate not only household items, but high fashion. And with these basic techniques at your fingertips, so can you . . .*

Quilting by hand is relaxing and satisfying because you can watch the design grow as your needle goes in and out.

Wadded quilting, sometimes known as English quilting, is traditionally worked by hand in running stitch. Often the designs are very intricate and seen to best advantage worked on large quilts; particularly beautiful examples come from Wales and the north of England.

Popular quilting designs and motifs have been passed down through the generations and you will find these old patterns available commercially – some in the form of templates or stencils.

Many geometric or pictorial motifs are adaptable to quilting, too, so there's plenty of scope for designing your own.

## English quilting materials

Most of the fabrics, waddings and threads used for machine quilting are suitable for hand quilting.

**Fabrics** Plain cotton fabrics are the easiest to work with because you can see the quilting design more clearly than on patterned ones. Shiny fabrics, which catch the light, give the most relief to the design.

The backing fabric for hand-stitched work should either be the same type as the top fabric, or it can be muslin or

*Below: A perfect present for a new baby, this hand-quilted cover is fully washable.*

calico – the latter is the traditional backing for English quilting.

**Needles** must be fine to avoid marking the fabric, and this applies to tacking needles, too. Betweens in sizes 7-9, even as fine as 10, are in common use and crewels are sometimes used. You will also need a box of fine lace pins.

**Threads** Quilting threads should be strong, and of the same type as the fabric. Strong, poly-cotton quilting thread is available in white and some colours, but if you need a thicker thread, good choices are DMC Cordonnet Spécial coton 20, 30, 40 or 50, Coats crochet cotton, or DMC pearl cotton. If the thread does not have a glazed finish, run it through a block of beeswax before quilting to help it to pass smoothly through the layers of fabric and wadding, and to make it stronger.

**Thimbles** It is well worth persevering to learn to use a thimble, to protect the finger constantly pushing a needle through several layers of fabric. Choose a large, comfortable thimble with a flat, indented head and wear it on the middle finger of your sewing hand. Some quilters use a second thimble on the hand underneath the quilt to guide the needle back up again when it has passed down through the three layers. Others use a leather finger guard or masking tape on the working finger.

### Transferring designs

The design must be marked on the fabric before it is attached to the wadding and backing. It is important not to use a permanent marker as the design may show between stitches.

For fairly intricate quilting designs such as the one overleaf, traditional methods used for transferring embroidery designs are suitable. These include the trace and tack method, dressmaker's carbon paper (following manufacturer's instructions) and the window method.

If the fabric you are using is translucent against the light, the window method is the simplest. Make sure the design tracing is marked in clear, black lines and trace it off on to the fabric with a dressmaker's chalk pencil, a well-sharpened hard pencil or a blue water-erasable marker (test it first on a fabric scrap).

Some geometric or repeat motif quilting designs can be transferred by making card or plastic templates of sections of the design which can be traced around. Another method is to make a stencil.

## How to begin

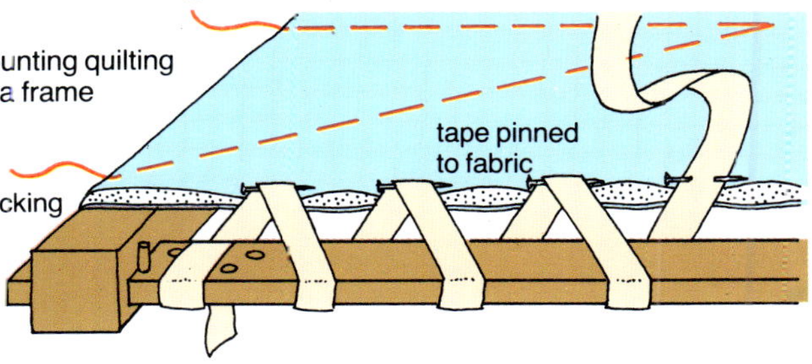


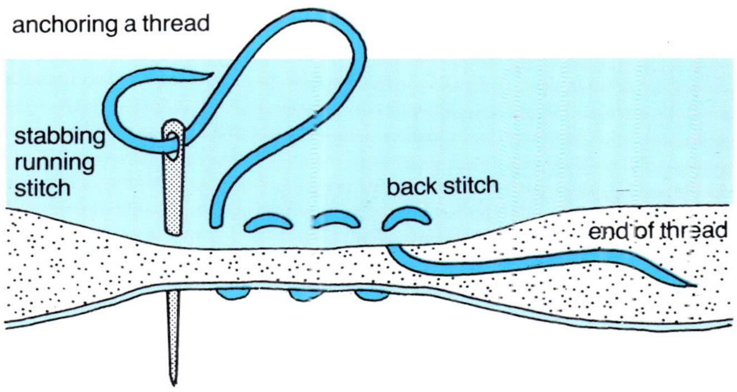


Small items such as cushions can be quilted using only your lap as a support. For larger work, use a rectangular embroidery frame or a special quilting hoop with a stand, to liberate both hands. To mount fabric on the hoop, simply lay the work over the smaller hoop and press the larger hoop over it to hold the surface flat, but not taut. If you stretch it too tightly the stitches will not sink deeply into the layers of fabric and the design will lack definition.

**Mounting quilting on a frame** An embroidery frame acts as a small quilting frame for a cushion or cot cover.

Attach the top and bottom of the tacked layers to the rollers on the frame. If the quilting is longer than the side stretchers, roll part of it over the rollers so it can be wound on as work progresses. Fix the rollers and stretchers so that the work is held firm but not taut.

To attach the sides of the work to the stretchers, tie a length of cotton tape to one end of one stretcher. Pin to the edge of the quilting, turn tape back over pin, wind round the stretcher and pin to the quilting again, 7.5-10cm/3-4in further along. Continue to the end of the quilting. Repeat on other side.

### Basic stitching techniques

As with machine quilting, the three layers – fabric, wadding and backing – must be well tacked before the quilting stitches are worked, especially when you are not using a frame. Lay the layers down in the correct order and smooth them out. Pin together with fine pins and tack in straight lines, radiating out from the centre.

The main quilting stitch is hand-sewn running stitch. Keep the sewing hand above the fabric, with the other hand underneath to guide the needle back into the fabric.

Running stitch can be worked either with a stabbing motion, one stitch at a time, or by picking up groups of four or five stitches – usually possible only on thinner layers, not with wadded quilting.

It is the evenness of the stitches that makes quilting pleasing to the eye, so make sure that your stitches (and the spacing between them) are all of equal length – about 2mm/⅛in for most projects. Begin stitching at the centre of the design and work outwards.

With each new length of thread, insert the needle into the top fabric and wadding some way from the stitching line. As shown above, bring the needle up where you wish to stitch, leaving a long thread in the wadding, and backstitch through the first stitch to anchor it securely. To finish off, make a small back stitch through the last stitch and run the thread through the wadding before snipping it off

# Hand-quilted cot cover

A delightful design of doves, hearts, leaves and flowers adorns this cot cover. The stitching is worked in white thread but you could use colours to create a bolder effect. All materials are made of polyester, so the quilt is fully washable.

**You will need**
1.80m/2yd white polyester satin or similar (122cm/48in width) *or* 2m/2⅛yd of 112cm/44in width
3.20m/3½yd polyester wadding (4oz weight) 122cm/48in width *or* 100cm/39in width
1m/1⅛yd muslin 122cm/48in wide *or* enough to cut a piece 116cm×100cm/46in×40in
Square or rectangular embroidery frame or quilting hoop to fit fabric
1 reel Coats Drima polyester thread
Crewel or between needle size 8

## Working the design

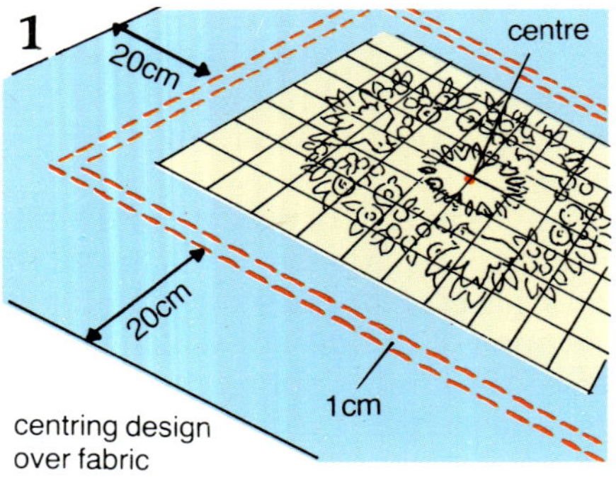


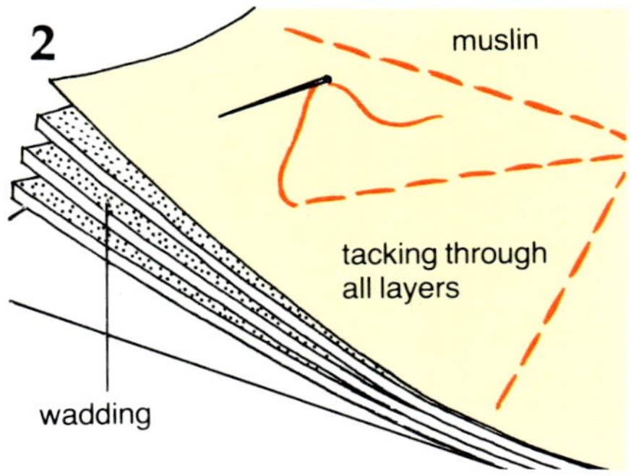


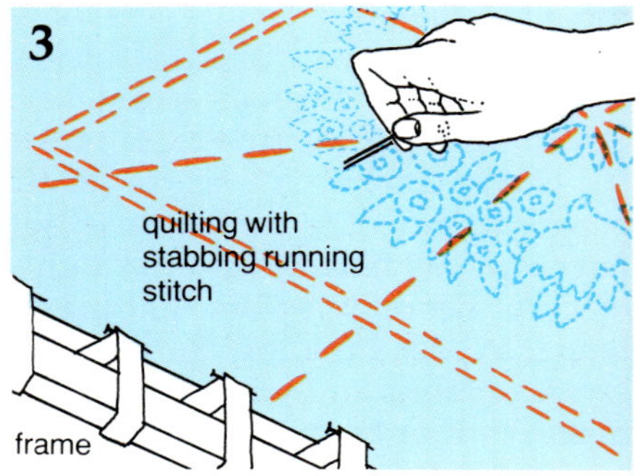


The small chart gives the complete quilting design. Enlarge it on to a grid of 5cm/2in squares on tracing paper, copying it square by square. The dove, heart and leaf motifs are given full size to help you.
**1** Trace off the motifs and, using the small diagram as a guide, position the tracings under your enlargement of the design and trace them in at the appropriate points to complete the full-size design.
**Preparing the fabric** Cut a piece of satin fabric 116cm×100cm/46in×40in. Fold it in half both ways, creasing lightly to make folds which cross at the centre point of fabric. This will help you to place the quilting design centrally. Transfer the design to the fabric matching the design and fabric centres.
Measure 20cm/8in from all four edges of fabric and tack or mark a border line all round the rectangle. Then tack or mark a second line 1cm/½in inside the first. Cut three 116cm×100cm/46in×40in pieces from the length of wadding.
**2** Lay them one on top of the other on the wrong side of the top fabric. Lay the muslin centrally over the wadding and tack thoroughly through all layers.

**Working the quilting** Mount the quilting on the frame, if you have one. If necessary, roll part of the design round the roller bars, but make sure you are able to begin the quilting at the centre of the design. (If you do not have a frame, work the quilting on your lap.)
**3** Work the quilting in stabbing running stitch (two movements) using the polyester thread – the wadding is too bulky to allow you to pick up several stitches at once. After completing the central motifs, stitch along the double parallel lines. Remove the work from the frame.

DESIGN EXTRA

## Bluebird basket cover

This pretty quilted cover can be worked on a small hoop. Pick out motifs from the cot cover.

**You will need**
For a round basket, diameter 20-30cm/8-12in
40cm/½yd polyester satin
40cm/½yd medium (4oz) wadding (use double)
40cm/½yd muslin for backing
Coats Drima polyester thread

**Working the cover**
Measure the basket diameter and add 10cm/4in to obtain fabric lengths.
To plan the design, draw round the upturned basket on tracing paper and trace off motifs in desired positions. The cover (right) has a central dove inside a ring of hearts, leaves and flowers. Draw round a saucer and position them along this line. Transfer design to fabric and work quilting as for cot cover. Cut out circle of quilted fabric allowing extra 1cm/½in all round for seam. Cut satin backing to same size. Place right sides together and sew, leaving opening for turning. Turn, slipstitching opening.

*Above: A quilted cover for a basket.*

## Trace patterns

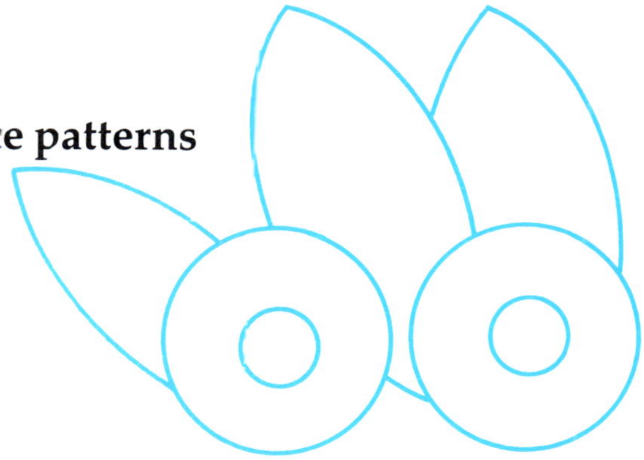

## Chart for quilting design

1 square = 5cm

## Making up and backing

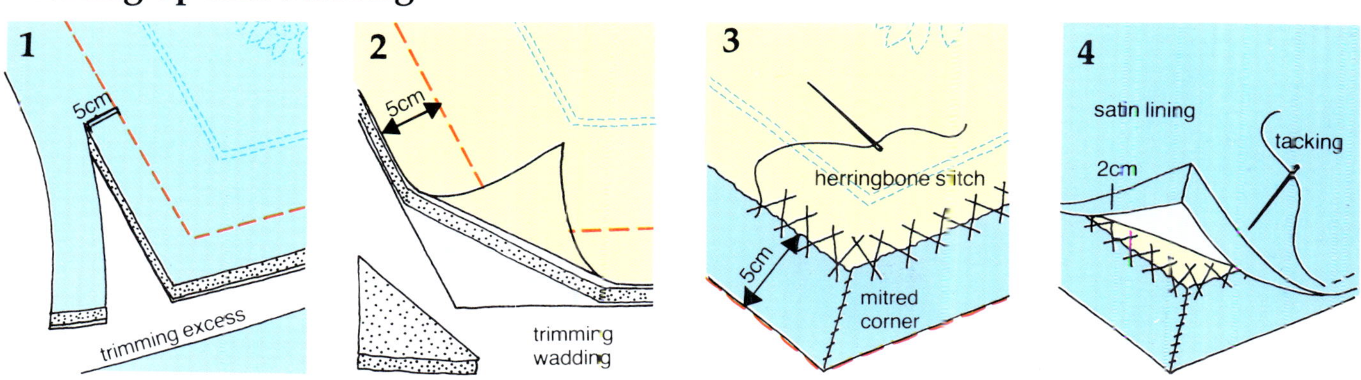


Measure and tack all round 8cm/3¼in outside the parallel border lines to mark finished edge of quilt. Remove all other original tacking.

**1** Trim fabrics and wadding to within 5cm/2in of the tacking.

**2** Trim the wadding only diagonally across each corner.

**3** Fold 5cm/2in to wrong side all round, mitring corners of satin and muslin. Tack in position. Slipstitch mitred corners and catch raw edge down all round with herringbone stitch.

**4** Cut a rectangle of satin fabric for the quilt backing measuring 96cm×80cm/38in×32in. Turn under 2cm/¾in all round and press. Tack to back of quilt close to outer edge and slipstitch in position all round.

# Trapunto

***Trapunto is an attractive form of quilting where selected areas of the work are padded, giving a raised effect to pictorial or geometric designs. The patterns are outlined in simple running or backstitch and the visual effect is varied by the amount of padding inserted.***

The technique is sometimes known as stuffed quilting and gives the effect of a raised design on a flat background. It is usually worked on plain fabric using the same colour thread. Two layers of fabric are stitched together and padding is inserted between the layers through slits made in the backing fabric. The slits are then sewn up. The quilting is usually hand sewn, but geometric and other simple designs can be machined.

## Materials and equipment

For successful trapunto, choose a closely-woven cotton or silk fabric in a pale or medium shade for the top fabric so that the design shows up well in relief. Lightweight fabrics can use the same material for the backing. Heavier or more openweave fabrics should be backed with muslin.

Pins and needles should be fine, and you will also need a small pair of sharp embroidery scissors for slitting the backs of the motifs.

Use a medium-sized knitting needle to help insert the wadding.

It is best if you choose a fairly simple design without too many tiny details; at the same time make sure the areas to be padded are not too large or you will have difficulty in making the work look even. Transfer this design to the right side of the top fabric as for ordinary English quilting. Water-erasable felt pens can be useful for this, but take care to make a fine line as the stitching is delicate.

## Working the trapunto

1 

2 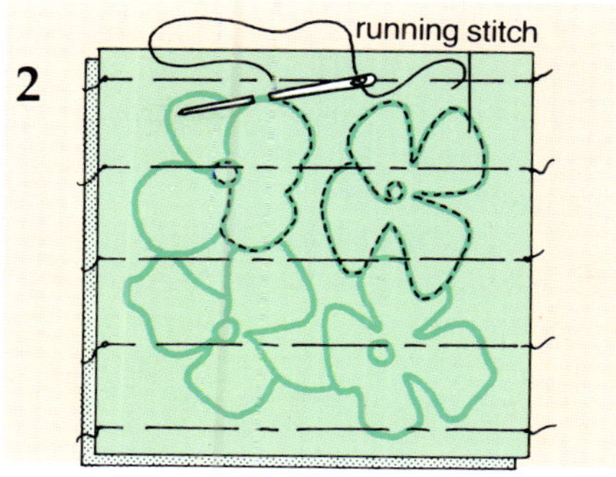


3 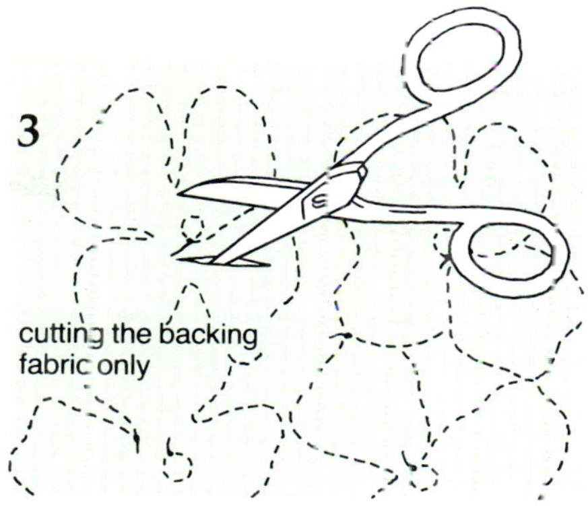


**1** Place the top fabric over the backing fabric. Pin and join the two together with lines of tacking stitches, about 7cm/2¾in apart, to cover the whole piece of fabric.

*Below: These beautiful trapunto designs are worked by hand on the cushion fronts before making up.*

**2** This type of quilting can easily be done in the hand, but mount the double fabric on a frame if you find it easier.
Stitch along the design lines in either backstitch or running stitch, making your stitches small and neat – they will have to hold the wadding securely in place later.

Begin each thread with a tiny knot. When the whole design is stitched, remove the tacking threads.
**3** Turn the work wrong side up. With a small, sharp pair of scissors, make a small slit in the centre of each shape to be padded, cutting through the backing fabric only.

4 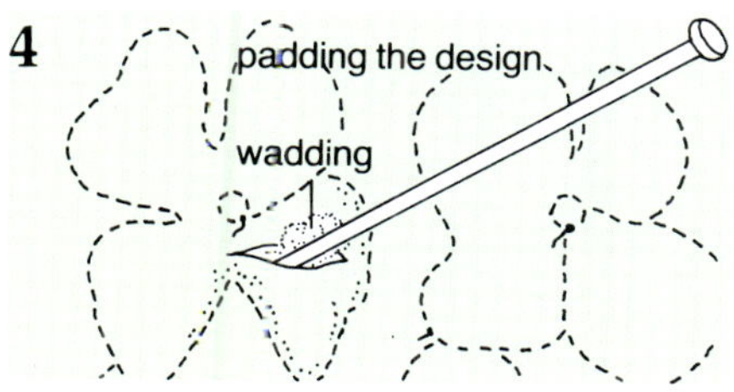


5 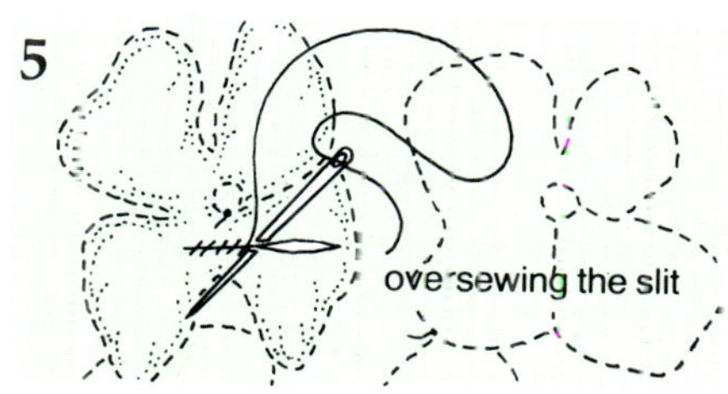


**4** Tease out a small piece of wadding and push it through the slit with the point of a medium-sized knitting needle; carry on doing this until the shape is evenly padded out on the right side, but not hard. Make sure you don't miss any corners.

Some areas can be padded out more than others but do not insert so much wadding that the unpadded background fabric puckers. Other parts of the design can be left completely flat.
**5** Sew up the edges of the slit with small oversewing stitches.

# *A pair of trapunto cushions*

These two cushions would look attractive either end of a window seat. The two scenes show inside and outside views of a window. You could make them from glazed cotton, polyester crêpe de chine or luxurious silk, but remember to match the thread to the material used.
Choose cool pale green and shell pink colours for a delicate look. Cream, yellow or palest blue would also look lovely.
The designs are worked partly in backstitch and partly in running stitch, and the amount of padding varies in different parts of the design.

### You will need for each cushion

50cm/⅝yd crêpe de chine (90cm/36in width, or more) in a pale shade
50cm/⅝yd backing fabric to match
1 reel pure silk sewing thread, to match crêpe de chine
10cm/⅛yd polyester wadding
18in/45cm square cushion pad
40cm/16in zip
Fine crewel or sharps needles
Tacking cotton

### Preparing the fabric

Cut both pieces of fabric in half to make two pieces 45cm × 50cm/18in × 20in. Enlarge the design on each chart to double the size (one square = 5cm/2in). Trace over the outlines in black felt tip pen on white paper, and lay one of the crêpe de chine squares over it, making sure the fabric is centred over the design. Pin in position all round the edge.

Trace the outline of the design on to the crêpe de chine using either a finely sharpened crayon just a little darker than the fabric, or a water-erasable embroidery marker. Test on a scrap of the fabric first.

**Working the trapunto cushions**
Remove the pins and paper, and lay the marked fabric over one of the squares of backing fabric.

Tack the two squares together as described on the previous page and carefully stitch the design in matching silk thread, working solid lines in backstitch and dotted lines in running stitch.
Turn the work to wrong side and insert wadding in those parts of the design indicated. Some parts are lightly wadded, some more fully to give more relief and texture.

**Windowbox design** Insert light padding into the outer window frames and the windowbox area. The flowers and leaves should be more fully padded so that they stand out in the foreground.
**Bedroom window design** Again, refer to the design to see which parts of the design are wadded. Heavy padding is inserted into the brush, bottles, necklace and part of

## Graph for windowbox design

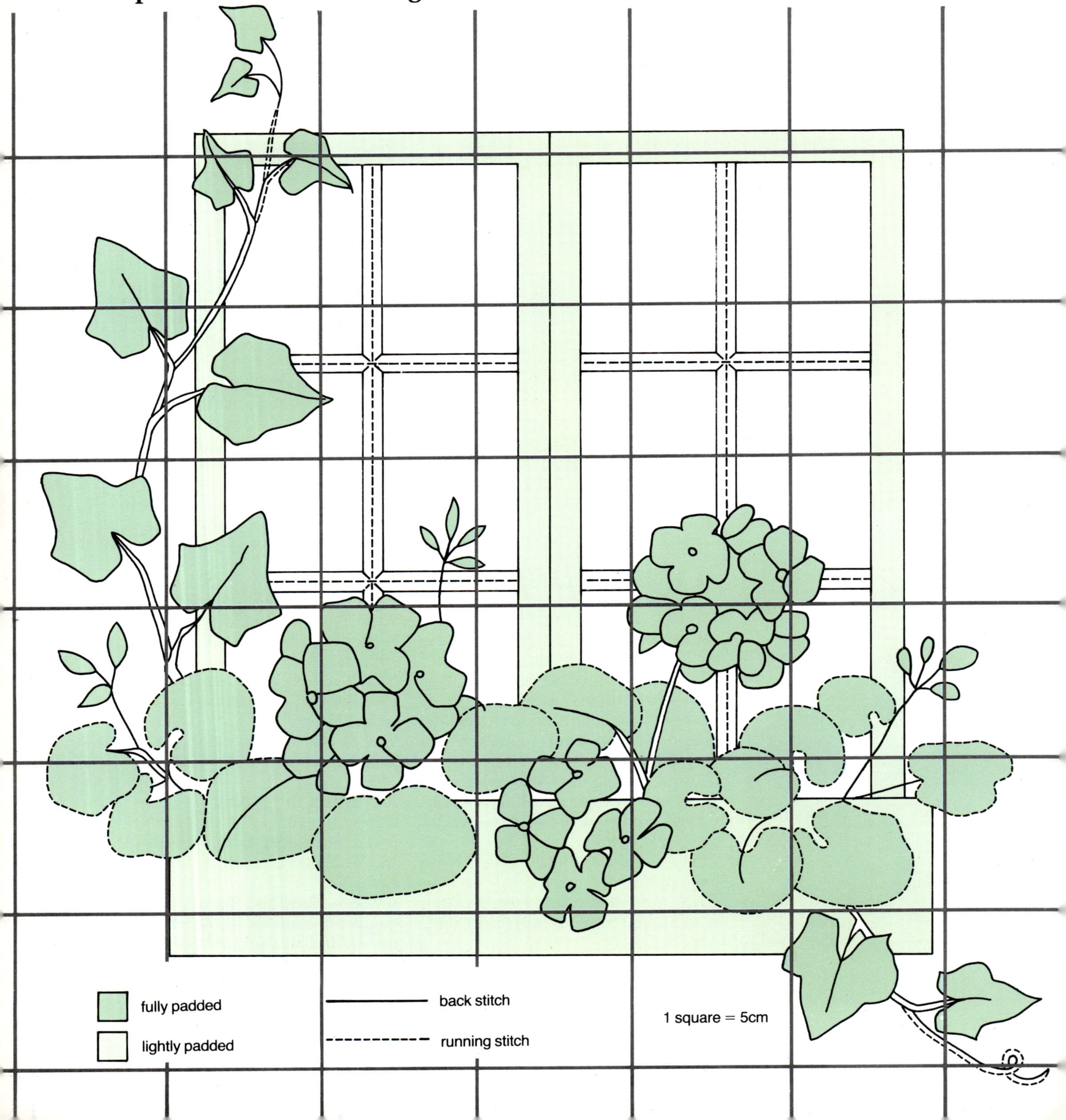

the curtains. Some of the curtain folds are lightly padded, while others are left completely flat.

**Making up the cushion**
Cut the remaining pieces of crêpe de chine and backing in half to make two pieces 45cm × 25cm/18in × 10in. With wrong sides together, tack the two pieces of backing to the pieces of top fabric.

**Insert zip centrally** between two long edges of these pieces.
With zip slightly undone, place right side of quilting to right side of back and stitch all round with a 1cm/½in seam (the size of the finished square will be 43cm/17in). Trim seams and corners, open zip fully and turn to right side. Top-stitch round seam 2mm/⅛in from edge.

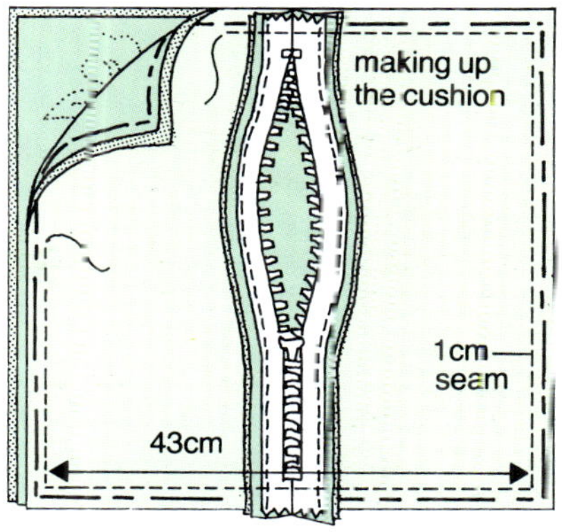


## Graph for bedroom window design

# Italian quilting for raised corded designs

***An intricate Celtic motif from the Book of Kells inspired this linear design which is particularly suitable for Italian quilting. Transfer the pattern to the delicate fabric by using pounce, and make an elegant cummerbund and matching bag.***

Italian quilting is sometimes called corded quilting and gives an attractive raised effect which is suitable for linear patterns. It is purely decorative and cannot be relied on for warmth and body. It is often combined with trapunto (page 56) and is used, for example, in floral designs where there may be a combination of linear stems worked in Italian quilting, and larger flower areas padded out in trapunto.

Like trapunto, the stitching is worked on a double layer of fabric tacked together and then the design is padded from the wrong side. The design is worked by hand or machine in parallel lines about 6mm/¼in apart and lengths of quilting wool or cord are inserted into the tubes formed by the parallel lines. The finished quilting is lined to hide the backing.

**Top fabrics** Italian quilting works best on plain fabrics with a sheen which shows up the corded design to advantage and therefore satin is a popular choice. The fabric needs to have a little more give than those normally used for other kinds of quilting so a fine silky jersey is also recommended. You could equally well use lawn or crêpe.

**Backing fabrics** Butter muslin or lawn are often used for the backing fabric. The quilting wool or cord is easily inserted through these soft fabrics.

**Cords** The cord inserted between the design lines may be a soft cotton cord or a special quilting wool. Wash both these before use – any shrinkage after quilting would cause the ground fabric to pucker.

**Threads** Try and match thread to fabric, using silk twist for stitching on silk, cotton thread for cotton fabrics, and polyester thread for synthetics.

*Right: An exquisite quilted cummerbund for straight or full-skirted outfits. Make a matching purse with a strap.*

## The techniques of Italian quilting

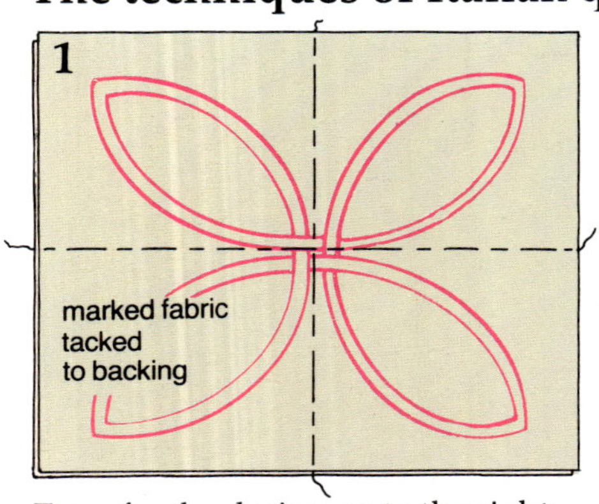


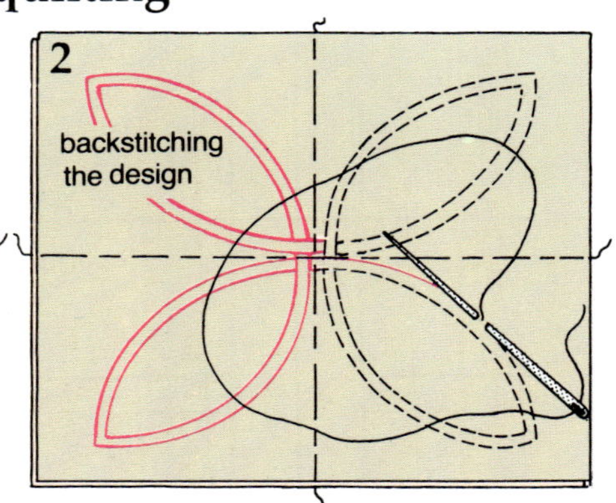


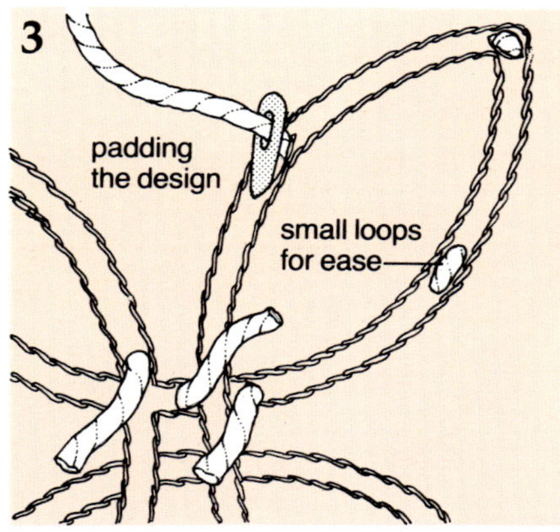


Transfer the design on to the right side of the top fabric using the prick and pounce method or tacking.

**1** Tack the marked fabric to the backing lawn or muslin with vertical, horizontal and diagonal lines. If quilting by hand, mount the two fabrics in a rectangular frame large enough to take the whole design. This leaves both your hands free for stitching.

**2** Stitch along the parallel lines of the design using backstitch or running stitch and a fine needle. If using running stitch, you may be able to pick up several stitches at once, rather than using a stabbing running stitch which takes longer. Make sure you finish off each length of thread securely on the back of the work. The cords cannot overlap – where one cord meets another the ends of one cord stop each side so that it looks as though it passes underneath the other cord.

**Using your sewing machine** If the design being quilted is not too complicated or curvy, it can be machined using a small straight stitch. In this case, do not mount the fabric on a frame. Work slowly and carefully, pulling all ends through to the back and finishing them off securely.

**Padding the design** When the entire design is stitched, remove the work from the frame. Working from the back, fill in the tubes formed by the stitching using a blunt bodkin or tapestry needle size 16 or 18 threaded with quilting wool or cord. To avoid piercing the top fabric, make the entry hole in the backing fabric very carefully using a stitch ripper. Insert the needle into the entry hole and after about 2.5cm/1in, bring it back through the backing fabric.

**3** Pull the wool or cord loosely through the tubes of the design, leaving a little showing at the beginning. Re-insert the needle in the same hole. At corners or on tight curves, bring the needle out and re-insert it in the same way, again leaving a little loop of the wool showing. This helps the tubes to remain full and not flatten, and also prevents the fabric round the design from puckering.

## PROFESSIONAL TOUCH

### Prick and pounce

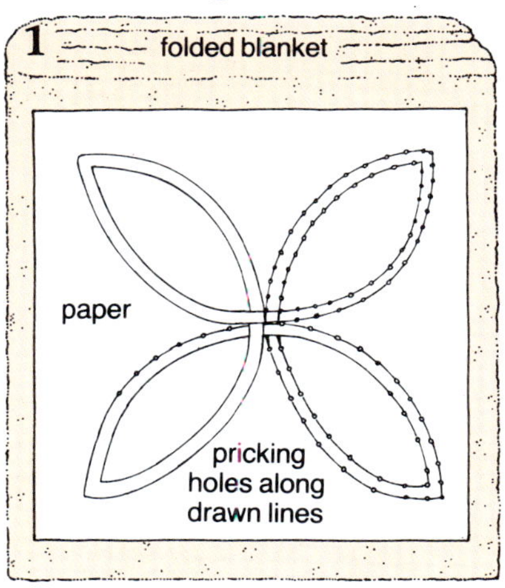


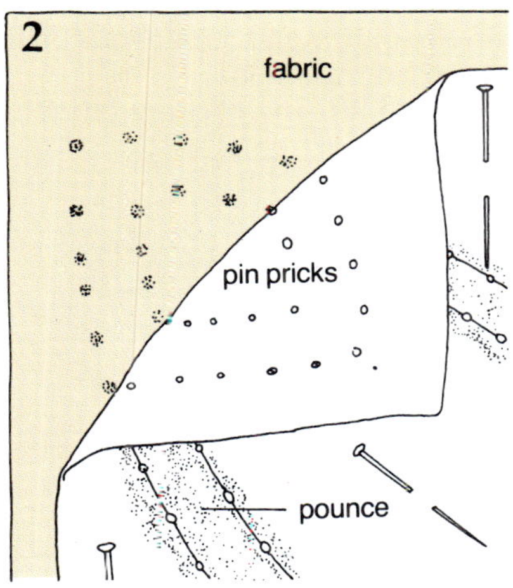


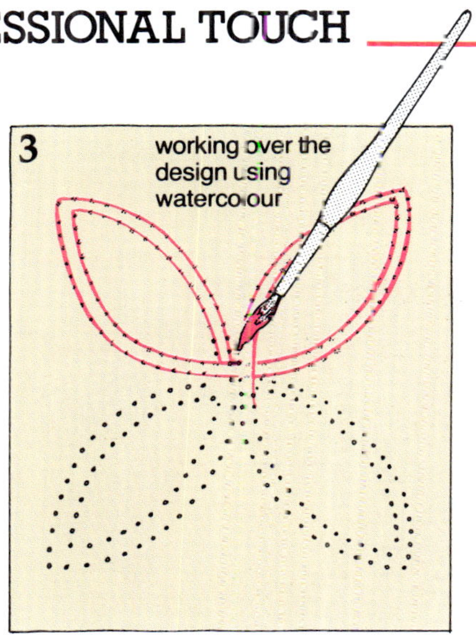


One of the best ways to transfer an Italian quilting design is the prick and pounce method. Marking with tacks is cumbersome for a delicate design, and dressmaker's carbon is indelible and may show on a light-coloured fabric.

**1** Draw the design on a sheet of firm paper and place it over a folded piece of blanket. Prick a series of holes along all the design lines – using a sharp needle, a stiletto or, if the design is not too intricate, by running along them with your sewing machine unthreaded and set to a long stitch.

**2** Pin the pricked pattern firmly in place on the right side of the fabric where the design is to be quilted. You will need a special marking powder called *pounce*. Take a small felt pad, or a rolled-up piece of felt, and rub pounce all over the design so it goes through the holes on to the fabric. Lift a corner to check that the design is clearly transferred before removing the tracing.

**3** Blow gently over the surface of the fabric to remove excess pounce. The design will show up as a series of dotted lines. Go over the design lines using a very fine paint brush dipped in watercolour slightly darker than the fabric or use a finely sharpened dressmaker's chalk pencil.

# Italian quilted cummerbund and matching purse

Treat yourself to the luxury of silk satin and make this cummerbund and purse for a special occasion. The design has been stitched in pale pink thread for emphasis. It shows up perfectly on the ivory silk satin.

**You will need**

**For cummerbund only**

30cm/⅜yd silk satin (any width)
30cm/⅜yd matching silk lining
30cm/⅜yd muslin/lawn for backing
15cm/⅛yd craft quality Vilene
15cm/⅛yd buckram for stiffening
2 hanks quilting wool
6 reels silk twist
Fine crewel needle
Blunt bodkin or tapestry needle
Pounce and felt pad (for marking design)
Rectangular embroidery frame (optional)
Stitch ripper

**For cummerbund and purse**

½m/½yd silk satin, width 115cm/45in *or* 1m/1yd of width 90cm/36in
70cm/¾yd silk lining (90cm/36in wide)
70cm/¾yd cotton lawn or muslin
35cm/⅜yd craft quality Vilene
8 reels silk twist
25cm/¼yd polyester wadding (2oz)
All other requirements are as for cummerbund only

**Cutting out the cummerbund**

Follow the cutting layouts carefully if you plan to make the purse too. The 90cm/36in width fabric is only suitable for waist measurements up to 86cm/34in. Above this use 115cm/45in-width fabric.

## Making the cummerbund

1
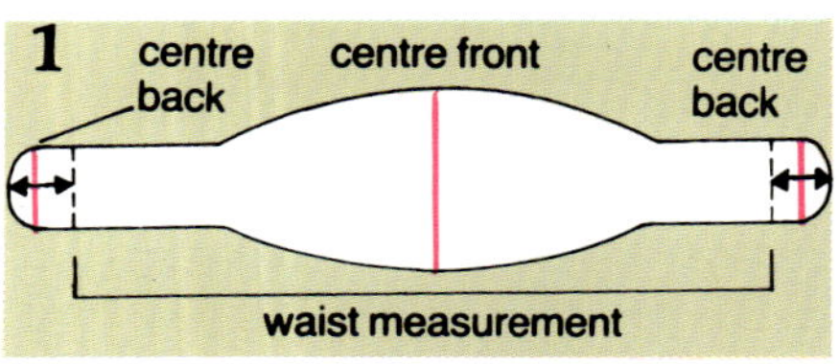


2
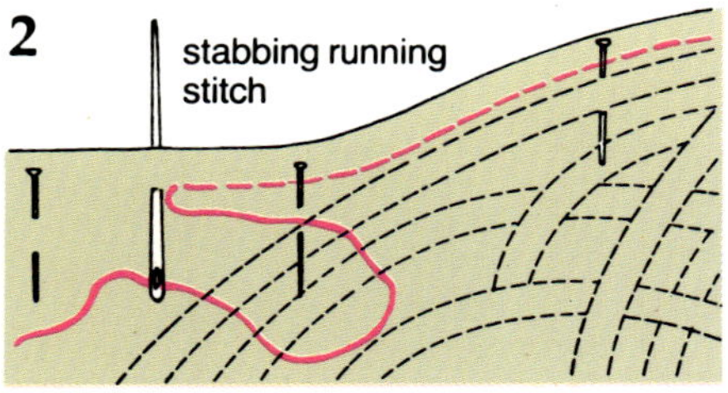


3
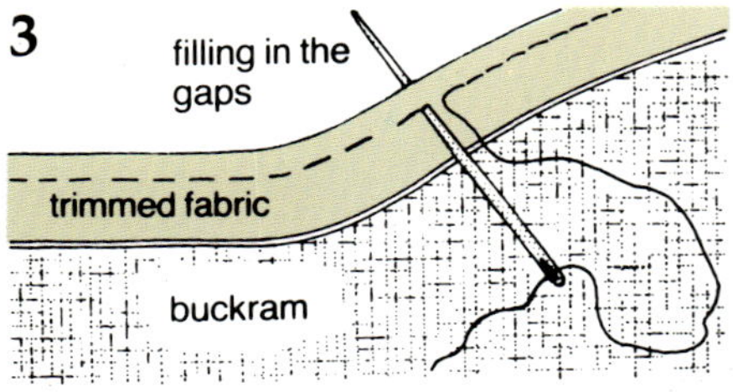


Make a paper pattern for the finished belt using the trace pattern outline.
**1** Extend each end equally until belt is 5cm/2in longer than your waist measurement. Round off ends as shown.
Use this pattern to cut a piece of Vilene and one of buckram to the finished size and tack them together. Pin the completed quilting with the backing fabric next to the Vilene. You will note that the quilting has 'shrunk' the design a little, leaving a small rebate between the quilting and the edge of Vilene/buckram.
Trim the quilting to about 4cm/1½in larger than the Vilene.
**2** Pull the satin and backing fabric tightly over the edge of the Vilene/buckram and work stabbing running stitch about 3mm/⅛in away from the edge, through all layers.
**3** When you have stitched all the way round the belt, cut away excess fabric at the back and work running stitch all round the edge again, filling in the gaps left by the

## Making the purse

1
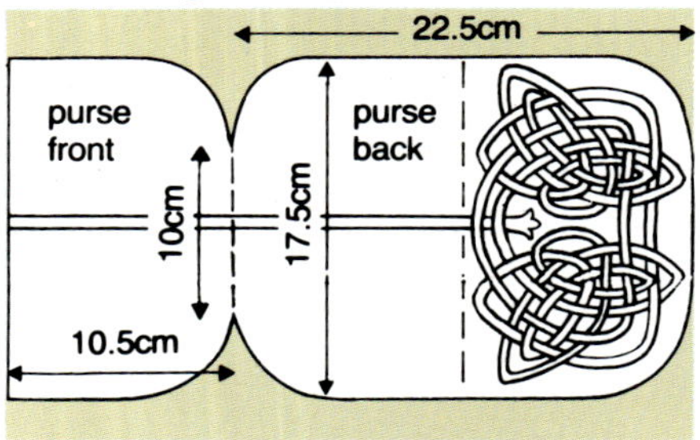


2
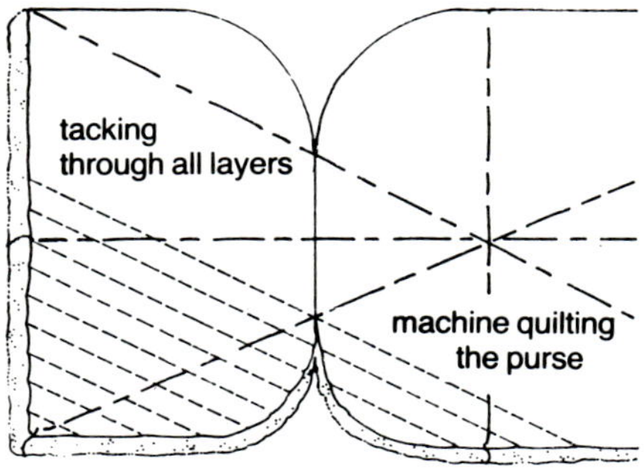


3
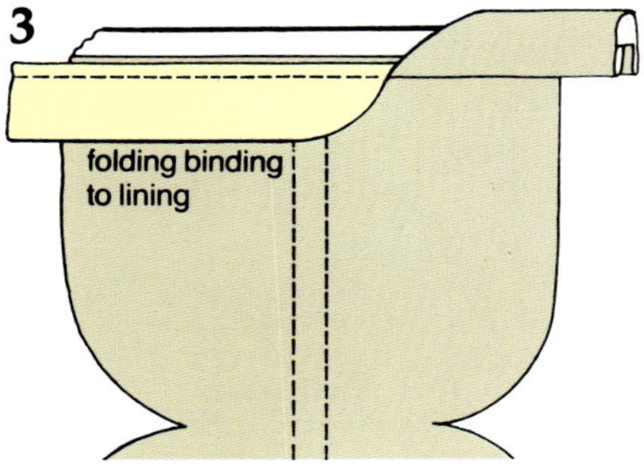


The purse has the Italian quilted design taken from the centre part of the cummerbund design on the front flap and a machine-quilted lining.
**1** Make a paper pattern following the dimensions in the diagram. Draw curved edges by eye, or use a saucer, or dressmaker's flexicurve. Cut rectangles 25cm×45cm/10in×18in from the satin and the lawn backing fabric. Use the pattern to roughly mark the purse outline with tacking stitches to help you position the motif. Transfer, stitch and quilt the design as described earlier. A single line of quilting runs down the centre of the purse, ending in a claw shape at front flap. Cut a purse shape from Vilene and cut two slightly larger ones from wadding and lining silk.
**2** Tack these together, wadding in the centre, and quilt all-over pattern by hand or machine.
Trim silk and wadding flush with Vilene and cut the quilted satin to the same size. Tack satin and quilted lining, wrong sides together.

**Finishing off** You need an 80cm/32in bias satin strip, width 3cm/1¼in, for joining and binding the purse. This can be cut in one piece if using 90cm/36in-wide fabric, or join strips to obtain right length.
**3** Bind top edge of purse front by placing right side of bias strip on right side of purse with edges matching. Stitching with a 6mm/¼in seam, turn binding to lining side, turn edge under, and slipstitch.
**4** Fold bag front and back together (lining inside) matching curved

Cut a satin rectangle 30cm×90cm/12in×36in. For waists larger than 81cm/32in, add the extra inches to the length. Cut backing to same size.
Fold a piece of tracing paper in half and trace the design on one half. Turn the paper and re-trace the design on the other half.

**Working the quilting**
Transfer, stitch and quilt the design as described on pages 60-61. Begin at the centre and work outwards and do not forget the line which runs round the whole design.

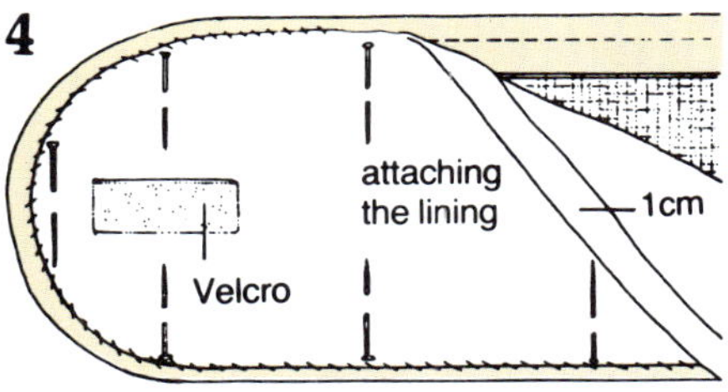


stabbing stitch. This will give the same effect as the backstitch on the Italian quilting.
**4** Use the paper pattern to cut a piece of lining silk, adding 1cm/½in all round. Turn under 1cm/½in, pin to back of belt and hem to border. Add two 4cm/1½in pieces of Velcro to the ends so that the cummerbund fastens with a 5cm/2in overlap.

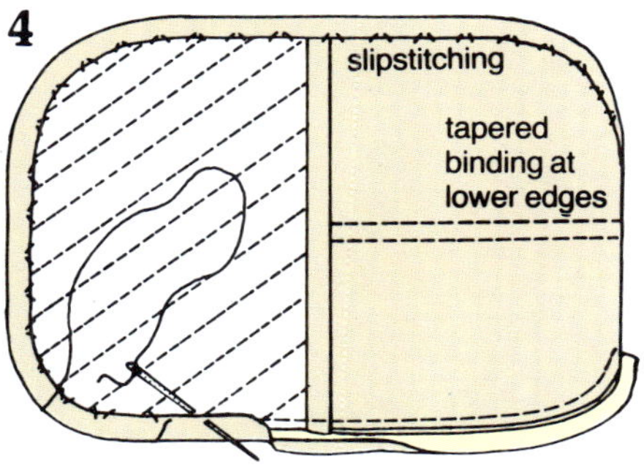


edges. Tack down sides. Place right side of strip on right side of back of bag and up round front flap and machine. Turn binding over edge and slipstitch, continuing round flap. Taper binding at lower edges.
**To make shoulder strap** Cut a 112cm/44in straight satin strip 5cm/2in wide. With right sides together, join long edges of strip taking a 1cm/½in seam. Trim seam, turn and stuff with four strands of quilting wool. Close ends and sew to lining at base of front flap.

## Cutting layouts for cummerbund and purse

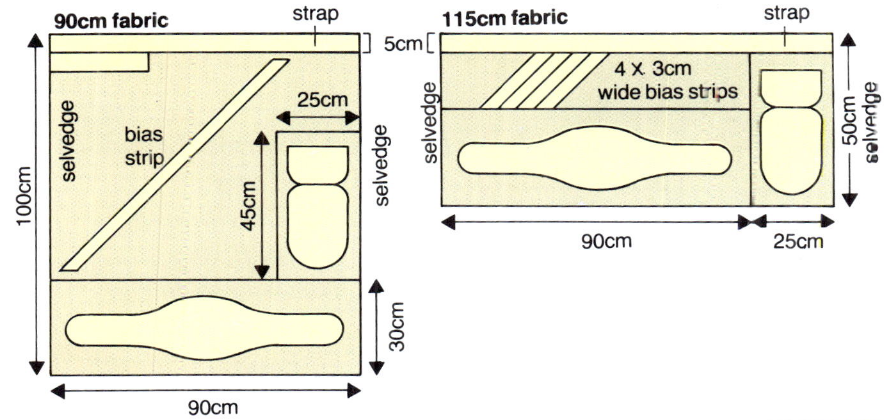


## Trace pattern

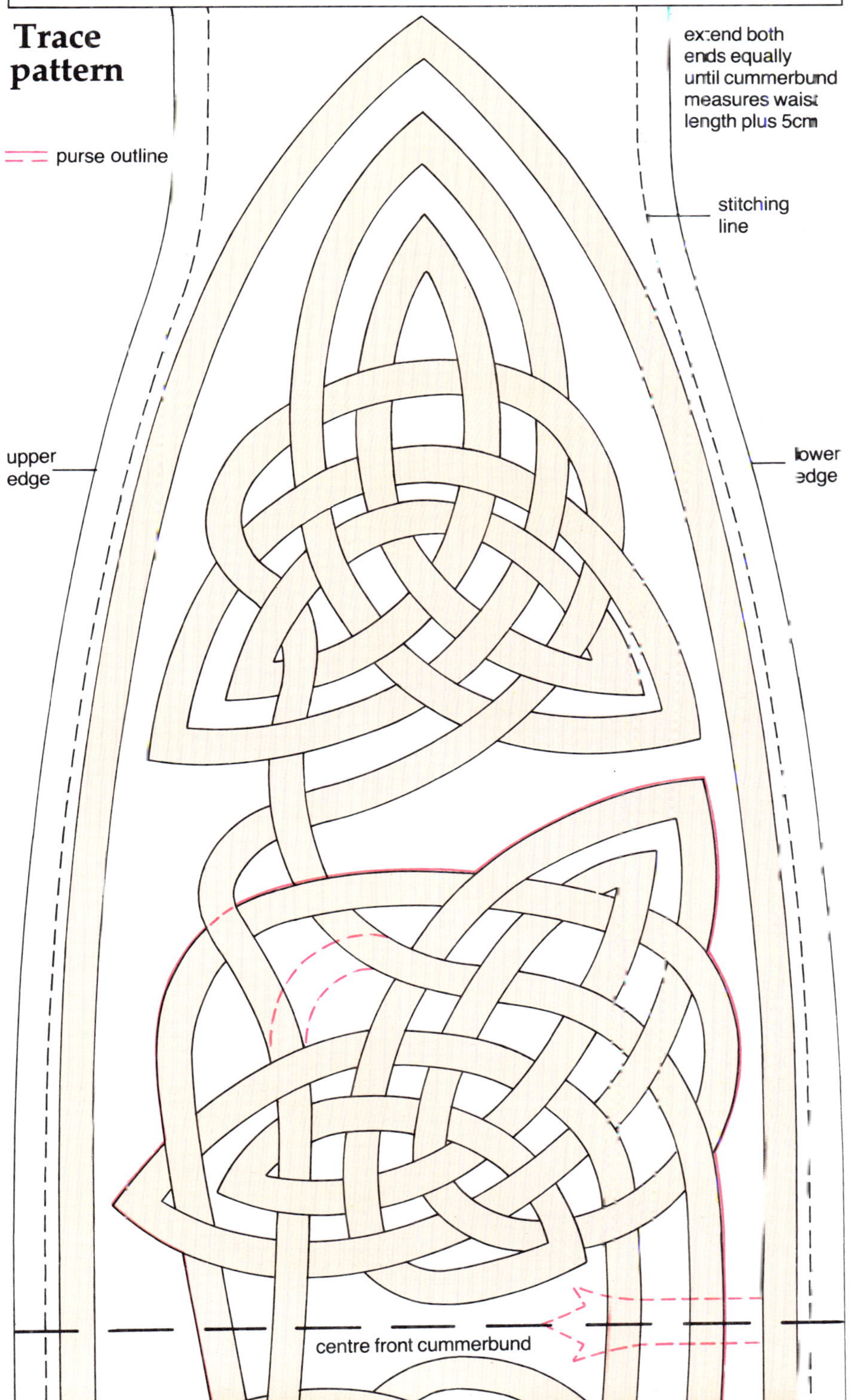

# Pillow and puff quilting for luxurious bedcovers

***Use these simple techniques to make a luxuriously padded pillow quilt for a full-size bed or a cosy puff quilt for a child's cot. Control the thickness by varying the amount and type of filling and edge the quilts with an attractive bound border.***

These two forms of quilting sound soft and soothing – and they are. Both are easy to do, and result in the most luxurious-looking, cosy throw-over quilts for beds or cots. You could also make softly padded cushion covers using both these techniques.

*Below: This cosy quilt is so easy to make using the pillow quilting method. Use alternate colours as shown here, or make it all in the same fabric, to fit a single or a double bed.*

**Pillow quilting** consists of a number of small 'pillows' (usually square) made up individually and then joined together along their finished edges. The pillows can be any size, but the smaller they are, the more stitching you will have to do.

Pillow quilting is just as neat on the back as on the front, so quilts are easily reversible.

Use firm cotton fabrics, lawn, or satin for real glamour. Fill each little pillow with a square of polyester wadding or stuff with washable polyester filling if you want to make a more heavily stuffed quilt. Remember to wash new fabrics first to avoid shrinkage. Any puckering would spoil the look of the quilting.

**Puff quilting** is similar to pillow quilting but it gives a slightly different effect – fuller and puffier. To achieve this look, make up pillows by stitching squares of top fabric on to smaller bottom squares to create fullness at the top. Fill the squares with polyester filling or folded wadding and seam them together. The top fabric squares can be up to 1½ times the size of the bottom ones – the top squares in the quilt featured here are 1¼ times the size.

The bottom squares can be made from muslin as the back of puff quilting needs to be lined to conceal the joins.

Although the basic patches are square, the overall finished effect is of raised rounded puffs.

## Pillow quilting techniques

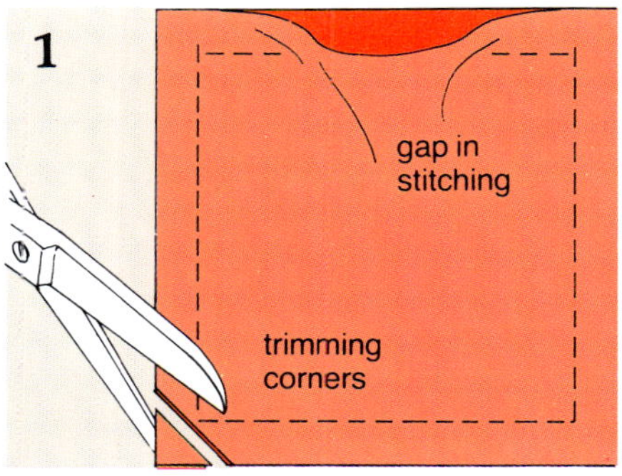


1 Cut out several square patches the same size from both fabrics.
With right sides facing, stitch top and bottom squares together in pairs around three sides, leaving an opening along the centre of the fourth. Trim corners diagonally.

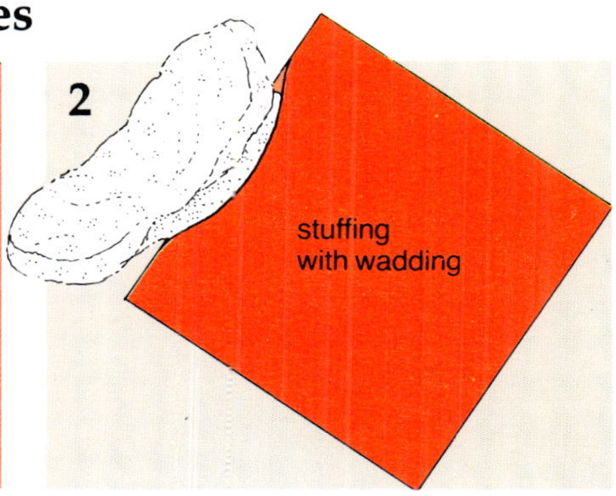


2 Turn pillows to right side and stuff each pillow with polyester filling, distributing it evenly.
Do not over-fill the pillows which would make them difficult to sew together.
For a flatter-looking quilt, use polyester wadding cut to the size of the *finished* squares. Neatly oversew the opening.

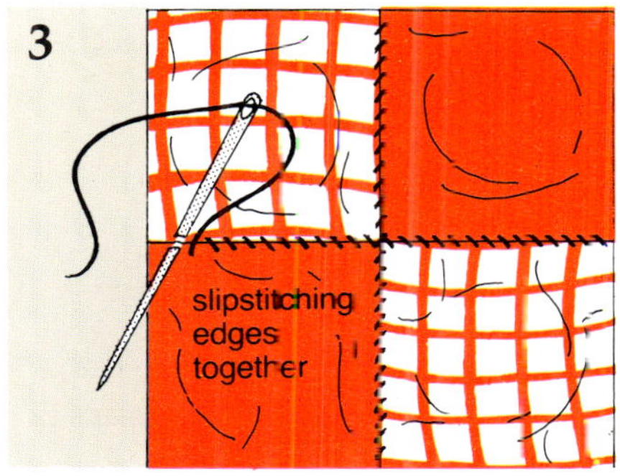


3 Join the finished pillows together along their edges in the correct pattern sequence, if you have planned one. To join pillows successfully, hold two with their edges butted up together and slipstitch invisibly by hand.
Alternatively, holding them firmly together, use a wide machine zigzag stitch to link them.

## Puff quilting techniques

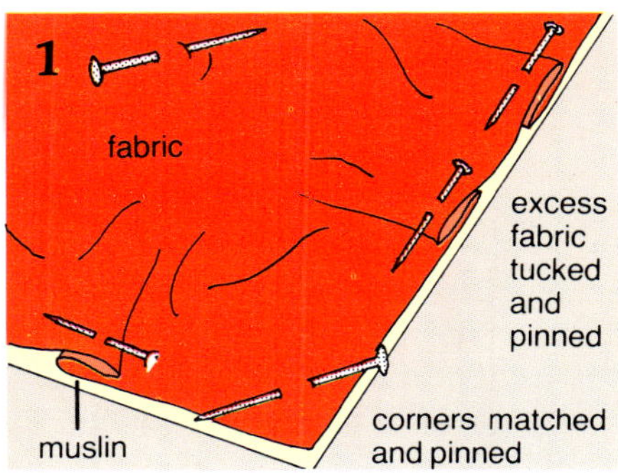


1 Decide on size of squares and make a template for both sizes. Use these to cut fabric and muslin (bottom) squares.
Lay a fabric square right side up over a muslin one, matching and pinning together the four corners.
Pin at centre of each side and fit the excess fabric by making tucks each side which lie towards the corners.

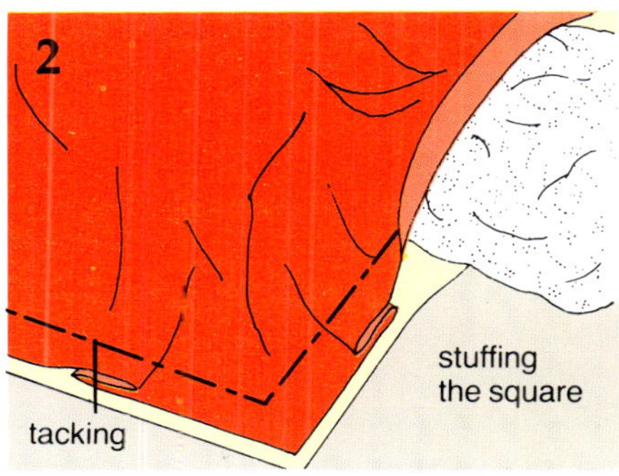


2 When all four sides are pinned, tack round, 1cm/½in from raw edges, leaving one side open between the centre and one corner for filling. (Tack the tuck in place on top fabric.)
Fill the puffed shape with washable polyester filling or folded wadding, pushing it in carefully until the spare fabric is filled up. Tack opening closed.

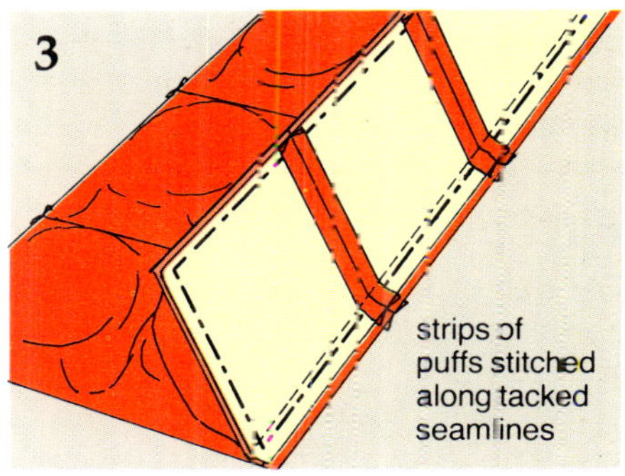


3 With right sides together, join the prepared puffs along tacked seamlines: seam together several puffs in a strip, make more strips and join these together lengthwise.
To line the work, cut backing fabric to the same size as quilt and with right sides together stitch together round edges, leaving an opening to turn through. Turn, and slipstitch opening.

## Pillow quilted cover for single or double bed

The quilt in the picture is made up from five different red and white printed fabrics, plus plain red, but you could also use patchwork pieced blocks, random coloured squares or squares all the same colour.

Fabric requirements given here are based on the design of diagonal checks as shown in the diagram. For any other designs, make your own calculations for the amount of top fabric required; each patch measures 32cm/12½in.

The single bed cover measures 145cm × 232cm/58in × 93in and the double is 203cm × 232cm/81in × 93in.

### You will need – single bed

Fabric requirements are based on 90cm/36in wide fabric (except backing and wadding)

1.30m/1½yd fabrics A and B, 1.90m/2⅛yd fabric C, 1m/1⅛yd fabrics D and E, 0.70m/¾yd fabric F

3.35m/3⅝yd of 150cm/60in wide fabric for backs of pillows

4.15m/4½yd 4oz wadding, 1m/40in wide

### You will need – double bed

1.95m/2⅛yd fabrics A and B, 2.60m/2⅞yd fabric C, 1.30m/1½yd fabric D, 1m/1⅛yd fabrics E and F

4.50m/4⅞yd of 150cm/60in wide fabric for backs of pillows

5.50m/6yd wadding as above

### Making up the quilt

Following the pattern chart for the number and arrangement of squares, cut out 40 (56 for the double bed quilt) 32cm/12½in squares from your chosen top fabric(s) and 40(56) from the pillow backing fabric.

Make up the 40(56) pillows, taking 1.5cm/⅝in seams when joining fronts to backs. Now cut 40(56) 29cm/11¼in squares from the piece of wadding and insert one into each pillow. Slipstitch openings and join pillows by hand, forming pattern as given in diagram.

**Optional binding** Cut binding strips for long edges from fabric B and C, 13cm/5in wide and slightly longer than the quilt – join strips if necessary to obtain this length. Lay binding strip wrong side up along right side of quilt with raw edges 3.5cm/1⅜in from edge of quilt and stitch with a 1.5cm/⅝in seam. Turn binding to wrong side of quilt, turning ends and remaining long edge under, and slipstitch in place. On top and bottom edges of quilt, machine along 5cm/2in from edge to balance side borders.

**Pattern for single and double quilt cover**

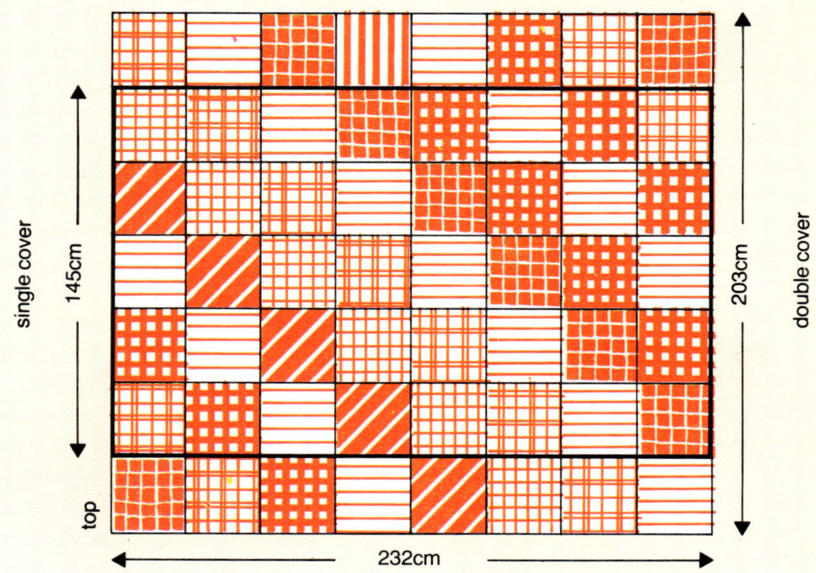


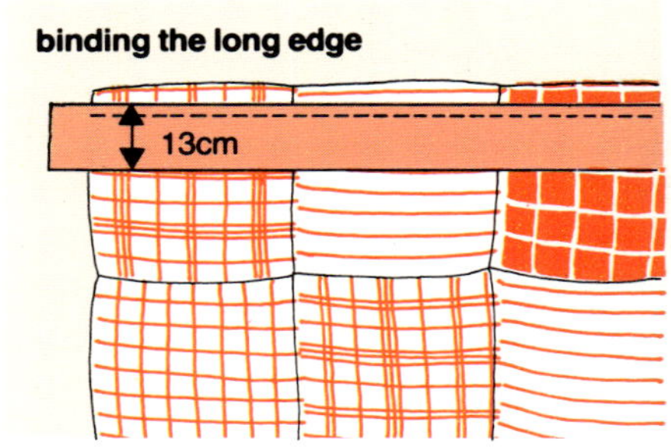


## Puff quilting for a pretty cot or pram quilt

Try out puff quilting by making a pretty quilt for a baby which is warm but extremely light and has a padded border. Use medium weight printed cottons – the ones used here are printed but you can choose plain fabrics in pastel shades.

### You will need

To make a quilt measuring about 60cm/24in square

25cm/¼yd each of 5 cotton print fabrics (any width)

90cm/1yd plain cotton fabric for backing and border (90cm/36in wide)

50cm/½yd muslin

1m/1⅛yd polyester wadding (4oz weight)

Matching thread

### Making up the quilt

Make two templates – 12cm/4¾in and 15cm/6in square. Cut 25 muslin squares using the smaller template and five squares from each of the printed cottons using the larger one. Join each cotton square to a muslin square taking 1cm/½in seams and leaving an opening in one side of each.

Cut 25 squares of wadding, 17cm/6¾in square. Fold the corners to the centre on each of these and slip one into each puff before sewing up the opening. Stitch the puffs together scattering the prints evenly.

From the plain fabric, cut a 62cm/24½in square for the backing. Lay the puff quilting right side up on the centre of the wrong side of this and machine all round, along outer seamline of quilting.

Cut four strips of plain fabric 8cm × 62cm/3¼in × 24½in. Join them together with mitred corners to form a 'frame', and leaving 1cm/½in unstitched at each inner corner

*Above. It's a good idea to pre-wash all the fabrics to check colour fastness.*

seam. Trim mitred seams.
**Lay the frame** right side down on the back of the quilted piece and machine round, 1.5cm/5/8in from outer raw edges. Trim corners and turn to right side.
**Finishing off** Cut enough 5cm/2in wide strips from remaining wadding to fill the border with a double thickness all round. Lay two strips of wadding inside the border along each side, fold over 1cm/½in on border strip edges, and catch in place along quilting seamline.

**making the frame**

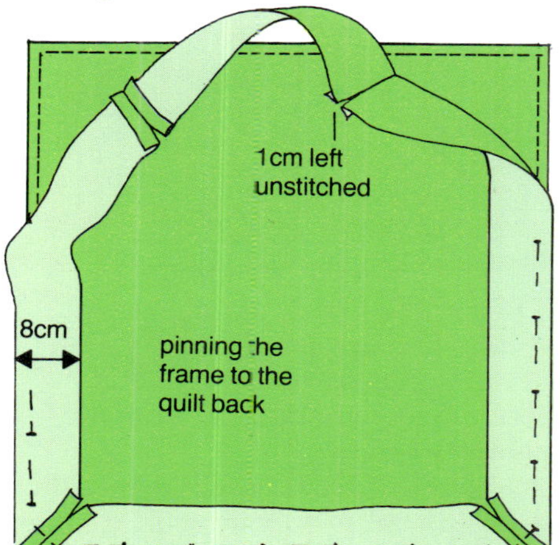


**finishing off**

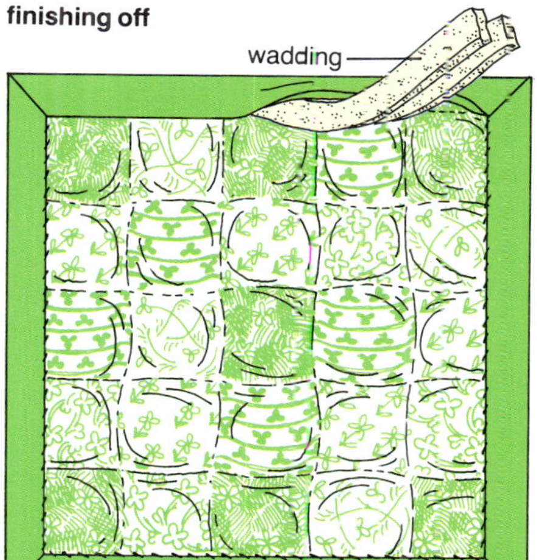

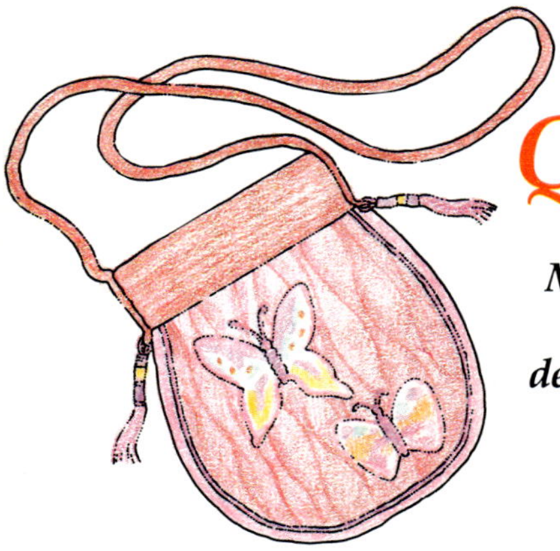

# Quilted waistcoat and bag

***Machine quilt your own fabric to make a really individual waistcoat and bag. The freestyle quilting design needs no prior marking on the fabric and is the perfect background for colourful appliqué butterflies. Tassel trims and piping threads add a lively finish.***

Quilted garments have been in vogue for hundreds of years. They are warm, often lighter than several layers of woollens, and can be stunningly attractive.

When making your own quilted clothing, remember that fabrics 'shrink' when quilting stitches are added, so never cut pattern pieces to their final size until the machine or hand quilting is completed. Either allow a few extra centimetres round the pattern piece edges when cutting out, or quilt a whole length of fabric and cut pattern pieces from this as usual.

## Quilted silk waistcoat

This waistcoat with its unusual machine-quilted design and shimmering appliquéd butterflies could be a collector's piece. Add the butterflies to any basic commercial waistcoat pattern.

Antung is good, firm silk suitable for quilting, but you could use tussah or surah silk or medium-weight cotton.

### You will need for waistcoat

Raspberry red silk (top) and pink silk (lining) fabric for waistcoat as stated on your pattern envelope. (Remember you need to cut the waistcoat out twice, once in top fabric and once in lining fabric).
25cm/¼yd multi-coloured swirling print silk for butterflies
90cm/1yd polyester wadding (2oz weight)
25cm/¼yd light iron-on Vilene
3.50m/4yd pink satin bias binding
Machine quilting foot (if possible)
1 large reel silk machine twist in purple, raspberry red and pink
1 ball Anchor pearl cotton in purple for embroidery, 1 ball in bright pink for waistcoat tassels
1 skein bright coton à broder for bag tassels
1 sheet of tracing paper

### Making the pattern

Trace off the half butterfly shapes given overleaf to make paper patterns. Use pattern pieces for the waistcoat from your pattern envelope. Following the cutting layout given in your pattern, cut out one back and two fronts in raspberry red silk with 2cm/¾in extra all round to allow for shrinkage in quilting. Cut out the same pieces in the pink lining silk.

## Quilting the pattern pieces

1

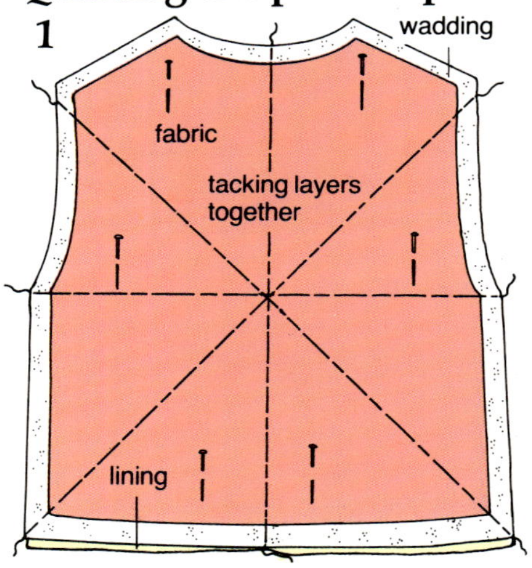


2

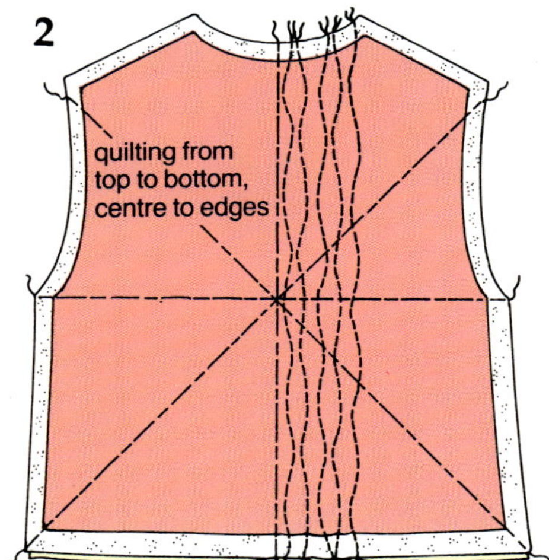


3

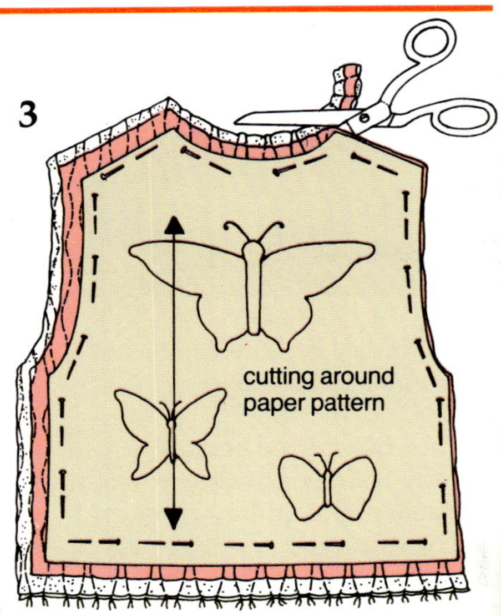


Lay the waistcoat back over the wadding, right side uppermost, and cut out the wadding slightly larger than the top fabric.

Lay down the back lining, wrong side uppermost, place the wadding on top, and the back top fabric (right side uppermost) on top. Pin.

**1** Beginning in the middle, tack a central line to top and bottom, one at right-angles to each side, and four others radiating out from the centre, as shown.

**2** With red thread in machine needle and pink in the bobbin, work gently curving lines of quilting on the right side. Quilt from top to bottom: begin in the centre back and work out to one side, then go back to the centre and quilt towards the other side edge. Repeat for the two fronts.

**3** Pin the paper pattern pieces over each quilted piece, and cut out to the correct size along cutting lines.

The advantage of quilting your own fabric is that you can quilt it in any pattern you like to make unique items, unlike anything available in the shops. Make sure the quilting pattern has enough stitching to anchor the fabric, wadding and lining together and give the garment stability. Garments which are to be worn often need all-over quilting designs with regular stitching.

The freestyle quilting pattern of undulating vertical lines which appears on the waistcoat and matching bag shown here is best used on a plain-coloured fabric, which will show it to its best advantage.

**Wadding** There are several different types and weights of wadding, so you can choose one appropriate to the project you have in mind. The two ounce wadding used for the projects shown here is very light, not too bulky and gives adequate relief to the quilting design. It is particularly suitable for decorative evening jackets, waistcoats or skirts which do not need to be particularly warm or thick.

**Seams** There are several ways of neatening seams on quilted garments. You can trim back the wadding by a few millimetres, turn the fabric edges under and hem to the backing fabric or you can trim the seam allowance down to 3mm/⅛in, press the seam open and stitch binding on the wrong side to cover the seam allowances. If you want to make the garment reversible, use a machine flat-felled seam.

**Raw edges** on the right side are best finished with binding. Choose matching or contrasting bias binding or make your own bias strips from leftover fabric.

**Decorative extras** Quilt a garment in a plain-coloured fabric and add appliqué, embroidery, beads or tassels.

*Below: A randomly quilted waistcoat – make it with or without appliqué.*

## Working the appliqué

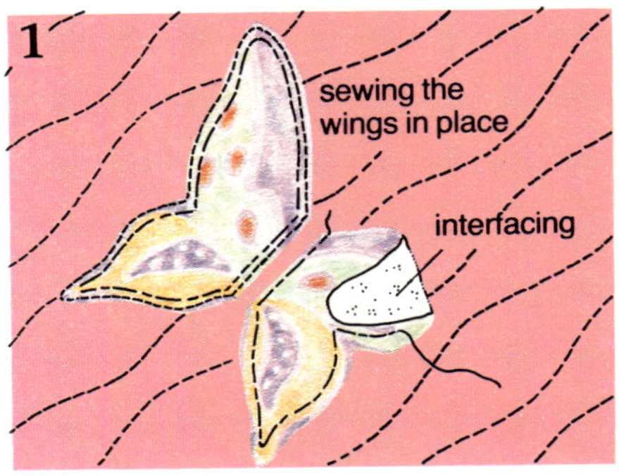


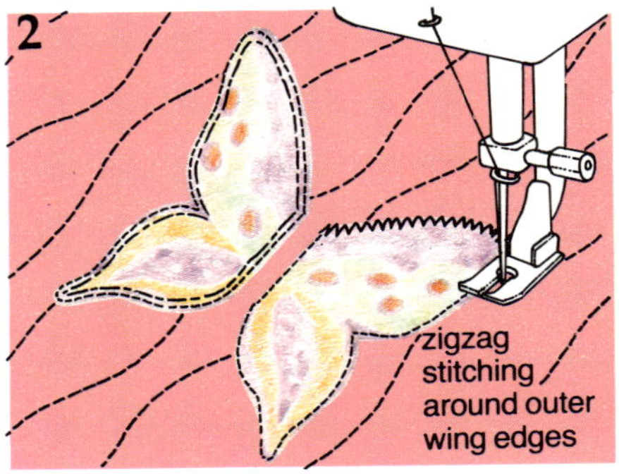


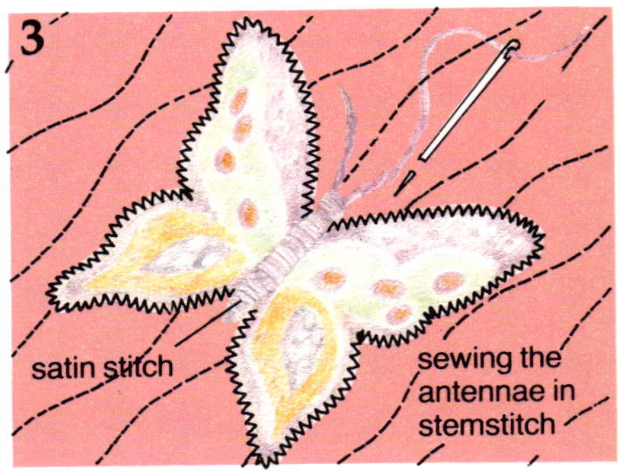


Cut seven butterflies from the printed fabric, cutting each wing separately but making sure that the fabric design is symmetrical for each wing in a pair.

**1** Iron the shapes on to light iron-on Vilene, cut round them and tack into position on the quilted pieces. Position the butterflies by eye or using the photo on the previous page as a guide. Machine straight stitch all round the wing edges.

**2** Change to a medium-width satin stitch and zigzag round the *outer* edges of each wing.

If your machine has a speed control, set this on slow to give more control when stitching round the tight corners on the wings.

**3** Using the purple pearl cotton, hand sew the butterflies' bodies in satin stitch to cover the raw inner wing edges – you can work an extra layer on the larger bodies to give them more relief. In the same thread work antennae in stem stitch.

## Trace patterns for half butterfly motifs

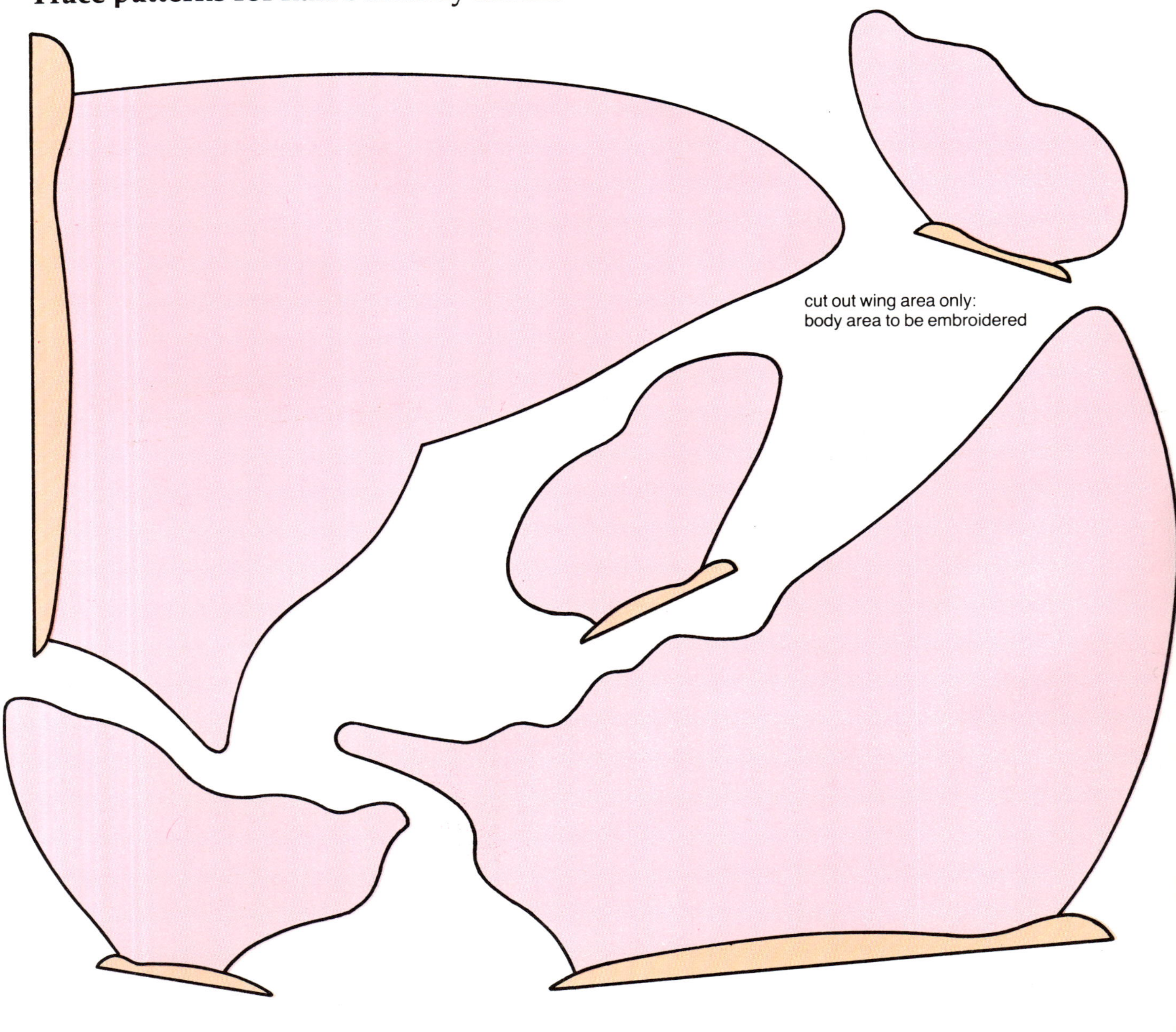

## Making up the waistcoat

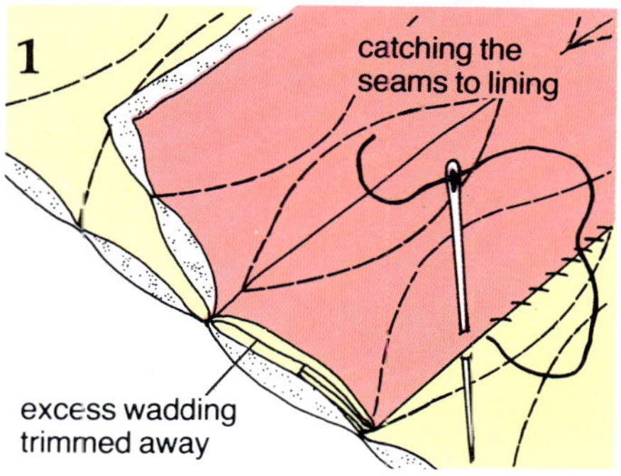


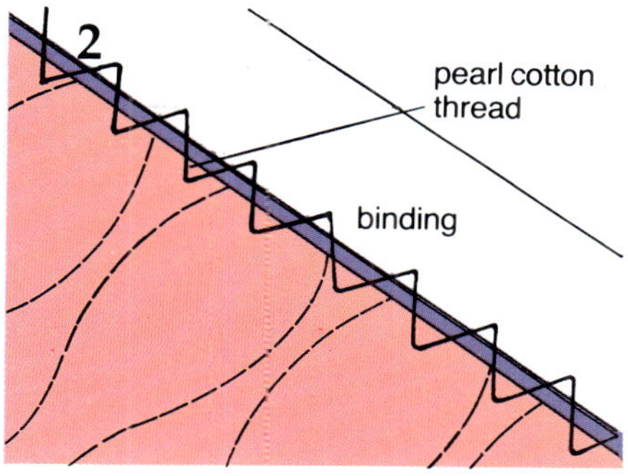


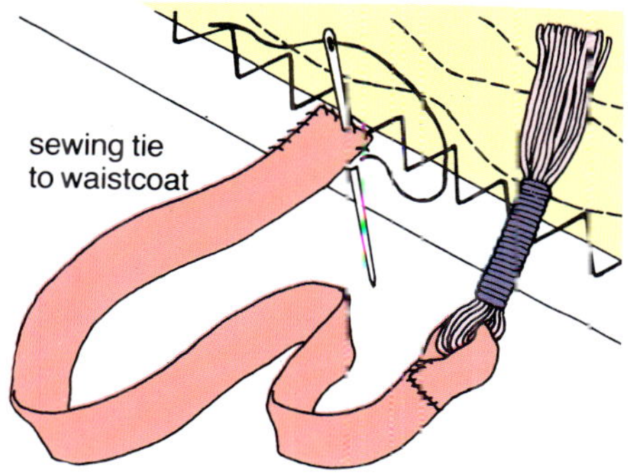


With right sides together, join the back to the fronts at sides and shoulders, with a 1cm/½in seam.
**1** Press seams open and trim away excess wadding from seam allowances. Fold over raw edges of each seam allowance and hem, catching on to lining.
**Binding edges** With right sides together, stitch one long edge of satin binding to all raw edges. Turn binding to inside and catch hem to lining.
**2** Lay one strand of purple pearl cotton along the inner edge of the satin binding and catch into place with purple thread, using a widely-spaced machine zigzag stitch.
Repeat along all the bound edges.
**Waistcoat ties** Cut a strip of fabric 3cm × 20cm/1½in × 8in. Fold lengthways, machine raw edges together with a 1cm/½in seam and turn inside out. Press, cut in half and neaten one end of each before looping through tassel and securing. Sew inside front edge.

## Matching quilted bag

This beautifully quilted, embroidered and appliquéd bag perfectly complements the waistcoat, but you could make it on its own as a special gift.

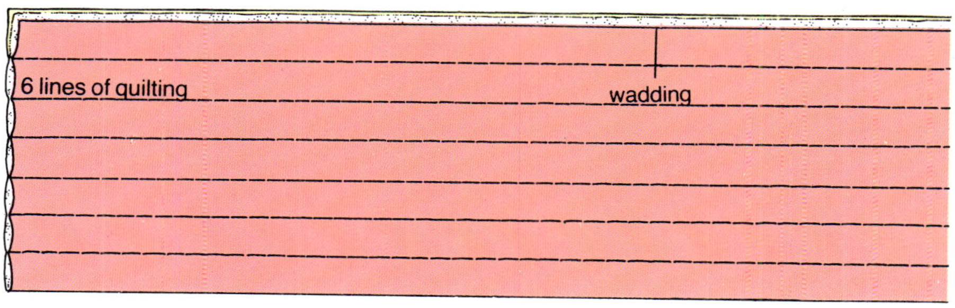


### You will need for bag only

25cm/¼yd raspberry red silk antung (any width)
25cm/¼yd pink silk antung for lining (any width)
25cm/¼yd polyester wadding (2oz weight)
Threads as for waistcoat
Machine quilting foot (if possible)
50cm/½yd pink satin bias binding

### How to make the bag

Draw round a 20cm/8in plate to make a paper pattern for the bag or draw a 20cm/8in circle using the string, pencil and drawing pin method. Measure in 3cm/1¼in at any point on the edge of the circle, rule a line through this point and cut off a section of the circle to give the flat top of the bag.
Cut out two raspberry red and two pink bag shapes. Quilt the pieces and add two butterflies to one side in exactly the same way as for the waistcoat. Remember to tack the fabric securely to the wadding and lining before quilting it. Place the two quilted pieces wrong sides together and tack round curved edges.
Tack satin bias binding round curved front edge of bag, right sides together, and stitch (do not bind top edge). Turn binding to back of bag and catch in place by hand.
Add the embroidery thread trim to the bias-bound edge as for the waistcoat.
From the raspberry fabric, cut a long strip 12cm × 34cm/5in × 13½in. Cut out a strip of wadding 6cm × 34cm/2½in × 13½in. Fold the fabric over the wadding to make the bag top and tack in place.
**Quilting the bag top** Machine six equally-spaced parallel lines lengthwise along the strip, using the quilting foot (if you have one) as a guide. Join end of strip with a 1cm/½in seam.
**Attaching the bag top** With right sides together, stitch strip round top of bag, with a 1cm/½in seam. Trim seam and neaten with overcasting zigzag stitch.
**For the strap** cut a long strip of raspberry silk 3cm × 115cm/1½in × 45in (you may need to join strips to obtain this length). Join long edges of strip with a 1cm/½in seam, turn through and press. Loop each end through a tassel (see above) and stitch to each side of the bag, beginning at lower edge of quilted band.

### Making tassels

Cut about 30 lengths of embroidery thread measuring 20cm/8in. Double them and pass bag strap or waistcoat tie through loop.

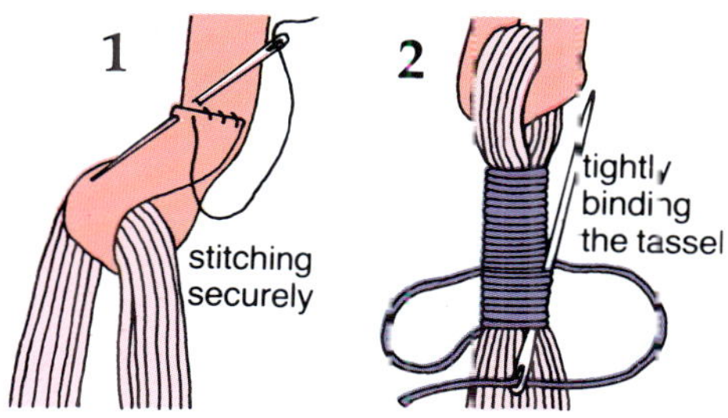


**1** Neaten end of strap/tie and stitch securely.
**2** Bind tassel tightly for about 3cm/1¼in from top using leftover embroidery thread in contrast colours. Finish by threading wrapping thread on a needle and sewing into tassel.

# Contour quilting

***This quilting technique adds a softly-contoured look to ready-printed fabrics. It needs no pre-marking, simply machine round the motifs to add definition to the shapes or hand stitch the outlines using decorative embroidery stitches if the design is more intricate.***

Contour quilting gives printed fabrics a new dimension. It adds emphasis to the pattern, and if wadding is inserted between the top fabric and the backing, the outlined design becomes raised and padded.

Instead of ignoring the pattern of a fabric and superimposing it with a completely unrelated quilting design, this technique makes the most of the pattern, whether floral, abstract or pictorial.

Use contour quilting to give that designer touch to cushions matching sofas and chairs, drop-in seats and stool covers, throw-over bed covers, bedheads and mats for dressing tables. Even parts of clothes such as dress yokes, cuffs and bodices can be contour quilted for effect.

## Choosing fabrics

Cotton, silk, satin or wool are all suitable for the top fabric. Glazed furnishing chintz looks particularly effective with a contour quilted design.

Lightweight fabrics such as cotton lawn or muslin are suitable for the lining.

Use a polyester wadding, or a cotton domette which is heavier, but thinner than the polyester. For articles which will require washing, choose polyester for practicality.

Examine the pattern of the top fabric carefully and decide which parts you will quilt round. With a floral design, for instance, you could outline each leaf and flower with stitches, or you could highlight other parts of the design such as a basket or some background stripes by quilting along their outlines.

Do not choose too intricate a design unless you intend to work by hand.

If the pattern repeat is very large and only one or two of the motifs will fit on an item such as a chair back or a bedhead, make sure you buy enough fabric from which to cut out the correct portions of the design and are able to position the motifs so that they are balanced.

Estimate the area of quilted fabric you need for the project in hand. As all-over quilting will 'shrink' the fabric, it is wise to be generous in the amount you allow.

*Right: This headboard combines two co-ordinated furnishing fabrics. Quilt a cushion cover, using any remnants.*

## Successful contour quilting

Follow the normal quilting procedure and cut wadding and lining fabric to the same size as the top fabric. Make a sandwich of the three layers with the wadding in the middle and pin together. Tack across the fabric diagonally, both ways, to secure the layers and avoid any puckering on the motifs.

### Stitching round the motifs

Fit a transparent presser foot on your sewing machine if possible. This helps you to see the design more clearly.

Begin at the centre of the piece of work using regular machine twist in a colour to match or contrast with the fabric. Leaving long ends of thread, lower the presser foot on to the fabric and start stitching using a small to medium length stitch. Work in the long ends afterwards by hand.

For extra emphasis, if desired, stitch round again close to the first stitching line. As far as possible, try to link motifs together without removing the work from the machine. When all the motifs are outlined, raise the presser foot, remove the work and cut the two threads, allowing enough to finish off. Pull all free ends of thread through to the back, knot them together and snip off. Remove the tacking stitches.

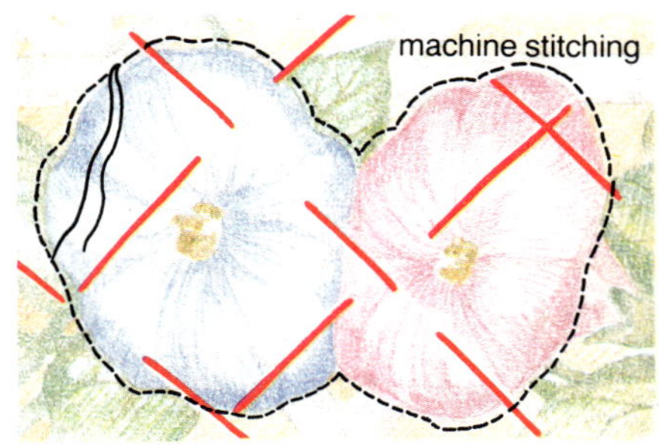


# A contour quilted headboard

Use a length of pretty bedroom fabric to quilt a headboard to match your furnishings. Most headboards can be covered by a simple slip-on cover and contour quilting gives a softly-padded finish to the front cover.

### You will need

Printed furnishing fabric
Polyester wadding (2oz weight)
Light backing fabric

### Cutting out the fabric

Cutting the fabric pieces to make the headboard is easy if it is a regular rectangular shape. For curves or fancy edges, make a template of the headboard front. If the board is more than 5mm/3⁄8in thick, it will need a gusset.

The only part of the cover which needs to be quilted is the front – remember it may shrink, so cut it out generously. Quilt the front before making up the cover.

### Quilting the design

Plan the quilting carefully. Do not give yourself too much work to do. If you begin quilting round every tiny detail on the fabric you may become discouraged halfway through the project.

Galleria L'Affiche Illustrée
Via dei Servi 69r · Firenze
OPERE DI GRAFICA
DAL 3 AL 30 APRILE 1982

## Working contour quilting by hand

As with any other type of quilting, there is no reason why you cannot work by hand, especially on smaller items. It is much easier to follow intricate design details with your stitching line to make really professional-looking articles. If possible, mount the fabrics and wadding on a frame before starting to quilt. Use running stitch, backstitch, or, for an attractive variation which gives a bolder line, chain stitch. Hand stitching gives you the opportunity to use an embroidery thread – pearl or stranded cotton perhaps – to really make the quilted parts of the fabric design stand out. Try using chain stitch to contour quilt the cuffs and bodice of a dress made up in a printed fabric. You could give the same treatment to waistcoats, jackets and skirt hems.

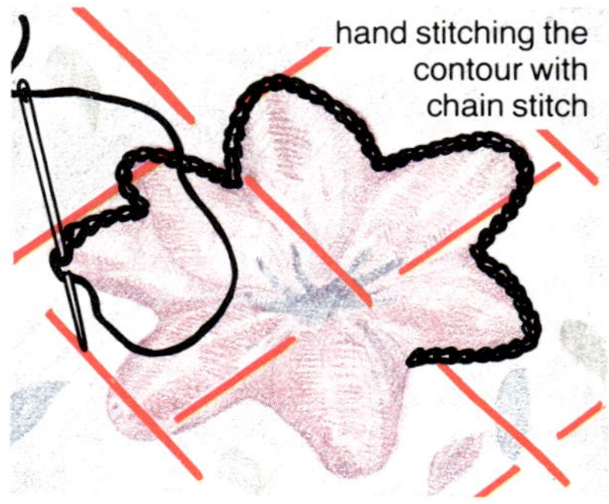

# Appliqué

*Appliqué is the name given to the technique of stitching pieces of fabric on to a background, either as simple, outline shapes or more complex designs built up from several pieces. They can be hand-stitched or machined into position and a variety of trimmings, such as braids, ribbons and beads, can be added for interest.*

*You do not have to buy fabric especially – a look through your scrap bag can inspire you to add that individual touch to soft furnishings and clothes. Patterns for the motifs can be copied from magazines. Or you can create your own pictures and designs in fabric.*

*The simplest forms of appliqué use patches of fabric to build up a picture which can be framed or used as a cushion cover. It can also be used to create a motif to highlight a jacket. In appliqué perse motifs are cut out from patterned fabrics and arranged in a pleasing design to decorate clothes or soft furnishings, and shadow appliqué adds a subtle hint of colour on a fine, see-through fabric. Appliqué can also be combined with patchwork to add emphasis to a fabric or with quilting to give a raised effect to the design.*

*This is one of the most versatile of needlecrafts. Whether stitched by hand or machine, it is restricted only by the limitations of your own imagination.*

# Simple fabric pictures

***If you have never tried your hand at appliqué, now is the time to start. It's a quick, simple and satisfying way to build wonderful combinations of shapes and colours into any design you choose. All you need to begin are some fabric scraps and basic drawing materials.***

'Appliqué' is the name given to the technique of placing pieces of fabric on to other fabrics and stitching them in place. This sounds like a very broad definition, but appliqué is an art with limitless expressions. It can be pictorial or abstract, bold and colourful or pale and delicate. Simple or complex designs can be created, depending on the number of different shapes you are laying on to the base fabric. You can also quilt the appliqué or add decorative embroidery to make your work extra-special. Appliqué has close links with both patchwork and quilting – techniques with which it is often combined.

Choosing the colours and textures of the fabrics and carefully planning an appliqué design is a skill in itself, and one which develops with practice.

## Using appliqué

The technique lends itself well to pictorial designs. Picture-painting with fabric is perhaps the most enjoyable and creative kind of appliqué.

As it is so quick to do, areas can be covered comparatively fast, so appliqué is also suitable for furnishings – cushions, curtains, tablecloths, towels and blinds, even bed-covers. Colour co-ordinating in the home becomes easy and fun.

Sensational effects can be achieved on clothes. Adding the right motif can turn skirt hems, dresses, T-shirts, baby and children's wear into eye-catching designer originals.

## Types of appliqué

Appliqué can be hand or machine sewn. The choice will often depend on the desired finished effect or the function of the article you are making. The applied shapes can have either raw or turned edges. In the following pages, you will discover several different types of appliqué and how and where to use them. You can design your own motifs or cut shapes from ready-printed fabrics adding embroidery, trimmings or beads for effect. This chapter concentrates on the simplest method – single and double layer appliqué without turnings – and gives patterns for a rag book.

## Fabrics for appliqué

The fabrics used in appliqué are all-important. Choose them according to the project in hand. Obviously, if it is going to need washing, you must use washable, pre-shrunk, colour-fast fabrics. It would be very disappointing if parts of the design shrunk or lost their colour after one wash.

Fabrics should be of a similar weight if possible – particularly for anything which will receive hard wear or repeated washing. For wall-hangings and pictures this is not a problem, so you can go to town with pieces of silk and satin, velvets and other non-washables. Unless you want a translucent effect, make sure the fabric is densely woven. If it is too flimsy, it can be backed with a firmer fabric or with light iron-on interfacing to give it extra body and prevent the ground fabric from showing through. Firm cottons are always a good choice. Felt is very easy to work with and does not fray but unfortunately it is not washable, so its use is restricted. Ribbon, braids and other trims can also be used to great effect in appliqué designs. For a novelty effect you could use lamé and metallic fabrics, or fur and pile fabrics.

## Other equipment

**Scissors** You will need two pairs – one for cutting paper patterns, and a sharper pair for the fabric itself.

**Pins, needles and thread** are also indispensable.

**Stiff paper** is useful for making templates (patterns), as is tracing paper.

**Graph paper** is needed for enlarging and reducing designs.

**Tailor's chalk** or a pencil is used for marking shapes on to fabric. You could also use dressmaker's carbon paper for this.

**Frames** A frame is sometimes useful for working appliqué, but by no means essential. If you do use a frame, do not over-stretch the base fabric –

*Right: Successful appliqué needs well-chosen materials. Look out for suitable scraps of fabric, lace and trimmings.*

keep all the fabrics at the same tension to avoid any puckering.

## Planning a simple appliqué

Shapes can be cut freely from the fabric, or else marked and cut accurately using paper patterns to enable you to repeat a design.

You can sometimes plan an appliqué design as you go along, but in general it's best to have a good idea of the effect you are after before starting work. Make sure that your chosen colours harmonize or contrast as you wish, and that none of the shapes is too complex. Remember that you can always add embroidery or machine stitching as part of the design. Books and pictures are a good source of designs for appliqué if you are not an artist. Try looking at young children's books for simple pictures with bold outlines.

## Enlarging and reducing designs

1

2

**1** Trace the lines of your chosen picture on to a sheet of tracing paper. Then stick the tracing paper over some graph paper so that you have a squared up drawing. (If the squares on the graph paper are very small, take a ruler and felt-tip pen and make an evenly squared grid on a larger scale using the graph paper.)

**2** Make a larger grid (smaller if reducing) on new graph paper. Copy the design on to it square by square. The design will be enlarged (or reduced) according to the relative scales of the grids. For example: copying a motif from a grid of 1cm/½in squares on to a grid of 2cm/1in squares doubles the motif size.

# *Appealing rag book for a baby or toddler*

The everyday objects that children see at home appear on the pages of this rag book. It would make a lovely present for any baby or toddler. Alternatively, you could cut out just one of the motifs and appliqué it on to the top of a pair of dungarees.

Using simple appliqué techniques, it is quick and easy to make in brightly coloured shapes. If you do not own a sewing machine, use non-woven fabrics for the motifs and secure the edges with overcasting or a decorative stitch such as cross stitch.

Use the shapes given overleaf, or incorporate any others your child would like – your dog or rabbit, for example. Try to avoid complicated shapes and too many design 'features'. Limit yourself to about four colours per page. The fabrics which you use for the motifs should be the same weight, or slightly lighter than the pages.

*Above: This brightly coloured rag book is an ideal first project in appliqué.*

**You will need**

Eight pieces of coloured cotton fabric of similar weight, each 22cm×27cm/9in×11in
Scraps of fabric for the motifs
Cotton thread in motif colours
20cm/8in soft iron-on standard-width Vilene for backing motifs
Pinking shears to cut page edges

## Making the patterns for the motifs

Outline motif shapes are shown in the diagram overleaf at reduced size. Enlarge them to the correct size as described on the previous page. Copy the square grid pattern on plain paper, making 2cm/1in squares. Or take 1cm/½in squared graph paper and mark up 2cm/1in squares with a ruler.

Cut round the outline shape of the motif to make a paper pattern for each. Cut the paper pattern into sections so that each colour has its own pattern piece. Where two sections overlap (shown by broken lines), you will need to make a tracing of one of them, and cut the other from the main pattern paper.

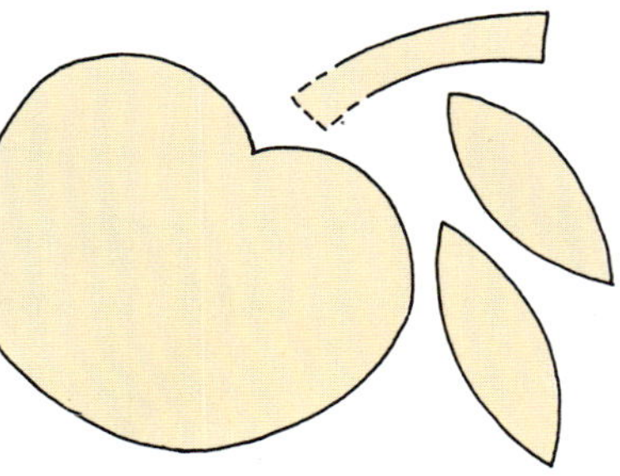

## Marking and cutting out the motifs

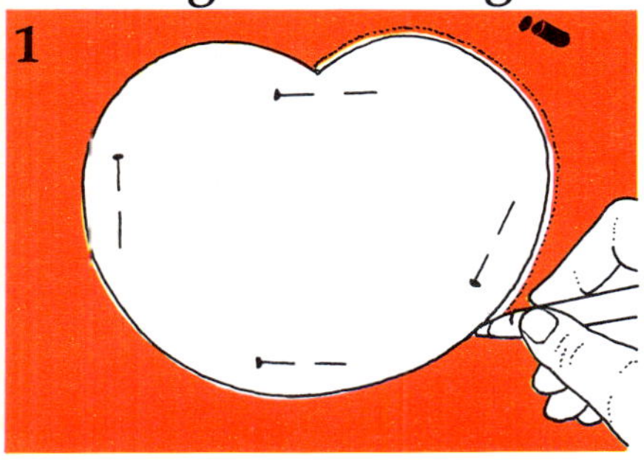


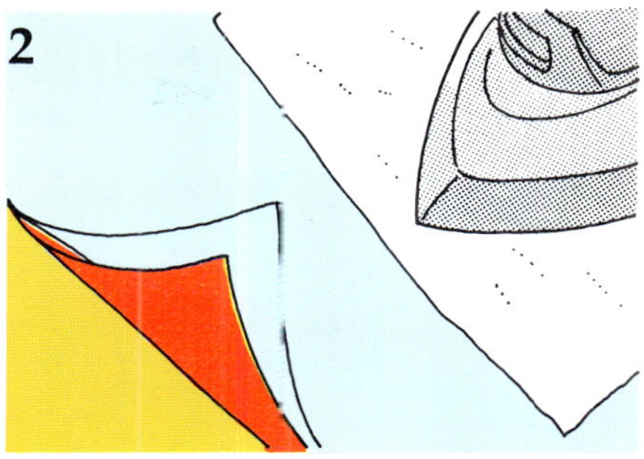

**1** Pin each section of the pattern on to the appropriately coloured or patterned motif fabric and mark the outline on to the fabric with tailor's chalk or a pencil. Try to position the pieces on the straight grain of fabric so that they will match the grain of the ground fabric.
Cut the motif fabric into a square or rectangle a few centimetres larger all round than the actual motif outline.
**2** Lay this fabric right side down and position on top a piece of soft iron-on Vilene interfacing, cut to the same size. The rougher, adhesive side of the Vilene should be facing the fabric. Cover with a damp cloth and press with a hot, dry iron. The Vilene will stiffen the fabric slightly and will also help prevent the raw edges from fraying when the fabric is cut.
**3** Carefully cut out the sections of the motif design round the marked cutting lines using an ordinary pair of scissors.

## Making the pages and fixing the motifs

To make pages, use pinking shears to cut out eight pieces of fabric, each 19cm × 24cm/7½in × 9½in. Choose different coloured cotton fabrics for each page, or very simple patterns such as checks or stripes. Position each motif centrally on the page, noting that sections with partly dotted lines must be laid down first. When the motif is complete tack sections in place. Using a small zigzag stitch, machine round all the raw edges with a matching sewing cotton to secure. Remove tacking. Add stitching lines for features such as the cat's whiskers, the hands on the watch, and the tips of the coloured pencils. Pull ends of thread through to the wrong side.

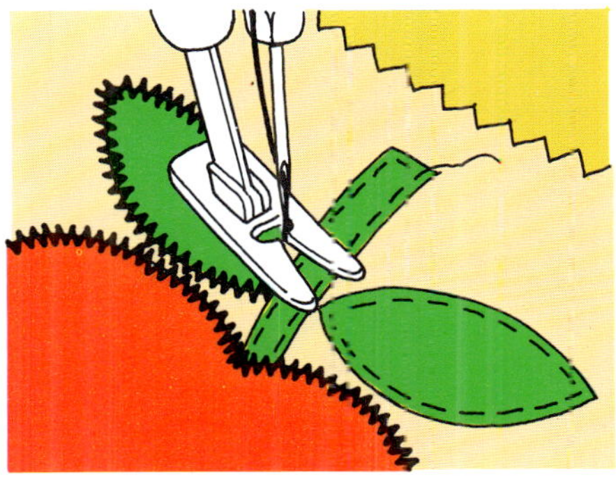

## Putting the complete book together

**1** Lay two pages right sides facing, and tack together down one short side. Sew, making a 1.5cm/⅝in seam. Trim seam to 5mm/¼in. Turn to right side and press to make a complete page with wrong sides inside. Repeat for remaining six page pieces to make three more pages. If necessary, iron with spray starch.
**2** Lay the four pages together, one on top of the other with pinked edges matching and tack through all eight layers of fabric on the unstitched short side. Sew through all layers with a 1cm/½in seam. Remove tacking.

1

2

## No pinking shears?

If you don't own pinking shears, proceed as above, but cut the pages to 22cm × 27cm/9in × 11in with ordinary scissors. Complete step 1 of *Putting the complete book together* and then press a 5mm/¼in hem to wrong side on raw page edges. Turn a further 1cm/½in to wrong side and machine with matching thread. Lay the four back-to-back pages together as for step 2, but join with a 2cm/¾in seam.

## Patterns for the eight motifs

# Appliqué motifs add an individual touch

***A simple appliqué motif or repeat design can freshen up an old favourite from your wardrobe or add a touch of individuality to a new purchase. Learn how to choose suitable motifs and how to hand sew them, slipstitching to achieve an invisible finish.***

An appliqué motif applied to a special garment adds an individual touch. Alternatively, an older item from your wardrobe, such as the black cotton jacket pictured below, can be given a new lease of life by the addition of some pretty motifs. These fans were made from some brightly coloured cotton remnants and a little embroidery and tiny ribbon ties finish them off to give that designer look.

Use this technique to co-ordinate your wardrobe by picking colours for motifs which will match with other separates. Choose fairly simple designs, such as fans, shells, leaves, fruit, stars and moons, and make sure that the ground fabric and appliqué fabric are compatible.

### You will need

Plain jacket (You could make your own or use a bought one.)
10cm/⅛yd remnants of two plain contrast fabrics
Matching sewing threads
Matching stranded cotton or pearl cotton
10cm/4in of 3mm/⅛in satin ribbon to match motif colours
Fine pins
Sharps needles size 7
1 chenille needle (for ribbon)
Dressmaker's chalk pencil
1 sheet tracing paper
Small ring frame (optional)

### Preparing the jacket

If the made-up jacket has loose front and neck facings, turn these back while you work the appliqué. If you are making up a jacket, work the appliqué before you attach the front and neck facings. Mark the seamlines with dressmaker's chalk for guidance when positioning the motifs.

*Below: The black ground fabric sets off the vibrant colours of the appliqué motifs.*

## Preparing and applying the motifs

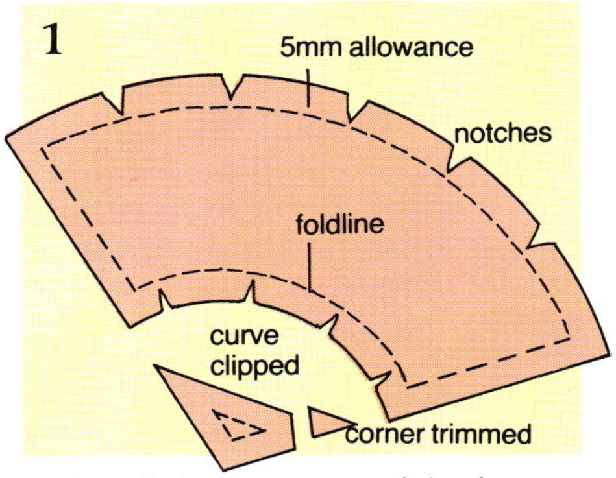


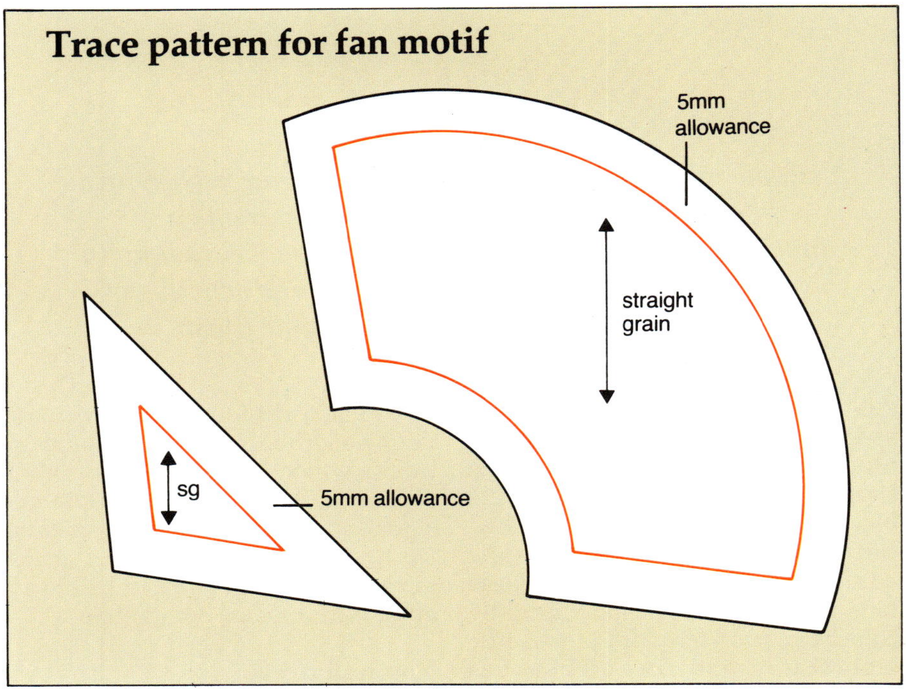


Trace off the two parts of the fan design and, placing the paper patterns on the straight grain of the fabric, cut out two fans, one in each colour.

**1** Clip the inner curved edges to help them to lie flat when turned under. Make sure you do not cut across the 5mm/¼in foldline. Cut out small notches along the outer curving edges. On the smaller triangular fan-base piece, trim all three corners diagonally to within 3mm/⅛in of the finished corner, to reduce the bulk. Turn under the 5mm/¼in allowance and tack the turnings in place.

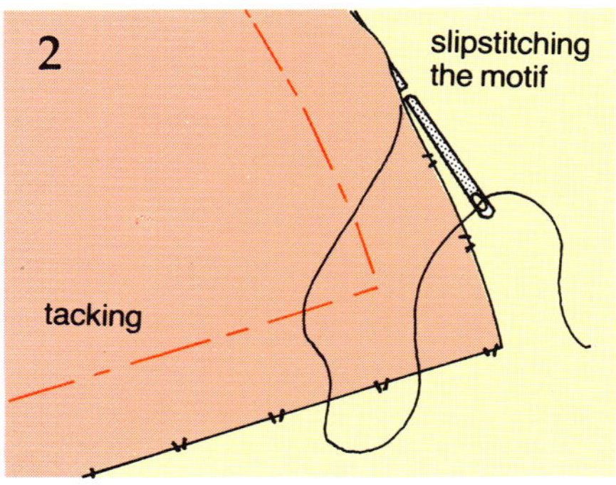


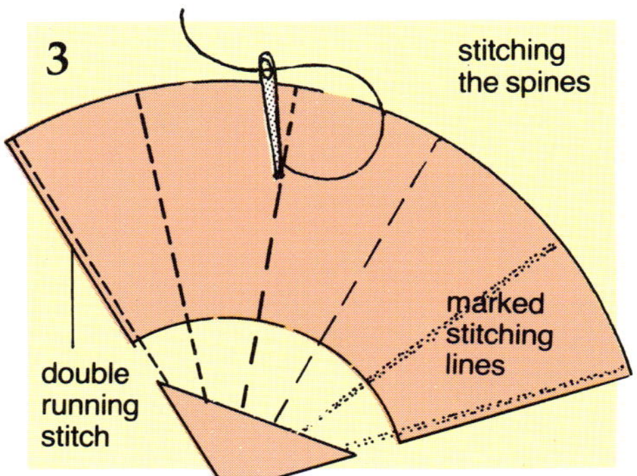


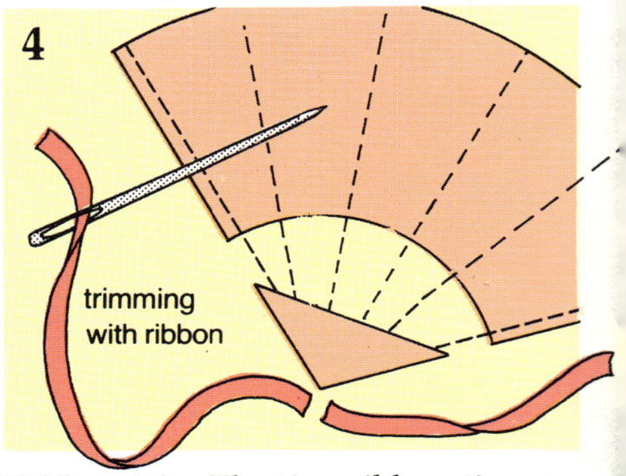


The base of the fan should lie about 1.5cm/⅝in from the lower curved edge of the main fan piece.

Pin and tack the motifs in place. If you have a small ring frame (11cm/5in), mount the ground fabric in this with the motif in the centre to avoid puckering.

**2** With a fine needle (sharp) and matching thread, slipstitch round the edge of each piece, so that your stitching is invisible.

To work slipstitch, pick up a tiny piece of the ground fabric, then run the needle through and along the folded edge of the motif, before making another tiny stitch in the ground fabric.

**Embroidery trim** Divide each fan into five equally-spaced sections and mark the spines between them with dressmaker's chalk pencil or fine tacking stitches. The two outer spines run along the edge of the fan and all the spines stop at the triangular base piece.

**3** With two strands of contrasting stranded cotton, or one of pearl cotton, embroider the spines in double running stitch.

First work a row of regularly spaced running stitches and then fill in the gaps by working a second row in between. This gives an effect similar to backstitch but is easier to sew on the double thickness of the fabric.

Do not forget the two outer rows along the edge of the fan.

**Ribbon trim** The tiny ribbon ties at the base of each fan are added when the jacket facings and hem have been completed. They help to hold the facings in place.

**4** With a chenille needle (large-eyed and pointed), thread the piece of contrasting ribbon (same shade as the embroidery thread) through from front to back. Bring it back to the front again and tie the two ends in a single knot, pressing with your fingertip to make it lie flat. Trim ribbon ends diagonally to 1cm/½in.

# Quick padded appliqué using bold motifs

*Develop your appliqué skills by making an amusing cushion for your favourite armchair. Add interest and relief to the design by slipping pieces of polyester wadding under some of the shapes, giving a quilted effect. Machine zigzag stitchery makes the appliqué hard-wearing.*

You can add interest and appeal to all sorts of appliqué designs by padding some sections with polyester wadding. Follow all the hints given on pages 76-77, and take extra care when securing the wadded pieces of the design.

As you can see, the zigzag stitch makes the armchair design look bold, bright and well defined. However, stitching with such a wide zigzag requires careful treatment. On tight curves where you continually need to stop stitching and pivot the fabric, work steadily so that the edges of the stitching line are smooth and even.

At a right angled corner, stitch up to the edge, raise the presser foot and pivot the fabric so that you begin stitching in the new direction directly in line with the edge of the previous row of stitching.

Where more than two lines of stitching intersect on the design, do not stitch three times over the same point, as the work will look too bulky: once or twice is enough.

If you don't have a zigzag function on your sewing machine, use a regular straight stitch and then finish the raw edges by hand, using satin or buttonhole stitch and stranded cotton in the appropriate colours.

*Below: The bold, appliquéd design on this cushion is simple to cut and stitch.*

# Cosy armchair motif cushion

This plump cushion looks even more inviting when the miniature cushions on it are padded with wadding. The entire cushion cover is backed with another layer of wadding to give it that extra bit of body.

### You will need

Main (ground) fabric: 1m/1⅛yd of 90cm/36in wide *or* 50cm/½yd of 112cm/44in or wider
Lining fabric: same as above
Scraps of four other plain or patterned fabrics (at least 20cm/8in for armchair motif and 10cm/4in for leaves and each cushion)
1m/1⅛yd medium weight (4oz) polyester wadding
Thread to tone with the chair, plant and both miniature cushions
35cm/14in zip fastener
Cushion pad, 50cm/20in square

### Planning the design

Choose fabrics carefully, picking firm, not translucent cottons. If a colour you need only comes in flimsy fabric, back it with iron-on interfacing before cutting out the pattern pieces. The ground fabric can be plain or patterned; here it is a fairly small red and multi-coloured print. An even smaller red and white print is chosen for the armchair, but they contrast well. Cut out the houseplant leaves in plain green fabric, or a simple, predominantly green print like this polka dot.
Make sure that the scale of your design is convincing – for instance, do not choose a design so large for the armchair that no pattern repeats are visible. It is helpful to make a coloured sketch first to be sure it works.

### Making the pattern pieces

Enlarge the armchair design given on the chart making each square 2cm/¾in to give the required size, and mark the design centre. Make a pattern piece for each section of the enlarged design by tracing this off and then cutting it into sections along the thick, black lines.

## DESIGN EXTRA

### Colour and design ideas

You don't have to copy the cushion design and colours exactly. Perhaps you'd like to make one for a pale, pretty bedroom – in which case, choose pastel fabrics and pale sewing threads. Or appliqué a design of bright primary colours to a plain black or white ground fabric. If you feel adventurous, have fun with the miniature cushions by making them different shapes, cutting them in shiny satin, or adding ribbon, lace or embroidery trims.
**Suit the cushion to the chair** A round cushion with a Victorian chair design (add beads or knots to a wadded button-back chair) could be trimmed with pretty lace to sit on an old-fashioned chair. And if you want to make sofa cushions, design a sofa motif and include more small cushions, or your cat sitting on it. The idea can be adapted in endless different ways.

# Making the cushion cover

1

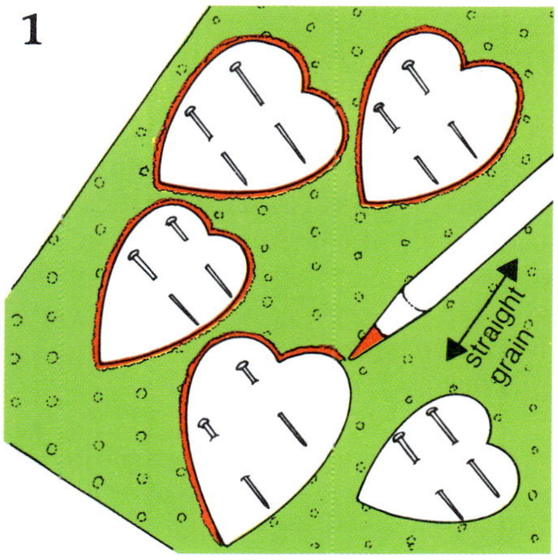


## Assembling the front

**1** Pin the pattern pieces on to the wrong side of the appropriate fabrics, keeping them on the straight grain as far as possible. Mark the outlines with a pencil or chalk pencil. Cut out. Cut main fabric into two 50cm/20in squares, and mark the centre of one of them by folding the fabric in half and in half again. Cut a further 50cm/20in square from the wadding.

2

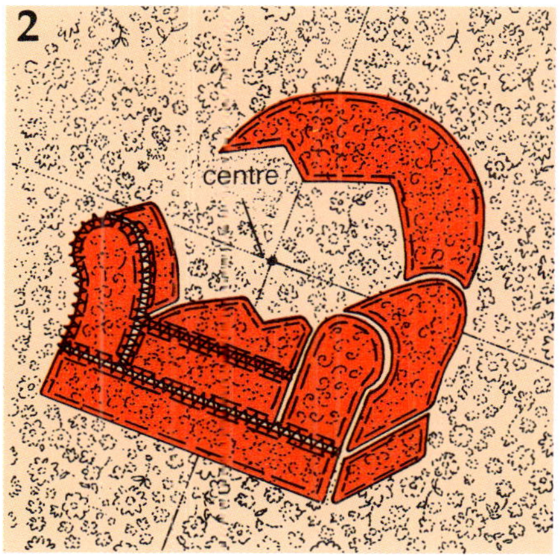


**2** Attach the chair shapes first, then the cushions, then the leaves. Following the chart, arrange the chair shapes on the right side of one of the main fabric squares. Make sure the centre point of the design is positioned over the marked centre of the main fabric. Pin the pieces so that the edges just touch and tack them carefully in place, close to the raw edges. Set the sewing machine to the tightest zigzag stitch (stitch length about 4mm/¼in) and machine round edges of the shapes, guiding the fabric.

3

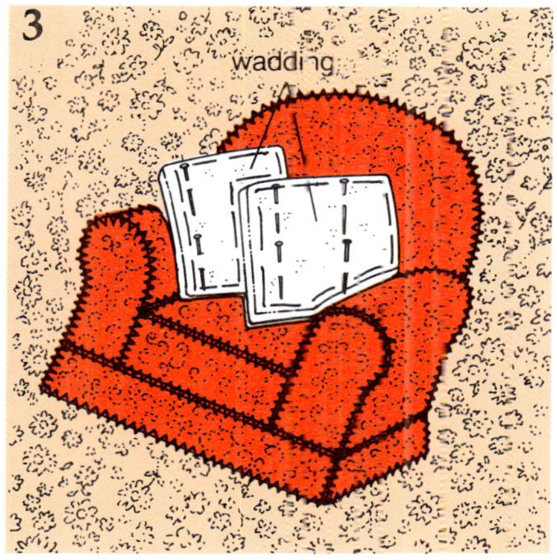


**3** Before appliquéing the small cushion shapes, cut two pieces of wadding slightly smaller than the actual pieces, to fit underneath them. Tack these in place on the ground fabric first to avoid any puckering.
Finally, add the leaves of the plant, tacking and stitching them in place as before. Remember to change the thread in your machine to the correct colour for each motif.

4

## Backing the front

**4** Cut lining fabric to 50cm/20in square. Lay it right side down with the 50cm/20in square of wadding on top. Place appliquéd cushion front right side up on these, pin, and tack with long stitches through all layers.
Set the machine stitch to a small straight stitch and carefully machine all round the outside of the chair and the leaves, very close to the zigzag stitching, using thread to match the ground fabric.

5

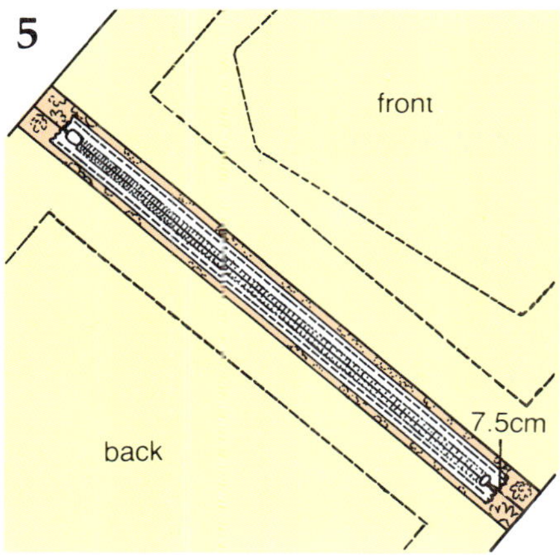


To secure the wadding, stitch all round the square, with a slightly longer straight stitch, about 9cm/3½in from the edges.

## Making the back

Make a sandwich of lining, wadding and main fabric for the cushion back. Tack them together and machine round about 9cm/3½in from the edges.

## Joining front and back

**5** Place front and back right sides

6

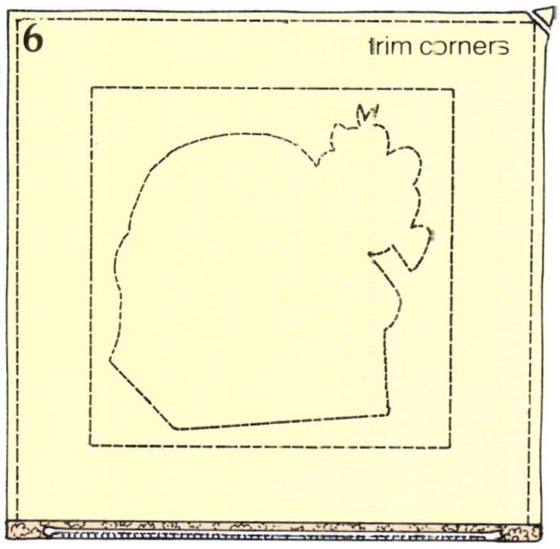


together. Along bottom edge only, tack and stitch a 1cm/½in seam, 7.5cm/3in in from each edge. Press seams open and insert zip in opening.
**6** Now place the right sides of the cushion front and back together and stitch the remaining three edges with a 1cm/½in seam.
Trim corners diagonally and trim excess wadding away from seams. Turn right sides out. Gently push out the corners with a closed pair of scissors.

# Floating balloon cushions

***Confident enlarging and reducing of designs is an important part of pictorial appliqué. The larger cushion shown here tells a story in pictures – the hot-air balloon appears at a different size in each panel, getting smaller as it slowly floats away.***

Beautiful appliqué work calls for a combination of skills. First, choosing suitable appliqué motifs and planning their positioning – which needs great care. Next, attaching the shapes to the ground fabric in the right order and with no puckers – thorough tacking will ensure this.

These balloon pictures include a stitched landscape. It is quite usual to embellish an appliqué with embroidery for the fine detail. Always finish the appliqué before adding any stitching either over or around the design. If your machine does not have a zigzag function, finish the edges of the motifs with buttonhole stitch then embroider the landscape by hand in stem or chain stitch, using a ring frame.

*Right: These appliqué cushions in two sizes are easy to make – choose pastel or primary colours for the balloon design.*

## Making the small balloon cushion

This pretty little cushion in fresh pastels is an ideal exercise in placing the appliqué pieces in the correct order, before you go on to make the larger cushion.

Try to obtain glazed chintz for the cushion cover and the motifs – it has a lovely sheen and can be found in most furnishing departments.

### You will need

50cm/½yd white cotton fabric, (width 112cm/44in or more)
35cm/⅜yd pale blue cotton fabric
20cm/¼yd cotton fabric remnants in pale pink, mid pink and yellow
35cm/⅜yd medium iron-on Vilene interfacing
Sewing thread in turquoise, white, yellow, pale blue, mid pink
1 sheet white dressmaker's carbon paper
40cm/16in square cushion pad
Tracing paper
Pencil

### Cutting the shapes

Enlarge the balloon grid design (on which one square = 3cm/1¼in). Trace off each part of the enlarged design on to the non-adhesive side of the Vilene.

From the colour remnants you need to cut one large pink circle for the balloon, two paler pink stripes and a pale pink balloon base. You also need two yellow sections for the basket, a white flag, and two white birds.

First, cut round each of the shapes on the Vilene, then iron these on to the wrong side of the appropriate fabric. Cut round the outlines carefully.

### Cutting the cushion fabric

From the white fabric, cut one 42cm/16½in square for the cushion front and two rectangles measuring 41.5cm×42cm/16¼in×16½in and 20.5cm×42cm/8in×16½in for the cushion backs. From the blue fabric cut four strips 7cm×47cm/3in×18½in for the flat border trim.

## Working the design and making up

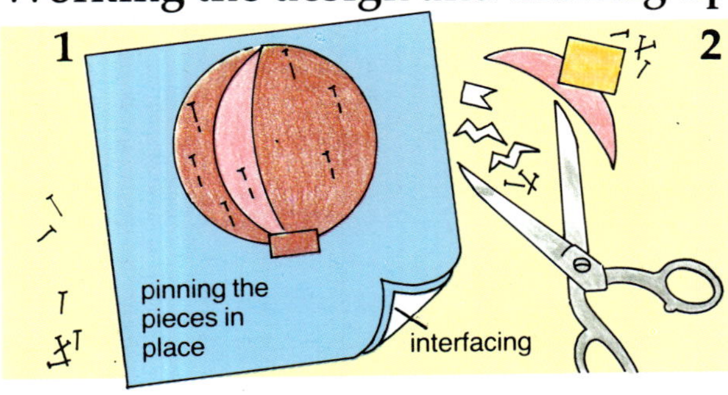

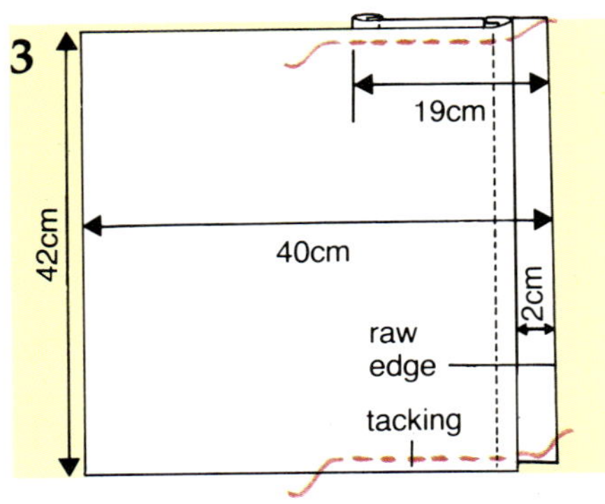


**1** From the blue fabric cut a 32cm/12½in square for the ground fabric and interface it with iron-on Vilene. Assemble the parts of the balloon design, laying down the large pink circle with the two paler pink crescent shapes on top to make the striped balloon. Use your tracing of the enlarged design to check the accuracy of positioning.

Pin all the fabric pieces in place and tack. Stitch round the raw edges with a close machine zigzag stitch using the following colours of thread; balloon parts – turquoise; basket – yellow; birds – white; flag – pink.

**2** Using dressmaker's carbon paper and your design tracing, transfer on to the fabric the balloon ropes, flag pole and scalloped line on the basket. Zigzag stitch the rope lines in turquoise and the other lines in pink.

Take the cushion front, press under 1cm/½in on all four edges of the ground fabric and pin centrally on to the white cushion front. Stitch round close to the edge of the blue square.

To make up cushion back press under 5mm/¼in, then turn under and hem 1cm/½in, on one 42cm/16½in edge of each of the rectangles.

**3** Tack the two pieces together with

4

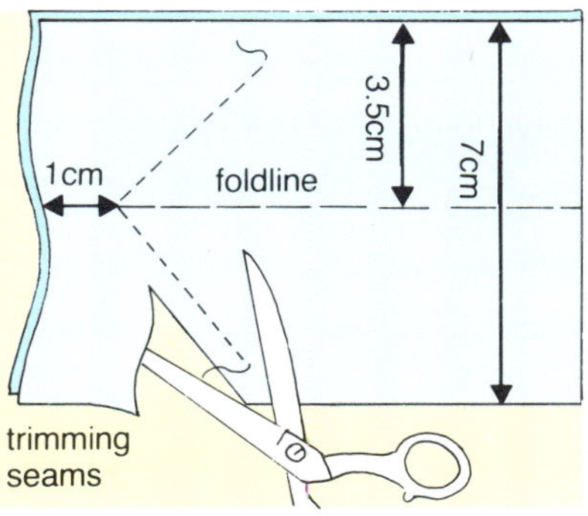


5

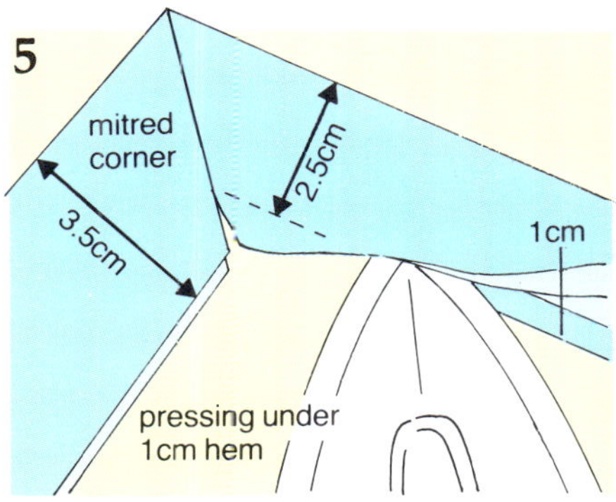


6

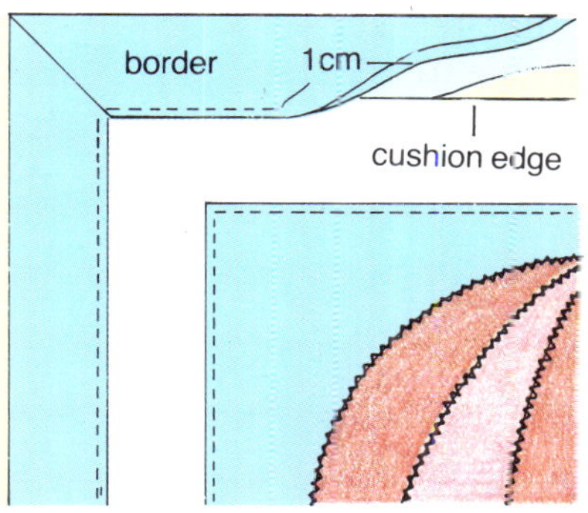


the long raw edge of the smaller piece projecting 2cm/¾in underneath the hem of the larger piece, to form a 42cm/16½in square, with a pocket for inserting the cushion pad.

The finished width of the blue border is 2.5cm/1in. Fold each blue strip lengthways, right sides together and press lightly.

**4** Open up the strips and join together two at a time with right-angled seams as shown. The corners of the right angles should lie 1cm/½in in from the ends of each strip. When all four strips are joined together to form a 'frame', trim back seams to 5mm/¼in, press open and turn whole border to right side.

**5** Press carefully and turn under 1cm/½in on all the raw inner edges. Tack the appliquéd cushion front and the back in place so that the back flap opens downwards.

**6** Slip the cushion edges 1cm/½in under the border. Stitch through all layers, close to edge of white strip on cushion front.

Insert cushion pad through back opening.

## Making the large four-panelled cushion

Children and adults alike will love this larger version of the appliqué cushion, following the balloon as it drifts further and further away. The four panels are divided by bands of white and the whole appliqué is bordered in the blue background colour. If you are not able to obtain an 80cm/32in cushion pad, it is a simple matter to make one.

### You will need

1.70m/2yds white cotton fabric (width 112cm/44in or more)
90cm/1yd pale blue cotton fabric
20cm/¼yd cotton fabric remnants in pale pink, mid pink and yellow
1.20m/1¼yd medium iron-on Vilene interfacing
Sewing thread in turquoise, pale pink, mid pink, white, yellow and pale blue
1 pack white dressmaker's carbon paper
Tracing or greaseproof paper

### To make the cushion pad

1m/1yd down-proof cambric and feather or feather/down filling
*or* 1m/1yd calico fabric and foam chip filling

### Cutting the cushion fabric

From the white fabric, cut one 82cm/33in square, one 81.5cm×82cm/32in×33in rectangle and one 20.5cm×82cm/8in×33in rectangle. From the pale blue fabric cut four strips 7cm×87cm/3in×34½in.
For the appliqué ground fabric, cut four 32cm/13in squares in pale blue and interface with iron-on Vilene.

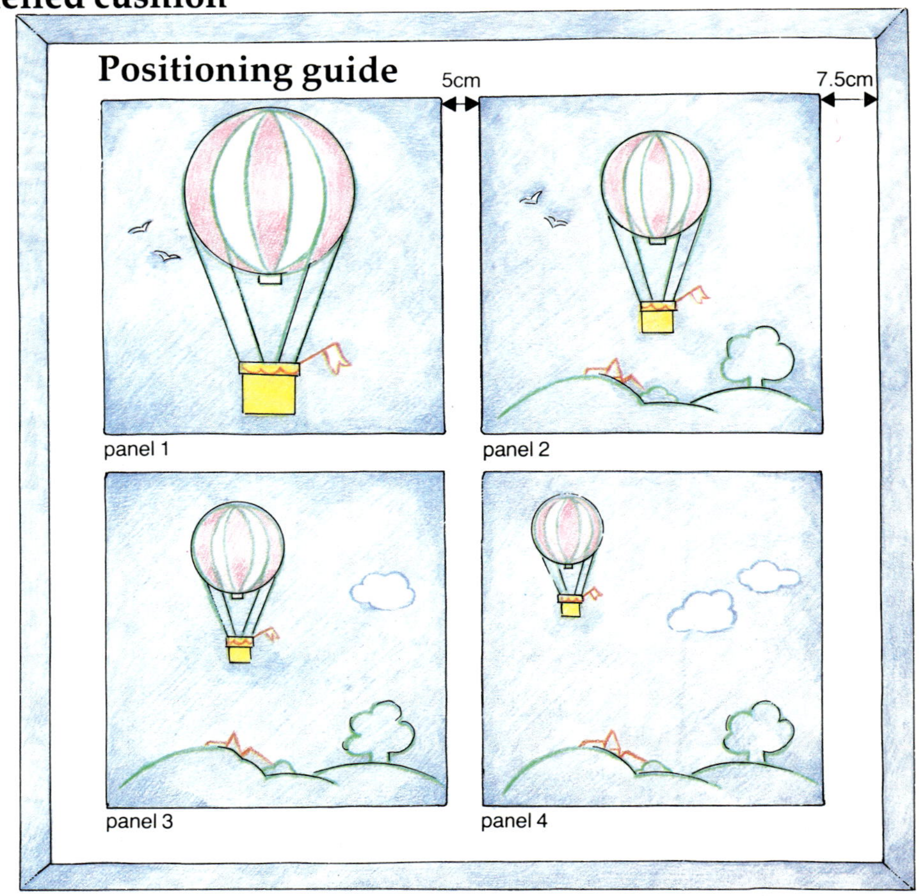


### Enlarging the motifs

The cushion design contains four panels, each with a slightly different version of the balloon in the landscape. The landscape appears the same size in each panel while the balloon is a different size in each, so the two parts of the design – balloon and landscape – are given separately. Enlarge the balloon motif to four different sizes

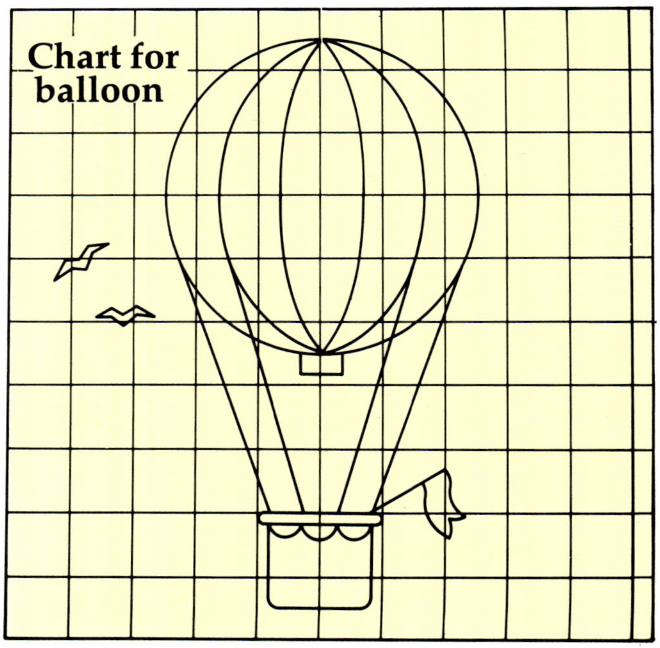


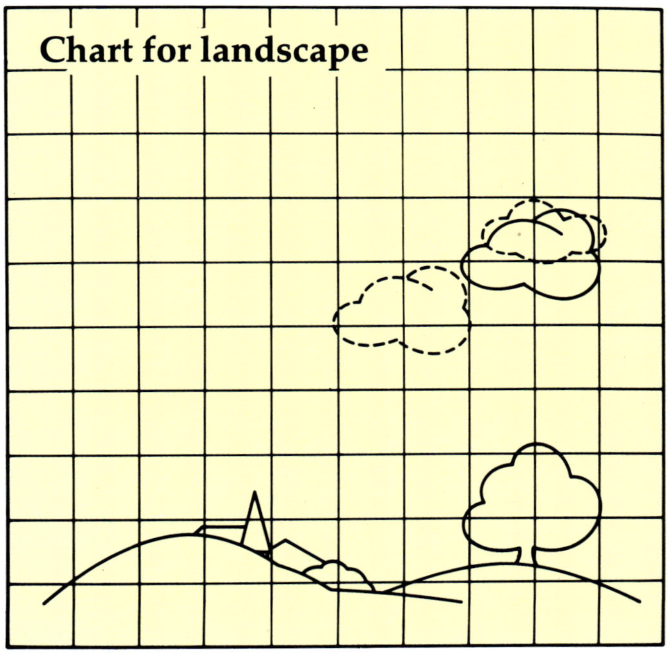

on to tracing or greaseproof paper as follows:
**Panel 1** Enlarge balloon with one square=3cm/1¼in, no landscape.
**Panel 2** Enlarge balloon with one square=2cm/¾in, enlarge landscape with one square=3cm/1¼in (no clouds). Position balloon 3cm/1¼in from top edge and 10cm/4in from right-hand edge.
**Panel 3** Enlarge balloon with one square=1.5cm/⅝in. Enlarge landscape with one square=3cm/1¼in. Include one cloud (bold outline). Position balloon 3cm/1¼in from top edge and 15cm/6in from right-hand edge.
**Panel 4** Enlarge balloon with one square=1cm/½in, enlarge landscape with one square=3cm/1¼in. Include both clouds (dotted outlines). Position balloon 3.5cm/1⅜in from top edge and 19cm/7½in from right-hand edge.

### Working the appliqué panels

Follow the instructions for the small cushion for the appliqué designs. Position the motifs on the four blue squares as indicated in the enlarging instructions. When adding the white clouds, stitch round them using pale blue thread. In addition, all the panels except the first one include the landscape design, enlarged as described above. Transfer the landscapes using white dressmaker's carbon paper. Outline with zigzag stitch: hills, tree and bush – turquoise; church – pink, house – pale pink.

### Making up the cushion

Press under 1cm/½in on all four edges of the four blue panels. Pin them to the large white square so that the distance between them is 5cm/2in and the distance of each one from the edge is 7.5cm/3in. Stitch round each panel close to the edge.
Make the cushion back in exactly the same way as given for the small cushion, turning in 1.5cm/⅝in along one 82cm/33in edge of both blue rectangles and tacking together to form a 82cm/33in square with a flap opening.
Join and attach the blue border strips as described for the small cushion – the method is exactly the same.

### Making a jumbo cushion pad

If you want to fill your cushion with feathers or feather and down, use down-proof cambric for the cover. Otherwise, use calico fabric and fill the cushion with foam chips.
Simply join two 84cm/33in squares of fabric taking 1cm/½in seams all round, leaving an opening in one side. Turn right side out, stuff and slipstitch opening.

DESIGN EXTRA

## Framed balloon picture

For an extra decorative touch, star-shaped sequins make a dazzling balloon. The white border acts as a 'mount' for the picture.

### You will need

50cm/½yd white cotton fabric
35cm/⅜yd pale blue cotton fabric
20cm/¼yd remnants in pale pink, mid pink and yellow
35cm/⅜yd medium iron-on Vilene interfacing
Sewing thread in turquoise, white, yellow and pink
Pink and silver star sequins
Carbon and tracing papers as for small cushion

### To make the picture

Cut a 50cm/20in square from white fabric. Enlarge balloon design with 1 square=3cm/1¼in. Work exactly as for the small cushion. Turn edges of blue square over 1cm/½in and press. Pin centrally to white square, leaving a 10cm/4in border all round and stitch close to the edge. Now scatter the sequins on to the balloon and hand sew them in place through all layers. Have the appliqué professionally mounted and framed.

# Shadow appliqué with added embroidery

***The delicate appearance of shadow appliqué has been used to great effect on this detachable organdie collar. The motifs can be hand or machine sewn and the technique is easier than it looks. A few simple embroidery stitches add detail to the design.***

Shadow appliqué is just like regular appliqué except that the motifs are applied to the *wrong* side of a sheer fabric, so that they show through as pale, shadowy shapes on the right side. The stitching which secures the shapes is worked on the right side by hand or machine, and helps to give definition to the design. Decorative embroidery stitches can also be

*Below: The back of this appliquéd collar is just as pretty as the front.*

added afterwards to complete the design.
If the finished work is hung against the light, the motifs will show up more boldly, so it's an effective decoration for sheer curtains or light roller blinds. It is not essential to have light behind the work for the motifs to show up. Beautiful designs can also be stitched on lingerie, mats, cushion covers for a bedroom – all sorts of delicate, pretty things for home and wardrobe.

## Materials and equipment

Suitable ground fabrics for shadow appliqué are organdie, voile and even gauze for very delicate work. The motifs for appliqué should be cut from plain-coloured, firm fabrics such as cotton lawn or cotton batiste. Do not choose anything too heavy or it will pull the ground fabric out of shape. The fabric must be colour fast or it will spoil the ground fabric.
Placing a coloured fabric behind a white fabric, however sheer, makes it much paler, so choose strong coloured fabrics for the appliqué unless you want a really subtle effect.
Use fine crewel needles and make sure you have a small sharp pair of scissors for snipping away the surplus fabric round the appliqué. The ground fabric can be mounted in a frame if you have one. This helps to prevent any puckering and maintains the tension of the fabric.

## Shadow appliqué step-by-step

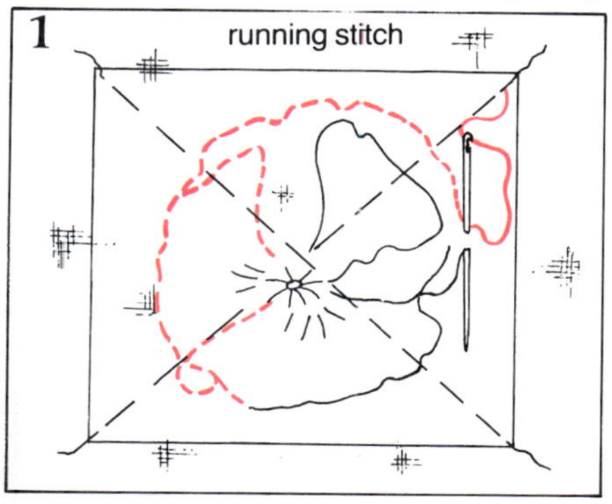


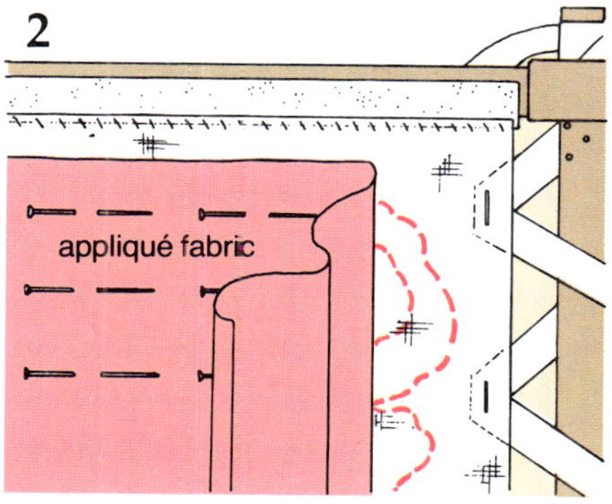


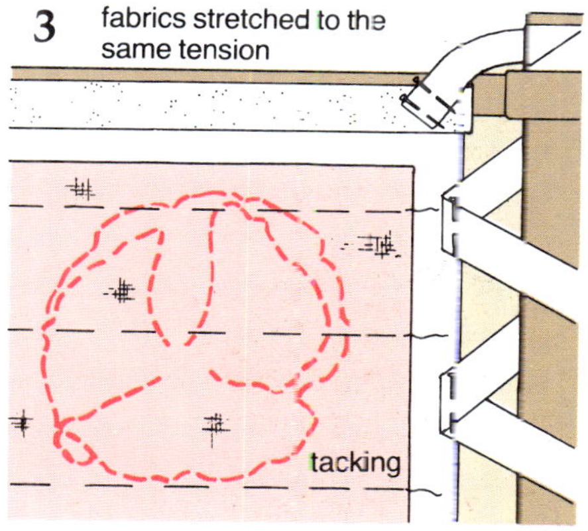


**1** Tack the ground fabric over a tracing of the design. Outline the design with small, neat running stitches without sewing through the paper. Do not knot the thread but leave loose ends at the back of the fabric. These stitches will be hidden by the stitched edge of the motif but it is important to keep them neat as they are not easy to remove later on. Remove the tracing and mount the ground fabric on a frame if you have one. Trim the ends of the threads outlining the design close to fabric.
**2** Pin a piece of the appliqué fabric to the back of the ground fabric, matching the straight grains of the two fabrics and covering the design.
**3** Tack the appliqué fabric in place, stretching it to the same tension as the ground fabric.

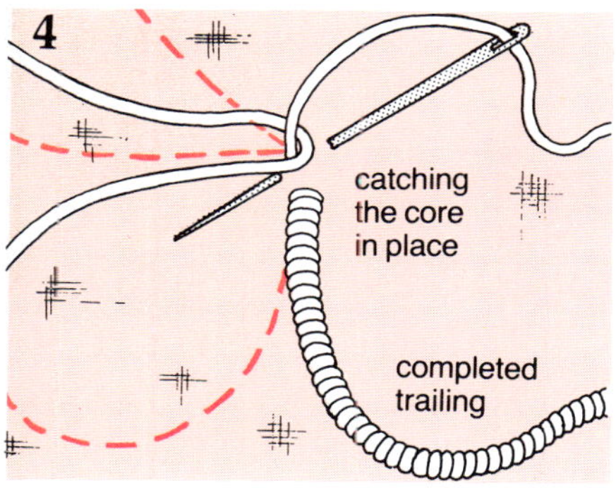


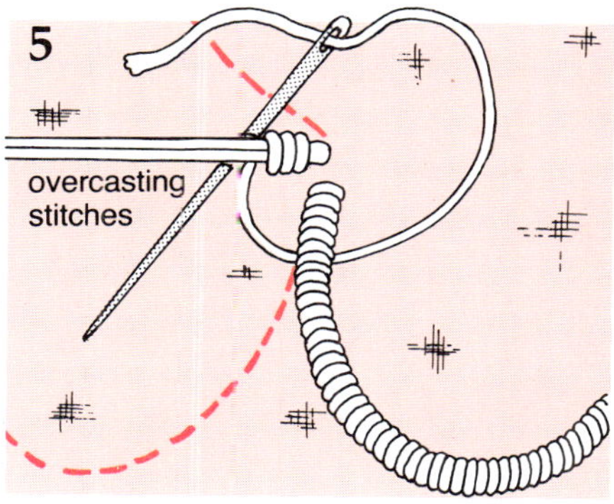


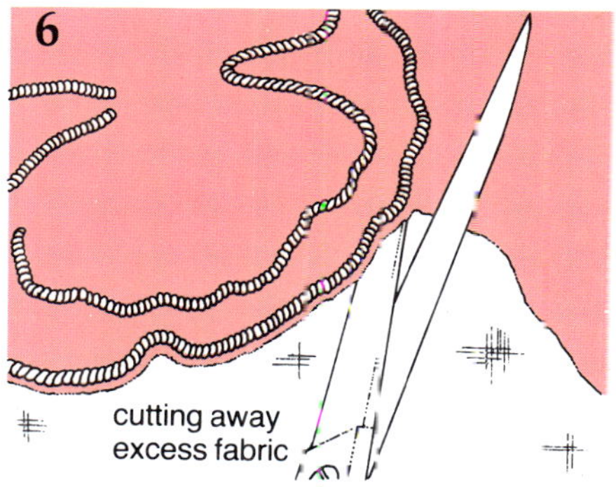


**Stitching the appliqué** Trailing (overcast stitch) is a good choice for work that needs to be washed. It gives a good firm outline and holds the appliqué securely in place with no risk of fraying. You could also use buttonhole stitch or, if you are using a machine, a narrow satin stitch.
Do not knot threads when starting or finishing – leave a tail of thread at the back of the work instead. Do not carry any threads across the back, from one motif to another, as they will show.
**4** To work trailing, cut a length of thread for the core at least twice the length of the line to be stitched. Fold it in half and catch in place with a small stitch over the loop.
**5** Hold the doubled thread in the direction of the embroidery with your left hand and work over it with small overcasting stitches. At the end, thread the core to the back of the work and snip off.

**Finishing off** Turn the work to the wrong side and remove the tacking holding the appliqué fabric.
**6** Hold the excess fabric tautly away from the stitching and cut it as close to the stitches as possible, using small sharp scissors. Take care not to cut the stitching or the ground fabric. Snip off any untidy ends on the back.
Pin the work out, appliqué side up, on an ironing board and press lightly with steam iron or damp cloth.

# *Shadow appliqué poppies on a detachable collar*

This beautiful organdie collar with its design of pale poppies and delicate white stitchery is surprisingly simple to make. A tie-on collar like this looks smart over a blouse, dress or jumper – tie it at the front or the back.

Organdie is a very fine fabric, so be sure to use the fine needles and tacking threads recommended. The finished collar is hand washable but you should check the red fabric for colour fastness.

### You will need

Commercial paper pattern for collar
1m/1yd white organdie or voile or the recommended pattern fabric requirement
Piece of red cotton lawn or batiste, about 15cm along straight grain × 41cm wide/6in × 16in
3 skeins white stranded cotton for embroidery
White cotton sewing thread No. 50 for tacking
Fine crewel needle (size 9 or 10)

### Working the appliqué

Trace off the poppy design on to the collar paper pattern piece, using a felt-tip pen. The trace patterns given are for the right and left-hand parts of the collar front. Match the dotted lines to give the design for the collar centre back. Cut two pieces of organdie to fit the paper pattern. The grain should run from the front to the back of the collar on each piece. Cut a strip of organdie 2cm × 90cm/¾in × 36in for the tie.

Pin and tack one piece of organdie over the pattern. Use fine white thread and small tacking stitches to outline the cutting edge of the collar, but do not sew through the paper pattern. Outline the petals, leaves and corn with small running stitches in the same way. Try to keep the work as flat as possible as you sew. Remove the paper pattern and mount the organdie in a frame if you have one. Cut the piece of red fabric in half, lengthwise along the grain of the fabric; cut one of these pieces in half lengthwise, again along the grain, so that you have two smaller pieces for each of the collar fronts.

Pin the red fabric to the wrong side of the organdie on the collar back and both fronts, covering the poppy flowers and matching the grain of the ground fabric. Tack firmly in place.

### Working the stitchery

All the embroidery is worked with two strands of stranded cotton.

Start with the poppy petal outlines in trailing.

The poppy centres are worked as oval buttonhole wheels with a few straight stitches radiating from the centre of each one.

When the appliqué is complete, turn the work to the wrong side, remove tacking and cut away the surplus red fabric as described on the previous page.

## Trace pattern for shadow appliqué poppies

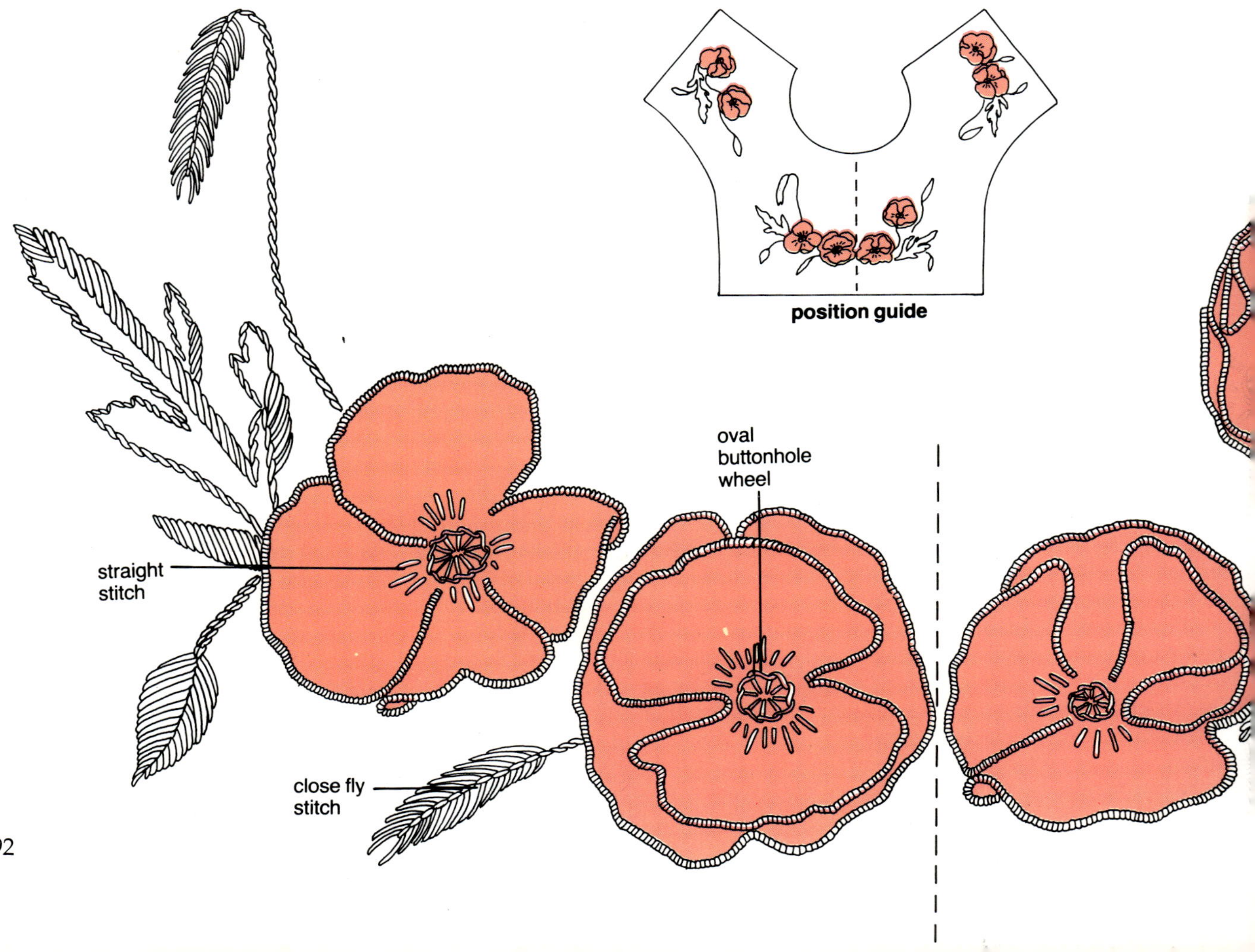

Now embroider the ears of corn, stems and poppy leaves in satin, stem and close fly stitch as indicated on trace pattern.
To give the satin stitch a firm edge, work over the outline stitches, stitching as close to them as possible.
Pin out the collar and press carefully.

### Making up the collar

Cut out the embroidered collar piece along marked cutting line. Using the paper pattern, cut a second collar piece from the remaining organdie for backing. With right sides together, seam the two collar pieces together along all edges except the neck edge. Trim seam allowance to 1cm/½in, and turn collar to right side. Press carefully.
If your machine has a decorative stitch facility, you could add a machine-stitched edging on the right side of the outer collar edges, to disguise the seam allowance. Use a thread that matches the appliqué.

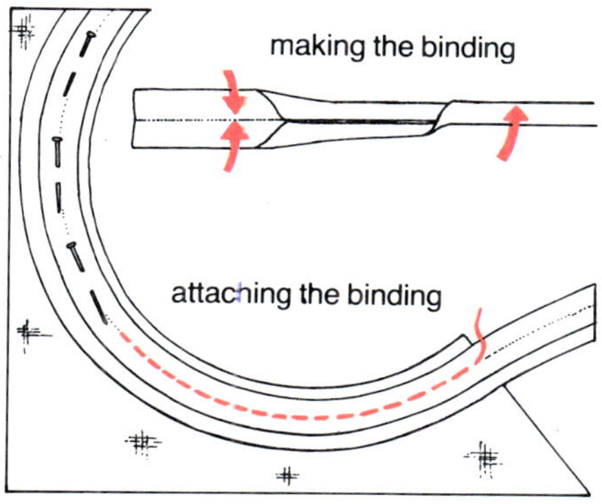


### Adding the tie/binding

Take the strip of organdie for the tie/binding. Fold in long edges to meet in the centre, then fold in half lengthwise and press.
Matching the centre of the strip with the centre back of collar, open out one side of the strip and place fold on right side of collar stitching line. Pin and stitch round collar edge. Trim seam to 6mm/¼in and press seam towards strip. Fold in strip ends and then fold strip in half lengthwise over collar edge and stitch the length of the strip through all layers and collar to finish ties.

### Stitches you will need

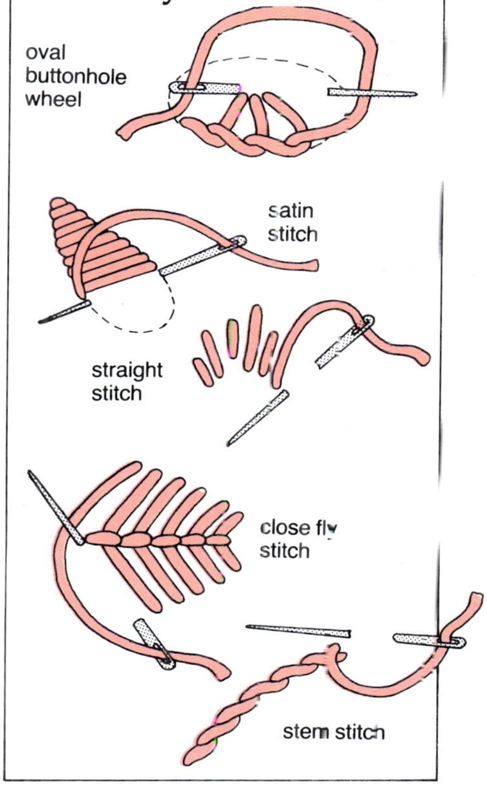


*Right: The two halves of the design (left) appear on the two collar fronts. Geometric appliqué designs could also be adapted for this type of collar.*

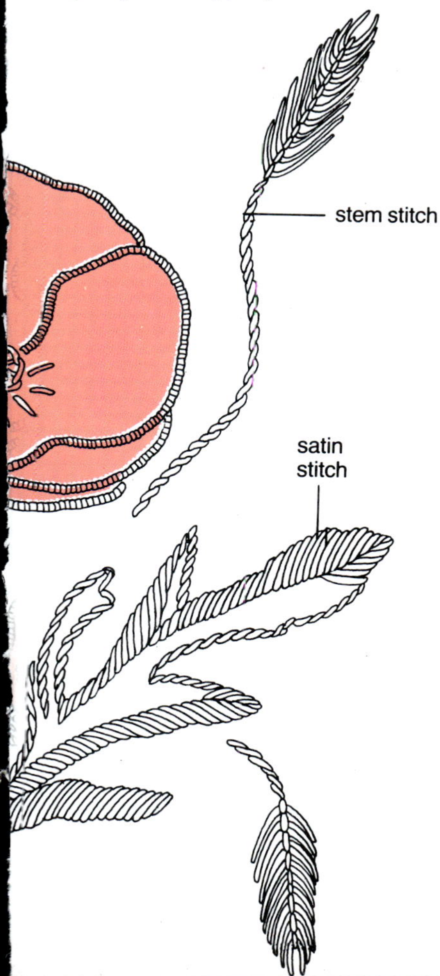

# *Appliqué perse to decorate soft furnishings*

***This appliqué technique was very popular in the nineteenth century. It is sometimes called broderie perse or cretonne appliqué and uses motifs cut from printed fabrics to build up a rich applied design on soft furnishings such as this collection of cushions.***

Appliqué was probably originally invented by the Persians or the Indians as a way of inexpensively imitating the effect of richer embroidered textiles. The particular technique known as appliqué perse (Persian appliqué) is fun to do and quicker than regular appliqué – the shapes are taken from printed fabric and so are already 'drawn' ready for you to cut out. You have to decide on the best arrangement of the cut-out motifs, and stitch them neatly in place on the ground fabric, usually with a machine satin stitch which gives a well-defined edge. If you don't have a swing needle machine, work by hand using buttonhole stitch.

Traditionally, motifs were always cut from printed chintz but any printed fabric will do, so long as it has a bold enough pattern and a close enough weave not to fray.

*Below: One length of fabric provides motifs for several cushions, each one using a different background colour.*

### Using the technique

This is a marvellous way of using up an odd remnant of furnishing fabric left over from making curtains or loose covers. You may not even have enough left to make up a cushion cover, yet you could use the remnant to create a unique design to decorate a plain cover with appliqué perse. Appliqué the motifs on to tablecloths, table mats, pillowcases, blinds and curtain hems. They can also be used to add a decorative touch to clothes and accessories.

### Planning the design

Wash and press your chosen piece of printed fabric to avoid shrinkage and to make sure the colours will not run on to ground fabric when washed.

Take a sheet of tracing paper and, using a thick felt-tip pen, trace off a series of motifs from the printed fabric – all the motifs which are bold enough to stitch round. Cut out the paper shapes and experiment with different ways of arranging them in a balanced design. Bear in mind the shape of the finished article when doing this. Motifs can certainly overlap, but don't make the design too complicated for yourself to stitch – more than two layers could be too bulky, especially if you are machine stitching round the motifs.

Your design need not resemble the original fabric design – create something completely different if you like. If the basic design is floral, have fun 'arranging' vases, baskets or bunches of flowers. Make a drawing of your completed design to refer to when appliquéing the motifs.

## Working appliqué perse

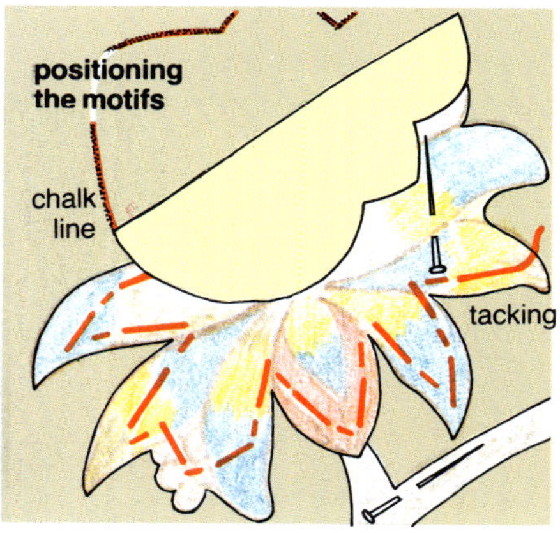


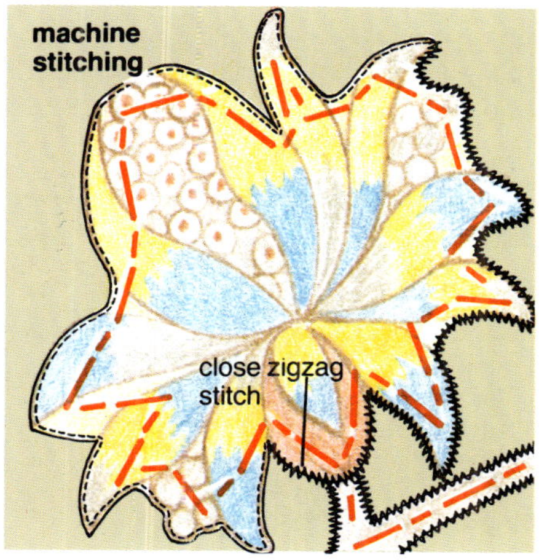


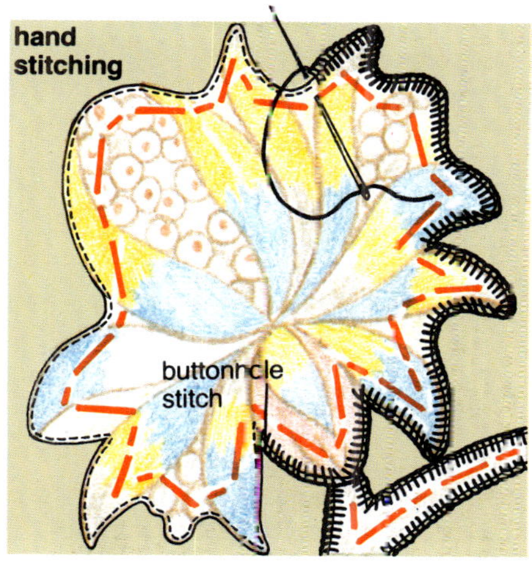


Using a pair of small, sharp scissors, cut out the fabric motifs along the outlines. Where an outline is too intricate, simplify it a little by ignoring some of the fine detail. Cut the appliqué ground fabric to the desired size for whatever you intend to make.

**Positioning the motifs** Using your tracing paper cut-outs, roughly mark the position of the appliqué motifs on the ground fabric by tracing round the shapes with a chalk pencil. If working by hand, mount the ground fabric in a frame if you have one.

Lay the fabric motifs on the ground fabric. Pin them in place and tack securely.

**Machine stitching** With the machine set to a medium straight stitch, sew all round the outside of the motif to anchor it securely. Using a close zigzag stitch and a thread to match either one of the motif colours or the ground fabric, stitch round all edges covering raw edges. Go slowly and carefully; some corners may need careful manipulation. Make sure you attach the shapes in the correct order for the design – raw edges of fabric and ends of thread should be neatly covered.

**Hand stitching** Tack round close to the raw edges of the motifs. Using stranded cotton, pearl cotton or coton à broder, work buttonhole stitch round raw edges with the knots on the outside. Make sure you keep the stitches close together to cover raw edges.

# *Cushions with appliquéd motifs*

The cushion shown here is decorated with motifs taken from a multi-coloured furnishing fabric. Plan your design to suit your cushion shape.

### Making up the covers

Work the appliqué design on the front of the cushion cover before making up.

Make bolster and large square cushion covers like the ones shown opposite from a half-metre/yard of plain cotton furnishing fabric.

Ready-made covers are easier to appliqué by hand. If you prefer to use your machine, you may need to unpick one of the cover seams to enable the fabric to lie flat.

### Stitching the appliqué

The appliqué is stitched using as many colours of thread as necessary to match the main colours in the design. Use a fairly wide satin stitch for leaves and flowers, making it narrower for stems.

# Index